Thomas Merton
poet • monk • prophet

THOMAS MERTON
poet · monk · prophet

Papers

presented at
THE SECOND
GENERAL CONFERENCE
of the THOMAS MERTON SOCIETY
of GREAT BRITAIN AND IRELAND
at OAKHAM SCHOOL,
MARCH 1998

Edited by
PAUL M. PEARSON
DANNY SULLIVAN
IAN THOMSON

P³P

Published in Great Britain 1998
THREE PEAKS PRESS
9 Croesonen Road
Abergavenny
Monmouthshire NP7 6AE
mail@p3p.org   http://p3p.org

Illustrations on front cover & p.211 by Lindsay Nevin

Designed & set in Joanna at Three Peaks Press

With thanks to Elizabeth Skelton

Printed in Wales
at Gwasg Dinefwr, Llandybie

A CIP record for this publication
is available from the British Library

ISBN   1–902093–01–1

Contents

"...I am glad to be able to tell someone at Oakham that I really bear the school a deep affection, with sentiments of gratitude that will not die... I never regret having gone to Oakham. On the contrary, I am very glad that I was sent there rather than to some larger school, for Oakham had something of simplicity and sincerity about it that one might look for in vain elsewhere."

THOMAS MERTON *to* C.J. DIXON,
November 9th, 1954

INTRODUCTION

T HE INITIAL EXCITEMENT OF any new venture can all too quickly pall and it is only in the years that follow that its true value and meaning can be seen. This is especially true as we approach the millennium with the pace of change apparently moving faster than ever and, with that change, instability and uncertainty appearing more widespread than in previous generations. Against this background, the monastic life, as seen through Merton's life and thought, can speak to the modern world of a stability, obedience and conversion of life which can paradoxically hold together change and movement whilst remaining focused on its one true point.

With the second general meeting of the Thomas Merton Society of Great Britain and Ireland at Oakham in March and the subsequent publication of these papers, the Merton Society moves from being a "one night wonder" to experiencing a sense of genuine growth and continuity. Our second general meeting brought with it many of the benefits of this growth and continuity, as well as generating its own feeling of excitement. Excitement at meeting at Oakham, a place with such strong Merton connections; excitement at the variety of people present who had come from far and near to celebrate the life and legacy of Thomas Merton; excitement of renewing friendships and making new ones; and the excitement of the excellent fare provided by the speakers and published here in this volume.

The conference title – Thomas Merton: Poet, Monk, Prophet – emphasises some of the central aspects of the life and thought of this most paradoxical of monks. The papers contained in this volume reflect Merton's wide and varied interests and his prophetic voice, which continues to speak from his Trappist silence thirty years after his untimely death.

Oakham School provided an ideal setting for this conference — a beautiful, tranquil location, good food and accommodation, and a welcome second to none. This volume cannot hope to capture that hospitality or the warmth and friendship shared by the participants, or the quality of the workshops, liturgies and poetry readings. It does, however, offer a broad and rich collection of papers which we believe will bring something of the unique flavour of the Society's gathering at Oakham to the larger Merton community, as well as witnessing to the growing maturity of the Society.

This growth and maturity is reflected in the atmosphere of our general meetings. In the brief time available in a single weekend, participants are able to build and share in the "hidden ground of love" Merton spoke about, and walk together, for a brief while, on our common "road to joy."

On behalf of the committee I would like to thank all those who worked to make the meeting such a success and to those who have enabled the publication of this volume, especially my fellow editors, Danny Sullivan and Ian Thomson. Finally, we hope that the experience of sharing together the insights of these papers will encourage many of you to join us for the third general meeting of the Society, *Thomas Merton: A Mind Awake in the Dark*, scheduled to be held once again at Oakham School, Rutland from 7th–9th April 2000.

PAUL M. PEARSON

Secretary

THOMAS MERTON SOCIETY
OF GREAT BRITAIN AND IRELAND

PRESIDENTIAL ADDRESS
A Day in the Life of Thomas Merton

CANON A.M. 'DONALD' ALLCHIN

LOOKING BACK OVER the two years since our first meeting at Southampton I can only rejoice at the steady development of our society during this time. I want, at the very beginning, to express my own gratitude, and I am sure the gratitude of all our members, to the officers and committee of our society, especially to Danny Sullivan and Paul Pearson, for all the work that they have put into the development of the society, to the publication of our admirable journal and to the preparation of this conference.

Once again we are delighted to have such strong support from the International Thomas Merton Society in the USA. It is a great joy to have with us Brother Patrick Hart from Gethsemani itself, the general editor of the Merton Journals. It is good that no less than three of those who have edited those journals are with us today. It is good too that Father Basil Pennington is able to be with us. I first collaborated with him in an ecumenical Cistercian conference in Oxford just twenty-five years ago. Amongst our other American visitors I must mention especially Tommie O'Callaghan, one of the trustees and one of Merton's closest friends, and Anne McCormick, for many years secretary to the Trustees and now one of the Trustees herself.

I had the joy of staying with the O'Callaghans in Louisville last October; I had gone to the opening of the new Thomas Merton Center in the library of Bellarmine College. It was a visit memorable for many things, not least for the fact that Bob Daggy, the former director of the Center, though critically ill, seemed to have a few days of partial remission in his illness. Thus he was able to enjoy the festivities, to greet many of his friends and above all to be present at the official opening of the new Center, which included the naming of a room in his honour. All those who knew him well have a sense of loss at the death of a man who was so generous with his time and energy, who was so careful and helpful as a scholar and who was so full of unexpected humour and zest for life. Like many others from many parts of the world my memories of Louisville and Bellarmine will always be associated with him. We are particularly happy today to have his successor, Teresa Sandok with us.

At our first meeting at Southampton, I said that we were bringing Merton home to England. Merton was of course never more than very partially at home in this country. But in his earliest years, Ripley Court and Durston House in Ealing, a school where I happen to have gone fifteen years later, were for a time a kind of home for him. The same thing would be true of this school during his teens. Here at least he could feel in part that he belonged. Our being here will, I am sure, help us to become more aware of what Oakham meant in Merton's life and how much he gained, of his initial formation as a writer of the English language, by his education in this place. This is where he began to acquire those skills as a writer which he was to develop throughout his life. It was not a very long life; it was cut short in full flight. But it was an extraordinarily full life; he lived every minute of it. That is what I want to think of in this address; the way in which, especially in his last decade, he filled his days with seeing and doing, with faith and struggle, with love and knowledge.

Some years ago, when I was working in the Thomas Merton Center in Bellarmine College in Louisville, I came across, in one of the working notebooks, two or three pages of notes which were dated Pentecost 1967. Merton was reading that day St. Jerome's Life of St. Paul of Thebes, St. Paul the Hermit. He made particularly full and detailed notes of the account of the meeting between St. Anthony and St. Paul which took place at the very end of St. Paul's life. It is a fascinating story, this meeting of the two old hermits, and it is one which was particularly important in the earliest centuries of the church in these islands. It is an incident which you can find depicted in prominent places on the high crosses in Ireland, from the eighth and ninth centuries. You can find it also on the Ruthwell Cross in Anglo-Saxon Scotland. You can also find it referred to with particular emphasis in one of the earliest theological praise poems in Welsh.

From the quality of Merton's notes and from the fact that he dated this entry, a thing which he didn't usually do, I felt that this reading had some rather special meaning for him. Perhaps, I thought, he was intending to write something about this moment in the life of the two first hermits of the Egyptian desert. It certainly seemed to me a highly appropriate subject for him to take for his study and meditation on the feast of Pentecost.

So, needless to say, when the appropriate volume of the journals came out, Volume Six, *Learning to Love*, the volume which covers the period of 1966 and Merton's love affair with M, one of the first things I did was to turn to this day to see what Merton had written in his journal. I was not at all disappointed, for I saw that the reading of St. Jerome had spoken to Merton even more deeply than I had imagined. But I found that he began his entry for the day, not with his reading but with the dawn. It is a brief but fine Merton dawn-scape:

> Lightning, thunder and rain, on and off all night, and now at dawn there is still more of it. The lovely grey-green valley, misty clouds sweeping low over the hills and forest out there in the south, iron-dark clouds heavy above them. The rainy gloom full of pale yellow irises and the cloudy white blossoming green masses of the rose hedge. I went out a while ago and a hawk flew fast away — it had been waiting on the cross or in the big poplar tree.

And then we come to Merton's reflection on the text of St. Jerome:

> As I have been asked to do a piece on Paul the Hermit, I re-read Jerome's *Vita* today. A work of art, really. With plenty of monastic theology in its symbolism. A beautiful piece of writing, with deep mystical and psychological implications so that whether or not it is 'historical' is irrelevant. It awakens a kind of inner awareness of psychic possibilities which one so easily forgets and neglects, the return to unity, to the ground, the paradisal inner space where the archetypal man dwells in peace and in God. The journey to that space, through a realm of aridity, dualism, dryness, death. The need of courage and decision. Above all faith, obedience to the inner voice of the Spirit, refusal to give up or to compromise.

And then one turns the page and finds a longer and deeper application of the text to Merton's own life, a passage not at all untypical of the second half of this particular volume. In that second part, one feels that Merton is reaffirming within himself the basic direction of his life, which the previous summer had so unexpectedly and so powerfully questioned, threatened and, in the end, renewed.

> What is wrong in my life is not so much a matter of 'sin' (though it is sin too), but of *unawareness*, lostness, slackness, relaxation, dissipation of desire, lack of courage and decision, so that I let myself be carried along and dictated to by an alien movement. The current of the 'world,' which I know is not mine. I am always getting diverted into a way that is not my way and is not going where I am called to go. And only if I go where I must go can I be of any use to the 'world.' I can serve the world best by keeping my distance and my freedom.

And Merton turns interestingly, from Jerome to Athanasius, and to the life of Anthony itself.

> In the *Vita Antonii*, 'virtue' is within us not outside us, and we find it when we return to our 'original nature' our 'natural state' the state proper to ourselves as we 'came into being' one might add our true identity in the mind of God. The soul, says Anthony, "came into being fair and perfectly straight," so the prophet says, "Make straight your paths unto the Lord God of Israel" and St. John the Baptist, "Make straight your paths"... So the job is (as St. John of the Cross says) "Keeping the strength of the mind, of one's thought and desires for God. Having received the soul as something entrustèd to us, let us guard it for the Lord that he may recognise his work as being the same as he made it."

So Merton has made his Pentecost around a return to two basic monastic texts of the early centuries, Jerome and Athanasius. He has summed up his meditation with a reference to St. John of the Cross. It has been, one might suppose, a quiet but full day of retreat and reflection.

And then we read on to May the 17th, the following Wednesday, and we are in for a good Mertonian surprise. Everything that I have quoted so far, together with the copious notes and translations from Jerome's life which I have not quoted, was written between, say, four in the morning, or whenever Merton got up, and about half past eight or nine. Because, as we find in the Journal entry for May 17th, the day had hardly begun.

> On Pentecost, drove in to Louisville with Reverend Father in the rain, found St. Thomas' seminary way out in the fields somewhere towards Cincinnati, walked in long halls this way and that and found a sacristy. And waited, and had pictures taken.

This is not going to be a day of silence in the hermitage. It is going to be a day of activity and celebration in Louisville. It is the day of Dan Walsh's ordination. Dan Walsh had been Merton's teacher back at Columbia and had followed him to Gethsemani, and he was now to be ordained in his sixties. For those days it was a late ordination and it had been largely arranged and promoted by the former Archbishop of Louisville, Archbishop Floersh, who had himself only recently retired.

Merton sketches in the event briefly:

The concelebration was fine... a great enthusiasm filled the large bright chapel, crowded with people, friends and students of Dan, including some former monks with their wives etc. Archbishop Floersh moved and moving. Dan nervous at one point. A great celebration though. Then we went on to the O'Callaghan's — this time I with a carload of ex-monks. The day stayed grey but we could sit in the yard at metal tables, where I talked too much, drank too much champagne and generally misbehaved, going against what I had in mind earlier Pentecost morning.

Now it really ought to be Tommie herself who should tell you about the Pentecost party. There were anxieties at the practical level, that it would continue to rain and that they would have to try to bring everyone into the house. But it didn't continue to rain. They could go out and sit in the garden. It was a great party, such as only the O'Callaghans can give, a party especially for Dan Walsh whom Tommie too had known since she was a student, and who was the person who had first introduced Merton to the O'Callaghan household. Tom was certainly very much there.

He gives us a more highly coloured account of the occasion in letters to his friends. In the letter to Jim Forest for instance he wrote:

Pentecost was a big day down here, as my old friend Dan Walsh was suddenly ordained, in his sixties, with all sorts of dispensations, and there was a lot of celebrating. In fact I celebrated on too much champagne which is a thing a Trappist rarely gets to do, but I did a very thorough job. At one point in the afternoon I remember looking up and focusing, rather uncertainly, upon four faces of nuns sitting in a row looking at me in a state of complete scandal and shock. Another pillar of the church had fallen.

Next morning Frank O'Callaghan presented Tom with an empty champagne bottle with a message tied round its neck, which said, "In memory of Father Louis, with apologies from Frank."

It had been a memorable and diversified Whitsunday, starting in the hermitage, continuing at the ordination, concluding with the party. It had been a day of celebration on many levels, inner and outer, divine and human, sacred and secular, sublime and ridiculous.

The following day was almost as full. I will describe it only briefly. In the morning Merton went to the Louisville Carmel and concelebrated with Dan Walsh.

It was deeply moving, a sense of light and joy and of spiritual reality, a most beautiful Eucharist ... I was very happy about it, preached homily,

later we had a half-hour or so with the nuns in their speak room and
again I talked too much, but everyone seemed very happy.

They lunched with the Fords, and Tom met some of the younger
priests who were teaching at Bellarmine.

"Later I went down to the Chancery and had a very good talk with
the new archbishop, McDonough..." Merton was relieved to find
that the Archbishop was happy about his writing and particularly
about his contacts with Muslims. The Archbishop was also able to tell
Merton that the Apostolic Delegate in Washington seemed highly
interested in his work.

But the day ends on a personal, not a public note, a note which
seems to draw together the disparate material of the two previous
days:

> Coming home late called M., who had had the day off, had been read-
> ing Robert Frost ("Bereft") and kept saying we should go on talking to
> each other as before (with love) and that she had dreamt of me. But I
> still have doubts about writing her with much affection, also frequently,
> and I know she has hesitations about our seeing each other — or at
> least about her driving down here. So it is calming down anyway; but
> I was glad to talk to her and on the phone she sounded happy.

So the storms of the previous May were subsiding. Just a week
before this entry Merton records that he had phoned her from the
airport and that she had told him of her intention to get married in
the autumn; and that they both had been happy and peaceful about
that decision. Certainly things were not yet fully resolved, but looking back, perhaps already Merton was beginning to see how much
he had gained from that new, if sometimes tumultuous experience
of love. Looking back now, after thirty more years we can surely see
in the continued and so admirable silence of M. a sign that for her
too, however painful and perplexing parts of the episode must have
been, it had not in the end been destructive or harmful.

Writing in his Journal ten years earlier, in 1957, commenting on
the theology of Bulgakov and Berdyaev, Merton says that our life is
called to be "a powerful Pentecost, in which the Holy Spirit, ever
active in us, seeks to reach through our inspired hands and tongues
into the very heart of the material world." Well, Pentecost '67, with
its ups and its downs, with its joys and its sorrows, had been a new
discovery of that constantly renewed, mysterious fact.

THOMAS MERTON
poet · monk · prophet

PANEL OF JOURNAL EDITORS

Chaired by

TOMMIE O'CALLAGHAN

with

PATRICK HART OCSO

LAWRENCE CUNNINGHAM

VICTOR A. KRAMER

CHRISTINE BOCHEN

PANEL OF JOURNAL EDITORS
Introduction

TOMMIE O'CALLAGHAN

GOOD AFTERNOON. IT's delightful to be here. Kentucky sends all of you her very best. Before I introduce the speakers I'd like to introduce a friend and a new trustee of the Merton Legacy Trust. As perhaps many of you know, we lost J. Laughlin in the Fall and the Trust and the Abbot have chosen Anne McCormick who many of you know through her rights work. If you have done any publishing or wanted to investigate further any of the Merton papers you have had to write to Anne McCormick to get permission. Well, Anne very happily has accepted the title of the third trustee of the literary estate. Anne, would you stand? [*Applause*]

This is Anne's first TMS meeting and she is very excited to know all of you and to become as proficient as you are on the Merton business. I'm not that proficient. So, without further ado, we will start with Brother Patrick Hart from Gethsemani who has been General Editor of the Journals and himself has edited Volume One and Volume Seven. He will speak about Volume One now and then he will speak about Jonathan Montaldo's volume, Volume Two, as Jonathan cannot be with us today. So, Pat...

PATRICK HART OCSO

Volume One: *Run to The Mountain* (1939-1941)

THANK YOU, TOMMIE and Ladies and Gentlemen. It's a great honour to be here especially to participate in this editor's panel at Oakham School where it all began for Merton. He began writing short stories here — in fact one of them was recently published in the Merton Seasonal – 'The Haunted Castle' – which is very much like Winnie the Pooh. Anyway I am fearful that if the archivist is here in our midst, he might say, "Come and see me afterwards. I've discovered some unpublished Merton Journals from his days at Oakham." This could disturb our Harper Collins publisher's schedule.

Anyway, we begin with the first of the Journals. This actually covers the period 1939-41 and consists of his pre-monastic journals. The first part is the Perry Street Journal. It begins with an entry of May 2nd 1939, so that's really the earliest entry we have of Merton's. It begins with an ungrammatical question. "This is May. Who seen any robins?" Interesting that he should begin this way with an ungrammatical question. The Journal reflects the life of a young intellectual living at Perry Street in Greenwich Village, teaching at Columbia where he received his Master's degree in 1938 on Nature and Art in William Blake and was contemplating a doctorate on the poetry of Gerard Manley Hopkins. In fact he had purchased in '39 or '40 the letters and journals of Hopkins. It never became a reality because he began teaching at St. Bonaventure. But the notes he took on Hopkins are there in the archive at St. Bonaventure's.

After his reception into the Church in '38 he must have discarded his previous journals. As he mentions,

> these are a few selections (in the Secular Journal) taken from a diary I kept when I was a layman, a graduate at Columbia teaching in university extension, later when I was an instructor at St. Bonaventure's. This was written like most diaries informally, colloquially and in haste. The whole diary filled two or three volumes. One of these still exists...

to quote Merton:

> ...the other three were thrown away or destroyed after I typed out a few excerpts which are given here along with part of the surviving volume.

Actually Merton was mistaken, because Mark Van Doren had deposited two journal volumes at St. Bonaventure covering this period. One was the Perry Street Journal. The middle was the Cuban Journal. The last was the St. Bonaventure Journal. We've always questioned in our minds what about the missing journal...there was no real journal from the Cuban episode. That was transcribed by Merton many years after Merton had entered Gethsemani. Actually he had given a manuscript to a Monsignor Fitzgerald who had kept all these transcripts for years and was retired and living in Florida. He wrote to St. Bonaventure and again this was before the Merton Center at Bellarmine College was begun, and said, "I have some journals of Merton that he kept in Cuba. Would you be interested in having these?" Of course Father Irenaeus [Herscher] said that St. Bonaventure were delighted and so were all of us when we discovered that he did have transcriptions that Merton had typed out and given to Monsignor Fitzgerald who had in turn deposited them at St. Bonaventure.

In going through these transcripts, there was a problem. Were they really raw journal or were they something that Merton had revised before publication in the Secular Journal? So there was only one way to discover definitively as far as I could tell and that was to check out the journals with Bob Lax. Now Bob Lax was a friend of Merton who had spent summers at the cottage at Olean, New York, and was in daily communion with Merton. And so I spent a few days with Bob Lax on Patmos where he had lived for about twenty years and we agreed, taking each page as it came along, that these were authentic primary journals from the Cuban period, and that they should be included in this first volume, Run to the Mountain. And then the third part was the St. Bonaventure Journal, written for the most part at St. Bonaventure's. Again it was Mark Van Doren who turned these volumes over to St. Bonaventure. The first person to actually discover them was Michael Mott. And thank goodness he did. With their survival established, we could include them in the collected journal project.

Towards the end of the journal there are references to the Baroness who had given a talk to the Friars of St Bonaventure under a lay apostolate. Merton was somewhat torn between a possible vocation to her work with the poor as a staff worker at Friendship House and a vocation to become a friar or a monk. The matter is finally resolved as the Journal closes and he departs from St. Bonaventure's for the Abbey of Gethsemani in the knob country of Kentucky where he would spend the next twenty seven years. And...

Volume Two: Entering the Silence (1941–1952)

To CONTINUE, I'LL say a few words about the second volume as Jonathan Montaldo who edited it isn't here. This journal was comprised of Merton's very earliest days as a monk of Gethsemani. In fact the first entry – he called it the novitiate journal – is dated December 12th, the day before he entered the novitiate — he became a novice and entered as a postulant on the Feast of St Lucy, December 13th. The Journal is in three parts again. The first part is this so-called Novitiate Journal which again he had entrusted to Sister Thérèse

Lentfoehr who kept her own archives of Merton's work. She decided
to turn her archives over to Columbia University in New York.

The second journal was a journal memoire and had to do with
the Abbot, Dom Frederick Dunne, who had received Merton into the
community. It was something that Merton had given to Father
Raymond Flanagan who was a fellow writer who was doing a
biography of Dom Frederic Dunne. So Merton wrote a note to Father
Raymond saying, 'Here are some notes which might be helpful in
your work if you can decipher, if you can read, them. So we have that
novitiate memoire which Merton gave to Raymond and it fills in a
nice gap there. Fortunately Raymond kept this in his files – he never
threw anything out – so we found that in our archives not too long
ago.

The third part is what was called 'The Whale and the Ivy,' the first
title that Merton gave to The Sign of Jonas, which comprises about half
of this Journal. It was published as The Sign of Jonas by Harcourt Brace
in 1953 but with lots of gaps, lots of editing, things taken out that
Merton himself edited out, and he used fictitious names...the monks
were given names other than their own. Merton dedicates The Sign of
Jonas, again the third part of the Journal edited by Jonathan Montaldo,
to the Most Blessed, Sorrowful Virgin Mary. I think Merton was
experiencing solitude, maybe some anguish and of course there was
the psychological searching he was doing into his own personality
and it was a time of entering into the silence, I think. The title was
good for that volume.

As Jonathan says, the editorial interventions in these journals were
minimal so he cut very little out, added as much as he could from
what was in the archives and, as he says, each emphasis, each ellipsis,
each parenthesis in this text is Merton's. In the translating and citing of
scriptural passages he used the Rheims Douai version and in these
early journals the editor appended to a text a daily schedule at
Gethsemani, which was rather helpful. The reader can figure out what
Merton was doing during his monastic day. A final word of advice —
and I'll quote Jonathan on this as he finishes his introduction...

> As you can, he says, reader, doubt everything you believe you already
> know about Thomas Merton and entrust yourself to his journals with
> an open heart. As Merton discloses and withdraws himself, as he
> masters and unmasters his world, as he names and renames himself,
> remain patiently with the paradoxes and the contradictions, the search

for simplicity becoming more and more complex as Merton's spiritual journey unfolds. Artist as he was, though, Merton seems to be speaking only and for himself. You will soon however find yourself embedded in his web of mirrors. The eyes smiling back at you as you read these journals will naturally be Thomas Merton's but often those eyes fathoming your eyes will be your very own.

LAURENCE CUNNINGHAM

Volume Three: *A Search for Solitude* (1952-1960)

I WAS AIDED IMMENSELY because the man who has the office next to me at the University of Notre Dame is an expert and editor of the Dead Sea Scrolls. He would look at photographs of tiny little fragments in Aramaic and I would ask him to try to decipher Merton's handwriting for me at times. He's a very famous palaeographer.

When Brother Patrick asked me to join the editorial team originally, I had received the Journals from 1956 to 1960, and then because Jonathan's volume was getting a little bit out of line in terms of size, I received partial journals from 1950 to 1953. I received these just at the time that I had been elected Chair of the Department of Theology at Notre Dame which has forty members — it's a very large department. And I made this wonderful discovery...for the benefit of anyone who is going to become an academic administrator, no one ever wants to see the Chair or the Dean before nine o'clock in the morning. They come toddling in at around about that time. So I would come into the office at around about seven and work on these journals for about an hour and a half or two hours every day, trying to get reduced to typescript maybe two pages which maybe would be one page which he wrote on these large legal ledgers. I think he had a very good sense of monastic poverty because he never wasted a line. Sometimes he would even write up in the top like a margin. Surprisingly enough, very, very few times did he ever cross out a line. He wrote rather fluently.

I want to make two points about the journals that I had, especially the journals between '56 and '60, because I think there are two somewhat independent but rather important themes in those journals. The one has to do with his own struggles to understand what it meant to be a monk in the twentieth century. There's a

famous line that I love from the great Cistercian writer André Louf.
He says, "What is a monk? A monk is a person who every day asks
what is a monk?" There's a lot on insight in that I think and Merton,
certainly between '56 and '60, was asking "What is a monk? What
does it mean for me to be a monk?" Now everybody who's read
Merton knows that he had certain dissatisfactions at Gethsemani. He
was not always a 100% cheerleader for the abbot. I didn't know the
abbot. I've only seen him at a distance at Gethsemani when he was
alive — I think he was in many ways a very wise man.

Merton was struggling during this period. Energised by his
meeting with Ernesto Cardenal, he gets this idea that he's going to
start a monastery in Latin America or Central America which is going
to be very simple and very plain. All through these journals there are
references to Merton looking up places in Colombia and places like
that where they might settle and he develops a few theoretical horaria
about how to spend the day and so on and so forth. Parenthesis from
the editor: a totally crazy idea, in my estimation. He couldn't learn
how to drive a car. How was he going to run a monastery in the third
world? But it does illustrate a point because what Merton was
attempting to do, I think, was to understand what it meant to be a
contemplative and at the same time somehow pursuing an
intellectual vocation that was going to have some particular
relevance to the world. I write in the introduction to my volume a
great insight that I got. The more he thought about this other project,
the more he would become, at least on one page, very critical of life
at Gethsemani, etcetera.

While I was working on the journals I was invited down to the
Abbey and there was no room at the inn and someone said would
you like to live up in the hermitage? Well, yes, indeed, and I spent a
week living up in the hermitage and I found in the hermitage a
mimeographed copy of Cassian's Institutes. And for lack of anything
better to do, I sat on the front porch of the hermitage and read these
Institutes and I ran across Cassian's analysis of acedia. And in there he
says, "...there comes a time in a monk's life (I would say there comes
a time in everyone's life) where one is tempted to be very dissatisfied
with where one is..." And Cassian who borrows this from an earlier
writer, Evagrius of Pontus, says — and he has wonderful descriptions —
he says, "The monk begins to look outside the door of his cell,
wondering whether anybody might come by that he could chat with..."

or, "he wonders about whether or not there might be some urgent reason why he should leave the cell and give spiritual direction to somebody," etcetera and "the more dissatisfied the monk becomes, the more he begins to criticise where he is living, insisting that it is impossible for him to advance in the spiritual life as long as he stays in this place, and how things would only be perfect if he could go somewhere else." And I'm looking at this and saying to myself, this is like a psychotherapist's folder on Merton in 1957, 1958, that it was a kind of a temptation that he had to go through when all of these elaborate plans fall through and Rome writes and says no exclaustration, no going to Latin America, no going to an island off the coast of Nicaragua and so on. Merton reads this letter on his knees and just drops the whole project and, in what I wanted to name the volume, he says, "I will find solitude outside geography." It's just a wonderful line but the editors at Harper did not think it as wonderful as I thought it! So it became something else.

That's just one point — this whole struggle for identity as a monk. Here's the other, and I'll be very brief. I think that, beginning in 1956, and I want to study this and maybe write something about it, Merton discovers a way of being an ecumenist in the broadest sense of the term. That is not only an ecumenist in respect of other Christians but an ecumenist in the sense of being in contact with the world and with the world's religions that I would call contemplative ecumenism. There are three instances of it in my journal. The first one is when he begins to read these wonderful Russian Orthodox writers who are publishing in French in Paris, mainly connected with the Academy of St Serge, the Seminary of St Serge — Paul Evdokimov, Vladimir Lossky and people of this nature. He has a paragraph in the journal which later gets reproduced in Conjectures in which he says, "I would like to be the person who reconciles, I would like by my study to reconcile the East and the West in my own heart by being appreciative..." And he's reading this stuff very critically. He gets a whiff of Gnosticism in Berdyaev but he has a great interest and a great tolerance for this. Parenthetically, I think it's connected to his great interest in sophianic themes, the theme of wisdom and so on which is also generating during this period.

Secondly, one of the reasons why he was interested in Latin America, and he writes this to Jaime Andrade, the man who makes the great statue of Our Lady of the Andes, he says, "I want you to make a figure of Our Lady that will move my novices to see that there is a larger America than North America, to reconcile North and South America, to give a great sense of identity for the Americas." So that was a second way and he thinks about this a great deal. It was also Jaime Andrade, by the way, who gives him the best advice about coming to Latin America. He said

> Your idea is not a good idea. The Catholic Church here is very reactionary and they wouldn't support what you want to do and all the intellectuals you want to talk to are Marxists and they hate the Church. It would be a fool's errand.

So that was the second thing. The third was his increasing correspondence with D.T. Suzuki and his interest in Zen Buddhism. Now again, parenthetically, I think his interest in Zen was not only because he thought it could teach him better contemplative methods but I think he also loved the aesthetic of Zen which was very much like the Cistercian aesthetic, very spare, almost an-iconic in a way. But as he begins to read Suzuki and he asks Suzuki to write an introduction to *Wisdom of the Desert*, (Suzuki writes it but it never gets edited with *Wisdom of the Desert*) Merton — and this is before the Second Vatican Council, says, "Gee, do I have to think of this person as a person who needs to be baptised in order to be saved?" He said "Am I not dealing with this person at a very deep level that is..." and you see a man struggling at a time when these were not fashionable issues and he says, "I can only enter the deepest dialogue with Suzuki as a dialogue of the contemplative or a dialogue of the heart."

So very briefly, maybe I've spoken too long, I would say this whole business of Gnostic, of what it means to be a monk...by the way, Paul Evdokimov, the Orthodox thinker, has a wonderful theory about interior monasticism which I think is a very interesting theme...that and this idea of contemplative ecumenism are the two great themes among many other themes that run through the journals. I would get irritated with Merton at times as I'm transcribing these things and wondering would I ever get done with them, but I would also say that it's a transforming experience to have been in his presence for the two years that I've worked on the journals.

VICTOR KRAMER

Volume Four: *Turning Toward the World*
Volume Five: *Dancing in the Water of Life*

I WANT TO CHANGE this subject just a little bit and say just a few things about these journals as journals which Merton, I think, pretty early on, was quite conscious of crafting, in a sense realising that he knew that these journals were most likely going to be published word for word. Now I need to give you just a tiny bit of background. I edited the period 1960 to 1963, *Turning Toward the World*, subtitled 'The Pivotal Years,' and I also need to say a few words about Volume Five which Robert Daggy edited, *Dancing in the Water of Life*.

In those journals, 1960 down to 1966, you have a Merton who is freer, a Merton who is able to write more, let us say, on his own, because his duties within the monastery are beginning to lessen and I think he has more time to think in terms of how he is going to write. In terms of how the seven volumes work together, the fourth one, 1960-63, is truly the pivotal moment in terms of the journals. Now, I had found a phrase within the journal: "...life moves on inexorably towards crisis and mystery..." and I had dreamt that we might call Volume Four 'Towards Crisis and Mystery.' Anyway the publishers wanted to call it by my subtitle *Turning Toward the World*. What I think is going on during this middle period is that he has worked through these years that Larry Cunningham was just talking about and I think that letter from Rome, that definitive letter saying 'You are going to stay put. That's it,' is a very important example of a moment where he's able just simply to say, 'OK, by virtue of obedience I will stay put. It's not necessary for me to go to Latin America. It's not necessary for me to do something else.' But it was necessary for him to work out how he was going to keep writing and simultaneously in some way as a writer turn toward the world and somehow to take this contemplative experience and figure out how to move that towards the world.

I want to talk about this decade just quickly, this decade in the middle, roughly 1953-1963 — which I think is the crucial middle period in his life where he is dealing first with what Professor Cunningham was talking about, the whole dilemma of what does it mean to be a contemplative, what does it mean to be a monk at this time and do you have to find a particular place or can you somehow make your place just where you happen to be, which is what he decided. But then once he's made that decision, he's still, because he is by instinct a writer, he's still trying to figure out how is he going to best write.

So what I want to do is just quickly go through some of these ideas and move towards the period which is in the middle, Volume Four, which covers 1960 through 1963. I want to say just a word about a few entries in the very middle of that book in December 1961 and January 1962. That's literally in the middle of the middle of these journals. If you read the journals through, the period between Christmas and January 1st is often a critical time for him because [it is a time when] he is kind of reassessing. As a kind of exercise I just looked at a few entries in that period — and you could also check this out at leisure in your own copy of Turning Toward the World.

Let me first just make a very quick point about the fact that we have, as editors, choosing titles, or choosing subtitles for divisions of each journal, probably created certain expectations on the part of the reader. You see Run to The Mountain, or Entering the Silence, or Turning Toward the World, or Learning to Love; and you figure that's what he's doing for those two or three years. I don't think it's ever quite that simple. It's very, very complicated and if, for example, you look at the journal for 1960-1963 –'my' journal — I call it 'mine' but it's his – and you watch what's going on, I headed the first year 'The Promise of the "Hermitage"' because he didn't even know what it was going to be. Was it going to be a meeting place for ecumenical conferences or was it going to be a place where he could live part-time or would it be a hermitage? Anyway, that's 1960, 'The Promise of a "Hermitage"' and it did finally end up being that but only many, many years later. I think I called the second section, 1961, 'The Need to Continue Questioning' — he might have the promise of a hermitage but he has to keep questioning. I called the third section, 1962, 'Seeking the Right Balance' — he realises he has to somehow combine whatever it is that he wants to do as a writer and what he wants to do as a contemplative and to combine these two things so that somehow he would not just be turned inward. I think there is something else going on in the Journals which is quite important and I think this is also true through most of Volume Three — and that is that this man is just constantly asking questions about himself. It's not exactly self-serving but you sometimes get very tired of it because he's constantly thinking what can I do about 'my' monastic vocation, 'my' vocation. And at some point, and it's probably already beginning in Volume Three, 1957/8/9, but gets stronger in the years to follow down through the middle sixties, he's forgetting about himself, he's not worrying about himself and he's thinking more in terms of what he can do to somehow turn towards the world. What I'd like to suggest is that we've imposed a structure on these journals and we could have the journals arranged in some other way.

If we just called them 'Father Louis's Journal' and arranged them in blocks according to the years in which he wrote them, you'd have a volume called 'Early Acceptance of Vocation,' you could have a volume 'Preparation for Ordination,' a volume, maybe 'Teaching Students' which would take you down through the Master of Scholastics period, and then a volume 'Guiding Novices.' Then you would have perhaps a volume beginning around 1963 which would be about writing about the world — as a monastic. You would have the period, 1964-5, about being a part-time solitary and then the seventh or eighth volume in this restructured, imagined way of publishing the journals in which you'd have him living full time as a hermit and full time distracted as a hermit. And finally you'd have the last year —'Traveller.' The point is that you wouldn't have these good titles that we've come up with and you wouldn't have the emphasis upon 'self.' You would have something that could be read differently. The journals wouldn't be so much our reading them as a record of what Merton does or encounters. They could be read then more as a kind of continual re-examination of what it means to be called to a dual vocation – silence and speaking – during this particular time in the United States.

Read this way, the journals would become much closer to Henry Adams's *Education of Henry Adams* where Henry Adams is writing about his life as an emblem of all lives. We would think of these journals much less than as a kind of record of observations. In other words, I think we've got something in the Journals which is much more crafted and much more sophisticated than what Henry David Thoreau did in his journals which is more or less a catalogue. Merton, I would maintain, is always selecting, selecting, selecting. Further, I think this becomes more and more obvious in the third and fourth volumes in which he becomes more conscious of the fact that every time he writes something down, he is going to be writing probably something that other people are going to read later. My point is that we don't have a diary here, we have very careful selections. We have a man who is becoming aware of the fact that he is selecting and therefore he is also becoming aware of the fact that he is responsible for choosing the words or crafting the sentences a certain way and so you've got a journal which is working on many, many different levels. This gets complicated by the fact that he really does feel a responsibility to move towards the world. You get a combination of all these things. I think it probably shows up best in Volumes Four and Five, because that's where he pivots, that's where he moves, but that's where he becomes more and more aware of the contemplative need.

In Volume Five, *Dancing in The Waters of Life*, you've got a straight chronology which Bob Daggy edited but you've also got two other things there. From another journal, he put in the visit that Merton made to New York City to visit D. T. Suzuki which is not part really of the journals proper but it's made to fit within Volume Five. In the same way, Bob Daggy includes the rough draft for an essay called 'Day of a Stranger.' Technically neither one of those are pure journal but they fit nicely into Volume Five. So again we're kind of giving a story and maybe what we need to be aware of is that Merton was very conscious of giving himself a story which is a very complicated one. Now, if you go and look at December/January 1961/2, you've got about fifteen good entries — you don't have a daily record, in a month you've got about ten good entries, usually. So you look at what's going on and it's very, very interesting.

In that period, mid-December 1961 to 1962, he's asking all kinds of questions about what's wrong with the world, how can he write about peace, why is he so disturbed, is he going to be delated again, somebody's reported him to the Abbot General, is he going to be able to write, what does it mean to write in these circumstances. This is during the Christmas season. He reads a prayer from the Nocturne office. He's amazed at what he sees there and he thinks about Christ's presence. He says the peace of Christ is here right now, right here. My job is not to preach about peace but to somehow be peaceful. But he keeps thinking about preaching. He keeps thinking about whether he is going to be censored...is he going to figure out a way to publish and so on.

And I was reading, and this is a quick parenthesis, the letters between J. Laughlin and Merton and this is very interesting. If you look at the same period, December/January, 1961/62, and you look at the letters that he is writing to his poetry editor, Laughlin, there is a wonderful long letter written in December where in effect he is writing to Laughlin and he is saying what am I going to do and can you help me figure out a way to publish essays which would have to do with issues of peace and of war and so on. Then you work through that period of December, just those few weeks. It's very interesting because he remains disturbed and unhappy with himself and with the world. But then he'll read Julian of Norwich and he says everything I need to know is right here — (December 27th 1961). Or you look at December 31st 1961, he says life is madder, madder and madder and he's about ready to give up. Then you look at the entries for January 2nd, 3rd and 9th, 1962, he's full of energy, not about publishing projects but about the beauty he sees right there in the monastery. He keeps turning to this 'peace' idea, peacefulness and how he can be peaceful. He, for example, at one point takes the word *majestas*, majesty, the Glory of God, and he then meditates just on that one word.

Now my theory, and it's just a theory, is that you could take these two months and you could watch this kind of roller-coaster event, up and down, and that's an example of how he's working just in two months. And you could do the same thing for Volume Four as a whole, 1960-63, up and down. And what you've got is a writer who's becoming more and more conscious of the fact that he has to somehow write because people are going to read this word for word later and he's going to have to write in such a way that it's interesting and therefore he's not going to put anything in the journal that isn't going to hold the reader's interest later.

There is a passage in Volume Three where he talks about what he's going to write, "I want to write a book about everything" and then he says that doesn't mean 'everything.' That means 'everything that somehow I've been involved in.' He talks about the cosmos and then almost immediately he talks about wilfulness. He says, "That's really the story," wilfulness; what he, Merton, chooses to do. So what I'm saying is that you've got a book, now seven books, which give us a story which he kind of structured, which we kind of re-structured as editors, but which is moving on many, many different levels. So it's not just *Turning Toward the World*, or *Dancing in the Water of Life*. I think it's the continual story of this monastic trying to figure out how he can remain contemplative while he's also thinking about all these relationships to the world. So you can run an experiment. You can just go and look at a little bit of December/January 1961/62. I think it all kind of comes together. But the same patterns are there in the earliest journal and I think they must also be there at the very end in the *Asian Journal*.

Christine Bochen

Volume Six: *Learning to Love*

I WAS THINKING ABOUT how different each of the approaches have been and I think mine will be different again, but in some ways responsive to all that I have heard. I wanted to share with you this afternoon something of the experience that I had in editing Volume Six, entitled *Learning to Love — Exploring Solitude and Freedom*. The volume covers the period from January of 1966 to October of 1967. It also includes by way of appendices two other works, one called 'A Midsummer Diary,' and the other a portion of Notebook 17, the first part of which is to be found in Volume Five. I've incorporated the segment dealing with the period from January until March. And so the volume sits as that.

I think you are aware of the fact that, as Victor was saying, Merton explored his relationship to the world now in a very different way and that is through the experience with one person. Most people picking up the volume, *Learning to Love*, will already be aware of the fact that in that volume Merton is speaking about a relationship most 'unmonkly' if we can call it that. And that is a very intimate and very intense relationship that occurred when he was hospitalised in April of 1966 and cared for there by a nurse with whom he fell in love. How well the cliché, of roller coaster fits because what we find in this volume is in fact an account of a relationship that raises him to the heights and brings him down to the depths. We find him elated and excited. We find him confused, bewildered, befuddled. And so it is a volume I think very much informed now by this relationship.

I'd like to say something about the work that I did as editor in selecting titles. I was working, essentially with one journal and so despite the fact that I agree with Victor's construction of the Journals and his recognition that there is a lead that each editor offers the reader, I think it is an important one and I have tried in offering the structure of that journal to be attentive to the cues and clues that I found in Merton's own text. And so I chose to describe and to introduce the four sections really with themes that I see emerging in each segment of the text. The first segment I call 'Being in One Place' and you will recall that Merton had rather recently moved to the hermitage – it was in the summer of 1965 – and he was in the first few months of 1966 tasting what he had longed for for so very long, actually since the time he went in to the monastery — a deeper silence and a deeper experience of solitude. He wrote in January of 1966, the end of the month: "...what matters is to love, to be in one place in silence..."

A wonderful quote. On the one hand it is, without Merton knowing it, a lead into the story that will unfold for him in the months that follow — what matters is to love. It is also a reminder that that love of which he speaks is not only the love of one particular other but the love to which he is called as monk and as Christian, the love which he experiences and tries to learn in the monastery which is the school of charity.

But he says "to be in one place in silence." Being in one place, as you have already been reminded, was not for Merton always an easy thing. Yes, physically and geographically he was rooted in this one place but if there is a vow with which he struggled, I think it is that of stability, the sense that there might have been another place, another way, another order, another location, in which he might be a more faithful monk. And so we see him in those first months of 1966 really dealing with now in a very intense way the challenge as well as the joy of solitude. It is certainly a joy. This is what he has wanted. And yet in that quiet and in that silence and in that solitude he encounters more than one demon. He has to sort out the experience of his own loneliness and he deals interestingly enough again with the Latin American temptation because once more there is the possibility of going to Latin America. Though he had resolved that issue years before, again there is just that little lead, a little hint that suggests, "Well maybe there..." But not for long. The hermitage was a place he would not easily have given up.

The second part of the Journal, entitled 'Daring to Love,' picks up on yet another few lines from Merton written in late April 1966, weeks after he met M.. And he writes, "I see more and more that there is only one realistic answer, love. I have got to dare to love and to bear the anxiety of self-questioning that love arouses in me until perfect love casts out fear." "I have got to dare to love."

That title 'Dare to Love' for the second section rose very easily from the page. It is in this segment that we deal with this relationship that Merton had with the woman referred to in the volume as 'M.' We see Merton enthused, excited, elated with this relationship. We also see him struggling to make sense of it, for certainly there is, in this, a contradiction. The contradiction is not love itself but a love which invites a kind of exclusivity of relationship which he had chosen to set aside when he became a monk. And so he is in this experience of a somewhat compromised solitude, if we might refer to it in that way, trying to deal with the simple, spontaneous total love that he has experienced for the very first time.

I have had the opportunity to give several interviews to newspaper and radio folk and inevitably the questions lead to the nature of the relationship and people are not too cheerfully disposed when I try to redirect the questions. I think that there is a way in which people come to this text preoccupied, if you want to say it, with the physicality of the relationship, whereas what I find striking and what I think is so present in Merton's experience is an intimacy he knows for the first time. And when I say 'intimacy,' I am referring to that sense of being known and knowing another and sensing that one is accepted as one is in a relationship. For Merton this was a new thing.

You will remember perhaps if you read Volume Five that, as he moved into those later years, he often reflected on an earlier period in his life, a period in which his relationships with women were hardly exemplary. And there was something of unfinished business there. For what he was discovering in this new relationship was something that he had not experienced, or let himself experience, before, and that is to open himself to the experience, to the sense of, intimacy. I think that readers will find this particular section reflecting some of the struggle and maybe more than a little bit irked with Merton who does revisit ground on occasion, moving back and forth ...and we move with him. Sometimes, some have said, in a way that makes you simply want to say, "Cut it out! Come on, let's get on with it..." And yet what I think we have here, even though we have some-one writing for an audience in one sense, is an individual, as he is writing, clarifying for himself where he stands.

By September of 1966, encouraged by the abbot who helped Merton to clarify where he stood, and also by his own sense of coming to terms with what was possible and what was not, we really see him moving to another period. And I decided to break the jour-nal with yet another subtitle at that point. I used the subtitle, 'Living Love in Solitude.' Merton was, at that point, trying to reconcile a relationship now transformed but not abandoned, and I think he was honestly trying to see how it was that he could carry the best of that intimacy, that sense of having loved someone and being loved by that person, into a new time and period in his life. We see him accepting responsibility for some of his behaviour which was again perhaps not exemplary, sometimes perhaps even petty, sometimes devious, sometimes informed by illusion rather than by clarity of truth. But in this period that sense of who he is really and the life to which he is committed come clearly into focus for him.

The fourth period, the fourth segment of the Journal, is entitled 'A Life Free From Care.' This time I was drawing on a metaphor that Merton used in the last talk that he gave to the novices before he moved into the hermitage. I was really impelled to capture that metaphor of a life without care by his resolve on December 31st 1966 to get his life back in right order. That sense of right order didn't necessarily mean as it might for me cleaning up my room or sorting that pile of papers which always seems to elude me but rather the 'right order' in the largest sense, being faithful now to what he saw to be his call and vocation and recognising that he must free himself from a kind of attachment and place his life in the providence of God. That is essentially a life lived without care. It doesn't necessarily mean carefree and free of responsibility, but it means a life rightly ordered. And we find Merton in 1967 returning to the norm, or to the normal, such as that might be for Merton, not necessarily our normal. But it is here that we see once again a very strong working writer, a very intense reader – this is the period in which he immerses himself in Camus for example – and we see that those references, very nice for an editor, which might have been lacking when he was so absorbed in this relationship, references to ideas and to what he is reading, now reassert themselves once more. We find Merton also, in this period, becoming increasingly aware of his own mortality, perhaps another turn of someone at mid-life. He's lost a few friends who have died and the message is not lost on him. So he has a certain sense, according to those last pages of 1967, that life is not without its end.

I won't speak at this point about Midsummer Diary except to say that it's one of those teacher tricks. I'm not going to talk about this but, in not talking, let me say Midsummer Diary is really what I have described as partly journal, partly love letter, that Merton wrote during a week in June. The relationship with M. was still intense and he not only recounts there something of what is in his heart at the time, but also, I think, writes some very profound and provocative things about the nature of solitude. I've often wondered what it would have been like for M. to receive this piece. The part love letter might have worked. The part journal reflection would have been a bit more mystifying. But it is a text, I think, which fits alongside the journal for 1966 and 1967.

I wanted to share with you two other things, if I may. One has to do with the nature of the handwriting. His got worse and mine has also. I have confessed in some other settings that I received the manuscript of this journal in 1993. I was working on the index for the volume of letters entitled *The Courage for Truth* and I could hardly finish that index because I wanted to get into reading the manuscript. But I have to tell you that when it first came I sat there, I think as any of us might have, kind of awed by the experience that I was really encountering a text raw. I mean I was seeing the thing that Merton had written once removed by photo-copying machine. And for a while I just sat there with this stuff on my lap thinking, you know, there's an issue here – an issue of relationship – because I knew what was in it. The fact that the story that I would read would not only be Merton's story but also M.'s. I trod a little lightly into the manuscript, reading a bit here and a bit there, but I finally settled on the fact that I could not, looking at the text, sit between it and in front of a computer or I would lose my mind. So I decided to rewrite the manuscript in my own hand. Now people who know my handwriting quickly said,"Christine, that is not progress!" But I have to tell you that I don't regret doing it because, as I did, I felt that story unfold. I felt that I had learned how to live with that journal a bit and to enjoy it as a reader not simply as a frantic typist. So for me that was a very good way to approach the text.

PATRICK HART OCSO

Volume Seven: *The Other Side of the Mountain*

THE OTHER SIDE OF the Mountain is not the title we chose nor was it Merton's title. Merton had chosen 'The Hawk's Dream' from Robertson Jeffers, a poem that he wrote, and he said that this should be the title for this volume but Harper Collins in San Francisco says it wouldn't fly. So we ended up with *The Other Side of The Mountain* which is very good because, as we'll find out from the text, very early on in the Asian Journal he has a quote:

> Last night I had a curious dream about Kanchenjunga. I was looking at the mountain and it was pure white, absolutely pure, especially the peaks that lie to the west. And I saw the pure beauty of their shape and outline, all in white and I heard a voice, saying – or got the clear idea of, 'There is another side to the mountain.'

and then he continues

> The full beauty of the mountain is not seen until you too consent to the impossible paradox. It is and is not. Nothing more need be said. The smoke of ideas clears and the mountain is seen.

It is autobiographical as far as I can see. So the seventh volume, like the first, was written in various notebooks and he was travelling as we know. The first was...he was in Cuba and Perry Street and St. Bonaventure's, so we had to put together three or four notebooks. The same can be said with the last of the journals.

It opens with the election of an abbot. The very beginning is dated the last months of 1967. There was the prospect of a new abbot with the resignation of Dom James Fox and Merton feared for the worst. He thought that one of the more conservative candidates would get elected which would mean the end of his hermitage, perhaps, or the end of his writing. So he had all sorts of worries and he just wasn't sure. But he did end up being a kingmaker. His candidate became abbot and it was Abbot Flavian Burns and of course Flavian was one of his students and they got along very well together. In fact Flavian had been a hermit and he was recalled from the hermitage to become abbot but he said he would accept it only for five years. He thought that if you can't do it in five years, you'll never do it. So he had five years as abbot and then retired.

But the first thing, I would say the most important thing that he did was, and perhaps Merton realised this, was that Flavian would give him some latitude and perhaps the chance to travel after all these years. And so Dom Jean Leclercq had arranged for an invitation, that he should come to Bangkok in Thailand where the Far Eastern superiors, the abbots and abbesses, mainly Cistercian and Benedictine, were meeting. And so he thought it would be a good idea for him to get a feel of Tibetan Buddhism especially. He had been in contact with Harold Talbott through Dom Aelred Graham of Ampleforth, who had put him in touch with a lot of his friends, which was very helpful. He began planning this trip to the Far East and making preparations for it. He had to take his shots and so forth, get his visa, and, above all, get some clothes to travel in. So he managed with Frank O'Callaghan's help to engage in purchasing some jackets and coats that he could put lots of film in and carry his camera because he was planning to document this trip with photographs. Laughlin had said if you do a book like the *Asian Journal*, we can publish it and we can defray the expenses of your trip. So I think he had a travel credit card or something from J. Laughlin to help expenses. One night, before he left, after he had had dinner at the Embassy Club with Frank and Tommie [O'Callaghan] and Ron and Sally Seitz, he went over with the Franciscan friars from St. Bonaventure's where the Merton Center used to be and was watching football. The Green Bay Packers had just beaten the Dallas Cowboys and Merton comments that it was 'damn good football.' He goes on to say:

> Football is one of the really valid and deep American rituals. It has a religious seriousness which American religion can never achieve, a comic contemplative dynamism, a gratuity, a movement from play to play, a definitiveness that responds to some deep need, a religious need. A sense of meaning that is at once final and provisional. A substratum of dependable regularity, continuity and an ever-renewed variety. Openness to new possibilities, new chances. It happens. It is done.

I was completely surprised. It was an autobiographical statement of Merton's life as a monk.

Anyway as the days grew closer to his time for leaving he was naturally excited about the prospect. First in May he took a little trip, a kind of experimental trip. I think Flavian wanted to see how he would handle travel in the States before he sent him overseas. So he went to New Mexico and then out to visit the Trappistines of Redwoods out along the California coast and he was looking for a possible site for a hermitage. Flavian had said 'You can have a hermitage far away from Gethsemani but it has to be in the United States. I don't want to be travelling to India or wherever. So he was looking in New Mexico, Christ in the Desert, then along the California coast as well as in Alaska. The Archbishop there was showing him various sites. He didn't especially like the grizzly bears as companions. However he was keeping all that at the back of his mind. He was going to Asia with the idea of returning and discussing the future with Flavian. People often said that he had no intention of coming back with which I completely disagree. He had every intention of returning and working things out because he had an abbot that he could talk to and would listen to his ideas. It doesn't mean that Flavian always agreed, but he would listen to Louie.

So he was off and I think that at the take-off, he says, "I am going home to the home I have never been in this body, where I have never been in this washable suit." He was excited and I remember he refers to the take-off as 'ecstatic' and meanwhile, when he was at the hermitage, he would look at the planes and he would be denouncing their sound barrier booms but once he got on board, he said it was like a pirouette, dancing on the runway ready for the take-off. He stopped in Honolulu and then went on to Calcutta where the poverty really hit him. But he was critical too. He was impressed by the people he met. But he met one Swami whom he said reminded him of Groucho Marx, manifesting contempt for his competitors. Merton comments, "Even his Kleenex is saffron." Merton noticed the detail. So he stopped in New Delhi and of course the great peak experience, I think, was those three interviews he had with the Dalai Lama. There were three hours they spent and they got to know one another very well on the deepest level. It was through Harold Talbott of course who stayed with him and managed to get a good translator. He had his first audience on November 4th, 1968 and then he returned on the 6th for a second, and then on the 8th for a third which, he says, was in many ways the best. By then, they knew each other very well and the Dalai Lama felt the same way. In fact, in the Dalai Lama's autobiography *Freedom in Exile*, he speaks of Merton as being the first Christian who introduced him to the beauties of Christianity. So it was a breakthrough for the Dalai Lama. They learned from one another.

So finally after Madras, Merton ends up in Bangkok and in his last entry in his journal, just two days before his death he writes to one of the monks,

> I think of all of you on this Feast Day and with Christmas approaching, I feel homesick for Gethsemani. But I hope to be at least in a monastery Rawa Seneng [in Indonesia] and then I look forward to being at our monastery in Hong Kong and maybe seeing our three volunteers there. No more for the moment. Best love to all, Louie.

Of course he never did get to Hong Kong nor to Indonesia as he had planned. Meanwhile he writes these lines in the Oriental Hotel in Bangkok just minutes before he left for the Red Cross Head-quarters on the outskirts of the city. By Christmas he was, after all, back at Gethsemani lying beside and along the abbey church, overlooking the woodlands and knobs that had become so familiar to him during his twenty seven years of monastic life at Gethsemani.

THOMAS MERTON
poet • monk • prophet

MAIN CONFERENCE ADDRESSES

ROWAN WILLIAMS

ESTHER DE WAAL

M. BASIL PENNINGTON OCSO

New Words for God:
Contemplation and Religious Writing

ROWAN WILLIAMS

I F YOU LOOK IN Merton's work for definitions of poetry or of the
poetic, you may sometimes be a little disappointed. As theologians
have often found, it is quite difficult to give positive definitions of
what matters most. You may find yourself defining more clearly by
negations, by saying what you're not talking about. And what I want
to begin with this morning is four areas which Merton identifies as
the sort of thing that poetry isn't.

And as a way of finding a path into what he thinks about
contemplation, I think this has its value. You'll see why, I hope. I'm
relying here mostly on two quite familiar pieces, both reprinted in
Raids on the Unspeakable: 'The Message to Poets' of 1964,[1] the short essay
that was read at a meeting of Latin American poets in Mexico City in
February of that year; and the 'Answers on Art and Freedom'[2] from
around the same time, also written for a Latin American audience.

Both texts clearly lay out not only what poetry isn't, but what it is
that poetry is against.

First of all, poetry isn't, and is against, magic. Poetry is not about
words that work. 'It is the businessman, the propagandist, the
politician, not the poet, who devoutly believes in the magic of words,'
writes Merton; 'For the poet, there is precisely no magic, there is
only life in all its unpredictability and all its freedom. All magic is a
ruthless venture in manipulation, a vicious circle, a self-fulfilling
prophecy.' Words that work, independent of their transparency to
truth, are magical words. They live without anchorage in reality. They
exist in order to exercise power, to control or develop a situation
according to the will of the speaker.

Of course, there is an immediate relevance here to some of the
unforgettable essays that Merton wrote in the middle sixties about
the language of war, which for him was a cardinal example of

magical language. You speak about war in such a way that the reality of conflict or of suffering is occluded. You speak about war in a way whose sole purpose is to create a consciousness like yours, another will projecting itself into the void. But I think too that Merton is casting a sidelong glance at some sorts of poetic self-consciousness, in the malign sense of the phrase, a poetic style that becomes self-referential, inclusive only of self. *That* sort of poetic freewheeling can be licensed as a parody of the unspeakable language of the state, 'The Ogre,' as W.H. Auden would have called it; but it isn't of itself the essence of poetry. And you might compare some remarks in 'Answers on Art and Freedom' on formalism...'a meaningless cliché devised by literary and artistic gendarmes...a term totally devoid of value or significance as are all the other cultural slogans invented in the   police station.'[3]

Poetry then may at times be parodic and playful in order to show up what magical language is like, to expose the evils of the magical language of the state, or the military machine, or the police station. And somewhere in the background here is an allusion ringing off to Auden's short poem, already mentioned, written in 1968 after the invasion of Czechoslovakia. It's about 'the Ogre' striding across a plain covered with ruin and darkness. The Ogre has mastered everything except speech.

> The Ogre stalks with hands on hips
> While drivel gushes from his lips. [4]

I think Merton's 'Unspeakable' and Auden's 'Ogre' have a good deal in common with each other.

Poetry isn't, and is against, magic and therefore, more generally, poetry isn't, and poetry is against, being useful, particularly that usefulness which we think of in terms of moralism. Here again, I'm turning to the Message to Poets:

> Let us not be like those who wish to make the tree bear its fruit first and the flower afterwards. A conjuring trick and an advertisement. We are content if the flower comes first and the fruit afterwards in due time. [5]

Useful moral poetry is an adjunct to something else. It might be there or it might not. Poetry isn't and can't be decorative in that way and in that sense it's never simply rhetoric. It is never simply about persuading someone to do something, or to think something. However significant the purpose, however good the end, poetry that is about defined goals, poetry that is functional, an advertisement, is

betraying itself. And that phrase, 'a conjuring trick and an advertisement' is very telling. Poetry which is an advertisement is poetry
whose point is not in itself. This means that authentic poetry is labour,
it's work, the doing of something which has its own integrity.

This leads me on to the third thing which poetry isn't and poetry
is against. Poetry is against any focus on the artist rather than the
work. To focus on the artist rather than the work is to draw our
attention precisely to the manipulating, controlling will that is the
enemy of all really truthful utterance. And I find myself turning, not
wholly accidentally, once again to W.H. Auden. Auden, as many of
you will know, was already a most austere critic of his
contemporaries' poetry when he was an undergraduate, and there is
a fine anecdote of an early encounter with Stephen Spender, who
burst into Auden's room one day to say that he intended to be a poet
when he grew up. Auden said, "You mean you don't want to write
poetry?"

This same emphasis comes out in a quite early letter to Mark Van
Doren, written in March 1948:

> I can no longer see the ultimate meaning of a man's life in terms of
> either "being a poet" or "being a contemplative" or even in a certain
> sense "being a saint," (although that is the only thing to be). It must be
> something much more immediate than that. I – and every other person
> in the world – must say "I have my own special peculiar destiny which
> no one else has had or ever will have. There exists for me a particular
> goal, a fulfilment which must be all my own – nobody else's – & it does
> not really identify that destiny to put it under some category —"poet,"
> "monk," "hermit." Because my own individual destiny is a meeting,
> an encounter with God that He has destined for me alone. His glory in
> me will be to receive from me something which He can never receive
> from anyone else. [6]

There is in this, of course, some of the ambiguous individualism
that shadows a good deal of early and middle Merton, but the point
stands. 'Being a poet,' 'contemplative' or whatever is not what it's
about, because this can direct attention once again to the will and
psyche of the artist constructing a self. And there is a fundamental
sense in which the will is inimical to art.

Finally then, the fourth thing that poetry isn't, and poetry is against,
is any sense of the self and its awareness that indulges the notion that
we have indefinite choices. Poetry is against the romanticism of a
will whirling in the void.

> The artist must not delude himself, [writes Merton in *Answers on Art and Freedom*], that he has an infinite capacity to choose for himself and a moral responsibility to exercise this unlimited choice, especially when it becomes absurd.

> If he does this then let him take my word for it. He will find himself with the same problem and in the same quandary as those monks who have vegetated for three centuries in a moral morass of abstract voluntarism. [7]

The sense of indefinite choice, that the artist is someone with an infinite well of creativity that simply has to be activated in selecting what is to be uttered, focuses our attention once again on the role not the work, because work is always about finite choices. Labour is to do this rather than that and to engage in the discipline and the limits of doing this rather than that. Work, labour, involves local commitment and specificity. Work is what has to be done in this moment, here and now, by this person, in the 'encounter' Merton speaks of in the letter to Mark Van Doren.

He speaks of 'this unique instant' in terms of 'the sense of water on the skin'[8] a very powerful image. The poet acts, works, in that moment of contact with truth. And in another of the letters, this time to Sister Thérèse Lentfoehr, written in 1948, where he was obviously thinking quite a bit about this business of role and labour, he writes:

> With me, I know what the trouble is. I come upon a situation and the situation seems to require a poem. So I write a poem. But the poem turns out to be not the precise, individual poem which that specific situation had demanded from all eternity but just "a poem." A generic poem by Thomas Merton that is something like all the other poems by Thomas Merton and which he drags out of his stock to fit on every situation that comes along. That is why *Figures for an Apocalypse* is a whole string of complete misses. All I can say is that the arrows were in the general direction of some target or other but I'd be hard put to it to connect the firing with the real object that was there to be fired at. [9]

You'll forgive me, I hope, for quoting Auden just one more time. Auden in his prose reflections on *Dichtung und Wahrheit*, (Poetry and Truth),[10] speaks of the poem that presents itself and to which you have to say 'Too late, my dear' and the one that comes along to which you have to say 'Not yet.' 'Be a son of this instant,' writes Merton again in one of the texts reprinted in *Raids on the Unspeakable*, this time one of the texts which emerge from his meditation on the Sufi mystic, Ibn Abbad, 'Be a son of this instant.'

So there are the four enemies of poetry; and a writing that avoids and resists those temptations and distortions will be, I want to suggest, religious writing. Now I hope you'll understand that as I develop these reflections, I'm using this phrase, 'religious writing,' to describe not writing about religious things but writing that is a religious activity; because what we have just been looking at, the four things that poetry isn't, provides us with one way into understanding what writing might be when it is a religious labour. A writing that resists magic and will in their various disguises is writing that will allow truth, allow God. Or to put it still more theologically it is writing that aligns my action with *what is being done* in my environment. This, I hope you'll see, is something totally different from passivity. Aligning one's action with what is being done in the environment is different from sitting there and saying 'let me be done things to.' It is to require from me that most demanding of all activities, the weaving in of my action with the action, the act, that is at work around me in the universe: not passivity, but an attempt, (to misuse the popular and rather horrible phrase), to be where action is. When we speak colloquially of 'being where the action is,' that's mostly the most appallingly trivial kind of aspiration we could have. Religious writing, poetry that is authentic religious writing, writing that is religious work, is very *precisely* an attempt to be where the action is, God's action, where *this* reality, me, my words, my perception, meet what is fundamental, God — the encounter spoken of in the letter to Mark Van Doren.

So that 'being a son of this instant' in the phrase Merton adapts from Ibn Abbad, 'is encountering and entering into that elusive 'there before us' quality of God's action, that active reality, or, indeed, to use the scholastic language which was not at all alien to Merton's thinking, that 'pure act' which is beyond both memory and fantasy, the active 'being' of the world now, in this moment. Religious writing is an open door to what God is doing in making and loving the universe — which of course God does in every moment. Religious writing, writing that is religious work, is part of our attunement to the doing of God, made real and concrete here in how we see and how we attend: a loving and acting, a perceiving without egotistic will, but without passive resignation.

Now it is that attunement to the 'pure act' of God that seems to me to be fundamental, in the last analysis, to all that Merton says about the activity of poetic writing. But it is precisely there that you touch the unity of what Merton has to say about poetry and what Merton has to say about contemplation. I don't think I need to labour the point too much, but in order to come around at it by another route, I'm going to step back a little and look at one or two of the things which the tradition tells us about contemplation. I'm going to look at St. John of the Cross for a moment, and particularly at a passage which grows and grows in my imagination as the years go by, in a passage in *The Ascent of Mount Carmel,* where St. John describes the process of contemplation, the process of growth into God's fullness, as a total restructuring of our inner life. Memory, understanding and will are transformed into hope, faith and love." The renewed self or heart or imagination which has embarked upon the contemplative journey becomes *hopeful.* It becomes open to God's future. It becomes faithful; that is it becomes trustful in what it can't perceive and control. It becomes lovingly attentive to the truth. All very splendid; and the bad news is, of course, that this entails the blockage and frustration of the ways in which our human faculties habitually work, the Night of the Senses and of the Spirit; because in this process the ordinary objects of memory, understanding and will disappear. That's to say, my awareness of myself, the way I build up a picture of myself from memory, self-perception, becomes blurred. I don't know quite who I am. My understanding meets a brick wall. I don't know what I am supposed to be engaging with. And my will goes completely down the drain, because there is no way in which I can impose what I want or prefer on the situation I am in. My only way through is for memory, understanding and will to become hope, faith and love. And it strikes me that this dismantling of the imagination and its reconstructing by the gift of God in darkness is by no means distant from what Merton has to say about overcoming the false poetic consciousness, about what poetry isn't, and what it's against.

Memory can be the conscious self-indulgence of a role, the clear sense of who and what I am. I am 'a poet'— and, one of these days, I'll get around to writing some poetry. False poetic activity is about justifying what is being done, being useful, getting people to do things, to have the right ideas and do the right actions. Faith is about justification by God and by Grace. The will can turn in on its own fantasies of being a kind of creative abyss out of which come constant, endless, infinite new things; and this will must be translated into the labour of love, attention to the instant, to what God does now.

It seems to me then that Merton probably could not have written precisely what he did about true and false poetry without, at the back of his mind, some very deep awareness of what the contemplative transformation involved. All real poets know that. Merton had read his John of the Cross, of course; and knew it better than most; so that, at the heart of what I want to say is that we will understand best the point of contact, the point of convergence between Merton on poetry and Merton on contemplation when we put side by side Merton's negative theology of poetry as expressed in the 'Message to Poets' and the negative vision of John of the Cross; both of them being about attunement to the act of God there before you in every instant, the act of God which neither memory nor fantasy, neither images of the past nor images of the future can capture; the act of God which can only be apprehended by a particular kind of costly openness, that refuses the comforts of memory and the comforts of fantasy in order to 'be' where we are.

And from that new imagination come 'New Words for God.' That bit of my title is more ambiguous than I realised it was when I suggested it. Obviously new words for God emerge from this process because, on the far side of what I have been talking about, God's act can be spoken of in and by my attunement to it, by words that make room for attention; which is why God is spoken of, and spoken for, or indeed just spoken, precisely in writing that has no explicitly religious content, because of the character of the writing as a labour of the instant. 'New words for God' then, on the far side of the negative theology, will be words that have room for the act of reality, the 'there-before-us' reality which is God's act in the present moment. And the religious writing that is, in the more obvious sense, words for God, will be precisely those words that escape the prisons, or the possible prisons, of memory and fantasy as we often use those categories.

Equally though, 'New Words for God' could be understood in a rather different sense. The poet and/or contemplative becomes herself a new word for God. In the act of challenge and suspension of the will, of the controlling ego, the life, the concrete identity of the poet and the contemplative, becomes itself Word, becomes itself a communication. It is God acting. Merton's own interest in the Eastern Christian tradition justifies some connections to be made here between this vision of the poet and the contemplative and the deep-rooted Eastern Christian idea that the 'logos' of each item in the universe is the utterance of the Logos of God in a particular and unique way. And I think back again to the letter to Mark Van Doren...

> [God's] glory in me will be to receive from me something he can never receive from anyone else because it is a gift of his to me which he has never given to anyone else and never will.[12]

We are to be 'new words for God' in that sense. And we are here celebrating Merton partly because of the belief, which I think most Christians share, that the lives of certain people will become, in a very particular sense, 'words for God.' This life, this identity, this face, this voice, this tonality of being, becomes a word for God to us, a word God addresses to us.

Poetry and contemplation, both identifying, sketching or pointing at what it might be for God to find words in the world, alike challenge other kinds of words for God, old words for God, safe words for God, lazy words for God, useful words for God. I taught Christian doctrine for many years and I'm not going to cut away the ladder on which I climbed; but it seems to me that Christian doctrine is there essentially in order that we may grasp how God acts in creating and transfiguring. Christian doctrine exists so that certain obstacles may be taken away to our openness to the action of God. We need Christian doctrine because we need some notion of what it is we are trying to be attuned to. Attunement to the void isn't very much use and out of that come other kinds of unspeakable language. But if doctrine doesn't make possible poetry and contemplation, then doctrine is a waste of time. It becomes purely and simply old, safe and useful. Which is where, (and this is not at all irrelevant to the matter of this conference), the poetic and contemplative touch the prophetic, because the prophetic is all about the diagnosis of dead words and false acts. And, if I may borrow a phrase that I used in another context recently, the prophetic task is to smell out death in a situation.

In conclusion: I've tried to sketch a negative theology of the poetic, and I've preferred that, as a way in, to a positive definition of the poetic not simply because I find Merton's positive definitions of the poetic occasionally a bit disappointing, but because most people who try to find words for God are likely to be more acutely aware of what it is they mustn't do than what it is they must do or say. This doesn't mean that we privilege inarticulacy or even silence. It does mean, though, that poetic and contemplative language, the struggle to find new words for God and to understand that the nature of religious writing, of writing as religious activity, is nothing if not a deeply self-critical enterprise, a living under judgement. But that is only another way of saying that these are activities which we can't begin to grasp or get any purchase on, without the vivid and sometimes frightening sense of what they are open to. The poet and the contemplative alike live under a very broad sky — which is sometimes a night sky. The attempt to build shelters or dig holes, the attempt to draw helpful charts of the sky which will allow you to find your way around, is a seduction that is always present. Perhaps the most important thing we can do if we are at all interested in the language of poetry and contemplation is to set up warning signs on our desks and our altars and our prie-dieux; yet to know at the same time that these are not warning signs telling us that about the punishments for making a mistake, but reminders of how very easily we become prisoners of the controlling will that we love and indulge — and how very bad prison is for any of us.

Notes and References

1. Thomas Merton, Raids on The Unspeakable [hereafter referred to as Raids] (Tunbridge Wells, Kent: Burns & Oates, 1977) pp. 118-124

2. Raids, op.cit. pp.125-135

3. Raids, op.cit., p.132

4. W.H.Auden: 'August 1968', Collected Poems, London: Faber & Faber, 1976, p.604

5. Raids, op.cit., pp.122-3

6. Thomas Merton, The Road to Joy: Letters to New and Old Friends ed. Robert E. Daggy [hereafter referred to as RTJ], (New York: Farrar, Straus & Giroux, 1989) Letter to Mark van Doren, March 30 1948, p.22

7. Raids, op.cit., p.133

8. Ibid., p.124

9. RTJ, op.cit., Letter to Sister Thérèse Lentfoehr, Nov.18 1948, p.189

10. W.H.Auden: 'Dichtung und Wahrheit' Collected Poems, London: Faber & Faber, 1976

11. The Ascent of Mount Carmel Bk.II c.vi.

12. RTJ, Letter to Mark van Doren, op.cit., p.22

Merton's Seeing Eye

ESTHER DE WAAL

W E ARE LOOKING AT Thomas Merton as monk, as poet, as prophet, and we could in fact go on and make that list much longer. This man eludes all categories. One might as well try to bottle fog, as his fellow monk Matthew Kelty said of him in a memorable epitaph after his death.

This is indeed one of the more extraordinary things about this extraordinary man: we all identify with him in so many differing ways and at so many different levels and different moments in our lives. It is as though we always manage to encounter the man we are looking for, are needing at any particular juncture.

My starting point now is the Merton of 1968. This is very appropriate in the year in which we remember that it was on December 10th, 1968 that he died in Bangkok. And if I start with the Merton of the *Asian Journal* that is particularly appropriate in my own life since this last year I have myself been both to the Philippines and to India. So I read again what it meant for Merton, the terms in which he undertook that journey, the frame of mind in which he set out, what it came to mean to him. In a prepared talk for Calcutta on monastic experience and East-West dialogue he said that he was not coming to India as research student or author, not to obtain information about other traditions, but as a pilgrim, to drink from the ancient sources of monastic vision and wisdom, not to learn more quantitatively but to learn more qualitatively, in order to become a better and a more enlightened monk. This asked of him that he learn from the East in terms of the East.

> "This exchange must take place under the true monastic condition of quiet, tranquillity, sobriety, leisureliness, reverence, meditation and peace – of nonhurrying and patient waiting."[1]

At first this eluded him. He catches the bewilderment that he feels in Calcutta (as any of us do for the first time in India) as he piles

up words, cascading words, which reflect his reaction in this
bewildering place.

> "How many purple flowers in the ponds. How many lotuses. How
> many long brick walls...all the cows and the slate-blue buffaloes...the
> sidewalk markets, the rickshaws, the fantastic and dowdy buildings,
> the tattered posters... Further and further into town. Buildings. Crowds.
> Rags, dirt, laughter, torpor, movement. Calcutta is overwhelming: the
> elemental city. with no room left for masks."[2]

This profusion of strange sight and sounds was also the first
impression of his visit to the Dalai Lama. Here he found a mountain
with a lot of miscellaneous dwellings, rocks, woods, farms, gulfs,
falls and heights. A succession of rimpoches each in his shrine-like
cell among tankas, flowers, bowls, rugs, lamps and images. [3]

How does one impose any sort of coherence? Any sort of
structure? At one point he uses the phrase "mandala awareness of
space." — he sees all this profusion gaining order from the seated
presences, burning with flame-like continuity, centres of awareness.

All this leads, as I think everything else in his life does, to that
encounter at Polonnaruwa. He gives us such a vivid picture of it as
he writes in the *Asian Journal* of setting out with the Vicar General
lagging behind, complaining, grumbling how much he dislikes
"paganism," saying that Merton will get better pictures in other places,
that the guides are all out to cheat them. The Vicar General represents
of course a total contrast to the sensitivity and openness of Merton,
who has taken off his shoes and is approaching barefoot: his is, in
contrast, the closed mind, and rather than see the statues he sits in
the shade and – what is so much less threatening – reads about them
in the guide book.

> I am able to approach the Buddhas barefoot and undisturbed, my feet
> in wet grass, wet sand. Then the silence of the extraordinary faces. The
> great smiles. Huge and yet subtle. Filled with every possibility,
> questioning nothing, knowing everything, rejecting nothing, the peace
> not of emotional resignation but of Madhyamika, of sunyata, that has
> seen through every question without trying to discredit anyone or
> anything - without refutation – without establishing some other argument.
> For the doctrinaire, the mind that needs well-established positions,
> such peace, such silence, can be frightening. I was knocked over with a
> rush of relief and thankfulness at the obvious clarity of the figures, the
> clarity and fluidity of shape and line, the design of the monumental
> bodies composed into the rock shape and landscape, figure, rock and

tree. And the sweep of bare rock sloping away on the other side of the hollow, where you can go back and see different aspects of the figures.

Looking at these figures I was suddenly, almost forcibly, jerked clean out of the habitual, half-tied vision of things, and an inner clearness, clarity, as if exploding from the rocks themselves, became evident and obvious...

The thing about all this is that there is no puzzle, no problem, and really no "mystery." All problems are resolved and everything is clear, simply because what matters is clear. The rock, all matter, all life. is charged with dharmakaya...everything is emptiness and everything is compassion. I don't know when in my life I have ever had such a sense of beauty and spiritual validity running together in one aesthetic illumination. Surely, with Mahabalipuram and Polonnaruwa my Asian pilgrimage has come clear and purified itself. I mean, I know and have seen what I was obscurely looking for. I don't know what else remains but I have now seen and have pierced through the surface and have got beyond the shadow and the disguise.[4]

Here Merton is showing us the qualities of dialogue, or openness. Here is his concern with light, with clarity. This is seeing through, seeing beyond, this is going beyond the half-tied vision of things. Everything, it seems to me, seems to lead up to this moment but perhaps most immediately those earlier journeys of 1968 which had taken him to the monastery of Christ in the Desert in New Mexico and to the sisters in the Redwoods in Northern California. We are shown this in what he wrote in *Woods, Shore, Desert*, the notebook that ends with the words: "Hang on to the clear light!"[5]

This is the end of a long journey which had begun when he entered Gethsemani on December 10th 1941, which was in itself the end of one journey, that restless searching, the wandering of the gyrovague. Then he was able to start another journey, the true, the interior journey, which is the real journey. This was a journey from a centred place, from rootedness, from the sense of belonging. Place is a vital element in the Benedictine and Cistercian traditions. Vital for they live under the vow of stability, and stability means being grounded "in one good place" as Merton himself put it so felicitously. A recent book by a monk of Gethsemani, Francis Kline, now abbot of another Cistercian house at Mepkin, is called *Lovers of the Place*, and at one point he writes this:

Taming the heart requires a sense of place. It roots not just the mind to a set of principles, but also the body to a piece of land. Each has an

important lesson to teach the other. Spiritual doctrine remains in the
head and not in the heart unless it is lived out in time in a given place.[6]

He then goes on to say:

> The heart of course also has its learning and longing beyond any given
> place, and looking beyond itself to God, becomes the place where God
> comes to dwell for longer and longer periods — so that the place
> becomes a garden, one in which the contemplative life grows. Not so
> much a translocation as a transformation of the same ground.

Merton found himself planted in a place of great beauty, and he
was profoundly aware of its beauty and its significance. He looked
outside himself, he looked beyond, and we can see both visually and
in words, in his photographs and in his writing, how he saw: his
awareness of shape and texture, of the relationships of things, above
all, his awareness of the play of light and dark, the play of shadow.
Everything in his monastic life built on what was already there in his
earliest years as the son of artist parents who had chosen, as Cezanne
did, to live in the south of France. On the very first page of *Seven Storey
Mountain* he wrote

> My father painted like Cezanne and understood the southern French
> landscape as Cezanne did. His vision of the world was sane, full of
> balance, full of veneration for structure, for the relations of masses and
> for all the circumstances that impress an individual identity on each
> created thing. His vision was religious and clean, and therefore his
> paintings were without decoration or superfluous comment, since a
> religious man respects the power of God's creation to bear witness for
> itself.[7]

When he was ten he lived for two years with his father, now a
widower, in the amazing small French town of St. Antonin, and again
he wrote almost lyrically of the experience of living in a small
medieval town where everything seemed to converge on the church,
where the spire of the church was inescapable wherever one was,
where the whole shape of the town and its surrounding landscape
seemed to be showing a contemplative vision.

> Here, everywhere I went, I was forced by the disposition of everything
> around me to be always at least virtually conscious of the church...The
> whole landscape, unified by the church and its heavenward spire, seemed
> to say: this is the meaning of all created things: we have been made for
> no other purpose than that men may use us in raising themselves to
> God, and in proclaiming the Glory of God... Oh what a thing it is to live

in a place that is so constructed that you are forced, in spite of yourself,
to be at least a virtual contemplative!"[8]

His Cistercian life deepened this sense of awareness of the visual.
For the counterpart to stability is non-attachment: the monastic knows
that this land is not for this generation but for generations to come:
there can be no sense of possession or ownership, but of
detachment. And with this goes a sense of listening to the land on its
own terms, letting it speak in its own voice, and as a result seeing
more acutely into the heart, the true essence. This is mindfulness,
attentiveness, awareness, which is found in all monastic traditions,
Christian or not. It is brought home daily to the Cistercian monk or
nun as they start each day with the office of vigils, whose name is in
itself a reminder of the urgent need to be vigilant, watchful, awake,
aware. It prevents going through life half awake and half asleep, with
the "half-tied vision." It is also symbolic in that it starts in the dark
and is a daily movement from darkness to light, from death to new
life.

Merton was himself never an artist as were Ruth or Owen. Yet he
had the opportunity to express himself visually as a result of a
fortuitous – or a God-Given – accident after the journalist, John
Howard Griffin, came to visit him at the hermitage bringing his
camera. Merton showed such a childlike delight in it that Howard
Griffin let him have it on loan and so Merton began to take
photographs. He approached this with that sense of reverence and
respect which is so fundamental to what the Rule of St Benedict has
to say about the handling of matter and of material things. Howard
Griffin also noticed a parallel with the way in which Merton handled
people, all those streams of people who came to visit him and talk
with him. He focused on them, gave them his full attention, so that
nothing seemed to be held back, and yet left them free to be their
own selves. He did not try to control, to manipulate, to alter the
other to fit his concepts. Already in 1948, in one of his earliest
expeditions to Louisville, he is writing of how he sees people in the
streets (a passage which is an anticipation of that more familiar
passage when he found himself standing on the corner of Fourth
and Walnut)

'I found that everything stirred me with a deep and mute sense of
compassion. Perhaps some of the people we saw going about the streets
were hard and tough — but I did not stop to observe it because I

seemed to have lost an eye for the merely exterior details and to have discovered, instead, a deep sense of respect and love and...I went through the city realising for the first time in my life... how much value people have in the sight of God.[9]

Loving and seeing, seeing and loving — Dante would say that seeing comes first: "The state of blessedness is based in the act of seeing, not of loving, which comes second." But the vital thing is seeing, not just looking — a distinction which sometimes has to be learnt, as his young friend Ron Seitz discovered as, each with their cameras, he and Merton walked through the woods...

> Tom would see me walking along in front of him, and stopping to hold my camera to my eye, snap, then move quickly someplace else and snap, always turning my head around looking for something to snap again and again, here and there, almost anywhere.
>
> "Stop! Stop!...enough. You take more pictures in an hour than Ansel Adams (you know him?) takes in a month — maybe two or three a day if you're lucky and something finds you... Hold up a minute, let's try something, maybe talk about just what..."
>
> And Tom would go on to teach me, when photographing (or any other time, for that matter), to stop looking and to begin seeing! — Because looking means that you already have something in mind for your eye to find; you've set out in search of your desired object and have closed off everything else presenting itself along the way. But seeing is being open and receptive to what comes to the eye; your vision total and not targeted...The same holds for listening as opposed to hearing ! —You can't approach sound or music already knowing or expecting what's to come, excluding all else surrounding it. That way you're making it do, not allowing it to be...[10]

In the photographs that he has left, Merton shows us something of the way in which he saw: how he saw the world around and the gentleness with which he handled it. For the two are interconnected: if you love a place then that place is changed by that love; if you pray in a place then the place is changed by that prayer. Here he is writing on October 12th 1947: "This whole landscape of woods and hills is getting to be saturated with my prayers and with the psalms and with the books I read out here under the trees...everything I see has become incomparably rich for me."[11] The outer and the inner landscapes reflect one another. Merton saw it clearly in the landscape of northern California, in the sea and the rocks, and he wrote of how his photography brought out "the great Yang-Yin of sea rock mist, diffused light and half hidden mountain...an interior landscape, yet there. In other words, what is written within me is there. 'Thou art that.'"[12]

Perhaps it is misleading to speak of Merton as a photographer. It was something totally natural for him because, as someone once said of the art of photography, it never makes the mistake of trying to turn from the material to the immaterial in hopes of conveying spirituality. This is simply of course the wholistic approach of the monastic way of life in its refusal to separate the material and the spiritual. The ordinary, the earthly, whatever is given, has an incarnational character. As he said it so simply himself, his camera was merely another tool for dealing with things everybody knows about but isn't attending to.

His notebooks give us short flashes in words of how he saw and felt the world around him. They are a comment on the way in which he took photographs, and both of them, the written words and the visual images, tell us much of the contemplative vision which lay at the heart of his life of prayer.

To go out and walk slowly in this wood — this is a more important and significant means to understanding, at the moment, than a lot of analysis and a lot of reporting on things "of the spirit." (March 2 1966)

One has to be in the same place everyday, watch the dawn from the same house, hear the same birds wake each morning to realise how inexpressibly rich and different is "sameness." This is the blessing of stability, and I think it is not evident until you enjoy it alone in a hermitage. (May 28, 1965)

Said Terce with great joy, overflowing joy, as if the land and woods and spring were all praising God through me. Again their sense of angelic transparency of everything, and a pure, simple and total light... It was all simple. But a simplicity to which one seems to aspire, only seldom to attain it. A simplicity, that is, and has, and says everything just because it is simple. (January 6, 1965)

The whole hillside was so bright and new I wanted to cry out, and I got tears in my eyes from it! (Feb 17, 1966)

In the afternoon, lots of pretty little myrtle warblers were playing and diving for insects in the low pine branches over my head, so close I could almost touch them... Sense of total kinship with them as if they and I were of the same nature, and as if that nature were nothing but love. And what else but love keeps us all together in being? (November 4, 1964)

There is in all things an inexhaustible sweetness and purity, a silence that is a fount of action and of joy. It rises up in wordless gentleness and flows out to me from the unseen roots of all created being...

Talking is not the principal thing. Nothing that anyone says will be that important. Here we do not feel that much needs to be said. We already know a great deal about it all. It is in all this that you will find your answers. Here is where everything connects.

Notes and References

1. Thomas Merton, *The Asian Journal of Thomas Merton*, New York, New Directions, 1973, p.313)

2. Ibid., pp.131-2)

3. Ibid., p.100

4. Ibid., pp.233-6

5. Thomas Merton, *Woods, Shore Desert*, Santa Fe, Museum of New Mexico Press, 1982, p.48

6. Francis Kline: *Lovers of the Place. Monasticism Loose in The Church*, Liturgical Press, Collegeville, 1997, p. 49)

7. Thomas Merton: *The Seven Storey Mountain*, New York, Harcourt Brace, 1948, p.38.Ibid., p.37

9. Thomas Merton: *Sign of Jonas*, New York, Harcourt Brace, 1953, pp. 91-2

10. 'The Way that Thomas Merton Saw' from Ron Seitz, *A Song for Nobody*, p.133

11. *Sign of Jonas*, op.cit. p. 69

12. *Woods, Shore, Desert*, op.cit., p. 42

Thomas Merton, Cistercian Monk

M. Basil Pennington ocso

Today, in the West, there is certainly a widespread interest in monastic tradition and the spiritual riches it has to offer. To what extent this is due to Thomas Merton, our Father Louis or Uncle Louie as some of his confrères fondly called him, could be a subject of considerable discussion. He has contributed to it, without a doubt, with millions of books distributed in dozens of languages. Other monastics have made their contribution: another Thomas — Keating by name, John Main, William Menninger, Benedicta Ward, to mention a few. While many from outside the monastic tradition have reached into it: Esther de Waal, Canon Allchin, Parker Palmer, William Shannon and many others.

This year, Merton's Cistercian family joyfully celebrates the 900th anniversary of the founding of Citeaux on March 21, 1098. Tom loved his Cistercian heritage. His writings give ample witness to this. I had opportunity to experience it personally as I worked with him in the founding of Cistercian Publications whose primary aim was to publish the Cistercian Fathers and Mothers in English and make the Cistercian heritage better known and more readily available. I think then it is a good time to look at Father Louis precisely as a Cistercian — in my estimation one of the truly great Cistercians of this century. I would even go so far as to say, in some real way, he is the Saint Bernard of our times.

When *The Seven Storey Mountain* suddenly became the astounding and totally unexpected success that it was and continues to be, his publisher, Bob Giroux, quickly signed Tom on to produce three more books. Tom in his own mind planned one of those books to be a volume about one of his favourite Cistercian Fathers, Aelred of Reivaulx. While he made considerable progress in preparing this volume, in the end it remained one of his unfinished works. It has

been published in five parts in *Cistercian Studies Quarterly,* a review Tom
was instrumental in establishing. Tom's study of Aelred is prefaced
by an overview of the Cistercian Fathers. With a conciseness and
clarity that characterized some of his more incisive writing, Father
Louis sums up the Fathers' literary physiognomy:

> The rich and elegant vitality of Cistercian prose – most of which is
> sheer poetry – betrays an overflow of literary productivity which did
> not even need to strive for its effects: it achieved them, as it were,
> spontaneously. It seemed to be second nature to St. Bernard, William
> of St. Thierry, Adam of Perseigne, Guerric of Igny to write with
> consummate beauty of prose, full of sound and colour and charm.
> There were two natural explanations for this. The first is that the prolific
> Cistercian writers of the Golden Age were men who had already been
> thoroughly steeped in the secular literary movements of the time
> before they entered the cloister. All of them had rich experience of the
> current of humanism that flowered through the twelfth-century
> renaissance...

> There is a second explanation for the richness and exuberance of
> theological prose in the twelfth-century monasteries of Citeaux. If
> contact with classical humanism had stimulated a certain intellectual
> vitality in these clerics, it also generated a conflict in their souls. The
> refined natural excitements produced by philosophical speculation,
> by art, poetry, music, by the companionship of restless, sensitive and
> intellectual friends merely unsettled their souls. Far from finding peace
> and satisfaction in all these things, they found war.

> The only answer to the problem was to make a clean break with
> everything that stimulated this spiritual uneasiness, to withdraw from
> the centres in which it was fomented, and get away somewhere, dis-
> cover some point of vantage from which they could see the whole
> difficulty in its proper perspective. This vantage point, of course, was
> not only the cloister, since Ovid and Tully had already become firmly
> established there, but the desert – the *terra invia et inaquosa* in which the
> Cistercian laboured and suffered and prayed...

> The tension generated by the conflict between secular humanism and
> the Cistercian humanism, which seeks the fulfilment of human nature
> through ascetic renunciation and mystical union with God, was one of
> the proximate causes of the powerful mystical writing of the Cistercians.
> However, once these two natural factors have been considered, we
> must recognize other and far more decisive influences, belonging to a
> higher order...

> It is the relish and savour that only experience can give that
> communicates to the writings of the twelfth-century Cistercians all the

vitality and vividness and impassioned sincerity which are peculiarly their own...

The White Monks speak with accents of a more personal and more lyrical conviction that everywhere betrays the influence of an intimate and mystical experience...

It is the personal experiential character of Cistercian mysticism that gives the prose of the White Monks its vivid freshness...

Since the theology of the Cistercians was so intimately personal and experiential, their exposition of it was bound to take a psychological direction. All that they wrote was directed by their keen awareness of the presence and action of God in their souls. This was their all absorbing interest.

I don't think any one would have any difficulty is seeing how well the Cistercian of Gethsemani described himself in describing his Fathers of old:

The rich and elegant vitality of Cistercian prose...an overflow of literary productivity which did not even need to strive for its effects... had already been thoroughly steeped in the secular literary movements of the time before [he] entered the cloister...had rich experience of the current of humanism...contact with classical humanism had stimulated a certain intellectual vitality...refined natural excitements produced by philosophical speculation, by art, poetry, music, by the companionship of restless, sensitive and intellectual friends merely unsettled [his] soul... The only answer...get away somewhere, discover some point of vantage from which [he] could see the whole difficulty in its proper perspective ... the desert ... seek the fulfilment of human nature through ascetic renunciation and mystical union with God ...

It is the relish and savour that only experience can give that communicates to the writings...all the vitality and vividness and impassioned sincerity which are peculiarly their own...

The White Monk(s) speak[s] with accents of a more personal and more lyrical conviction that everywhere betrays the influence of an intimate and mystical experience...

It is the personal experiential character of Cistercian mysticism that gives the prose of the White Monk(s) its vivid freshness...

All that [he] wrote was directed by [his] keen awareness of the presence and action of God in [his] soul(s). This was [his] all absorbing interest.

In 1953, on the occasion of the 800th anniversary of the death of Bernard of Clairvaux, Merton undertook, largely on his own impetus, to publish an English translation of Pope Pius XII's encyclical honouring the Master of the Cistercian School, providing the twenty-two page document of the pope with a ninety-page introduction. Again we are struck at how well Merton describes himself in speaking of his Father Saint Bernard:

> Yet like other complex and many-sided characters, he suffered a rapid and disconcerting fragmentation at the hands of his fame. Perhaps he was too great to be remembered in his entirety. It has ended with history celebrating one side of him, theology another, piety a third, his own monastic Order a fourth.

This morning I am admittedly seeking to bring forth one side of this great man or perhaps more truly the foundation or inner core which expressed itself so diversely in his multifaceted life. Merton in introducing the encyclical on Saint Bernard goes on to write:

> Not the least of the services that have been performed by this publication is the return to the whole and integrated picture of Saint Bernard, with emphasis not on the secondary and accidental phases of his career, but on the most important thing of all: his sanctity, his union with God, his conformity to Christ by perfect charity, and his teaching inspired as much by his study of Scripture and the Fathers as by his own experience of mystical union.

This short paper cannot hope to accomplish so much. But may it fill out the picture of Father Louis by showing his teaching and life as inspired by his study of his Cistercian Fathers and most notably Saint Bernard, whom Merton saw "as an organ of the teaching church and a sure witness of Christian tradition" and yet as one who "struck an altogether new note of hope and encouragement...in spirituality... the clean fresh sweetness of the fields and the forest." How all this appealed to and reverberates in Merton! He also notes of Bernard (as can be said of himself):"There were, indeed, times in his life when he had to be angry in the cause of justice. And he could be splendidly angry."

Yet another note Father Louis makes in regard to Bernard can be applied to himself:

> The essentially monastic character of all Saint Bernard's writing is what gives it a very special quality of its own. It is this character that especially recommends his books to us now, in an age that is proving

itself hungry for the spiritual provender that has lain hidden, all these centuries, in Christian monasticism.

This little book, *The Last of the Fathers*, is undoubtedly Father Louis' crowning tribute to his great White Father whom he hails as "the greatest man of his time."

If we discount a couple of small volumes of poems, *The Spirit of Simplicity* is the first volume published by Merton. It is the work of a young man, still in temporary vows as a Cistercian. It was assigned as a simple translation job, the third volume in a series, The Cistercian Library, inaugurated by Dom Frederic Dunne. But the enthusiasm of the young monk turned it into a significant volume, gracing the General Chapter report which he was to translate with a rich spiritual commentary, as long as the translated report and far more significant — a commentary that was as much Saint Bernard's as it was Frater Louis.' Dom Frederic could not have been surprised at this for it was he himself who had urged the gifted young man to read all of Saint Bernard, a task beyond the capability of most in those days when Bernard was largely available only in the tightly printed columns of the Migne edition in the *Patrologia Latina*. What is surprising to mature students of Saint Bernard is the incisiveness with which the young monk drew out from the Saint's very extensive and rich corpus those passages which are commonly accepted as holding the essence of Bernard's theological anthropology and mystical theology. And these include not only what today might be thought of as the more obvious passages, those in the final sermons of Bernard's commentary on the Song of Songs, but a rich array of texts from many other sermons and treatises.

Frater Louis sums up Bernard's teaching:

> The soul was created in God's image and likeness. St. Bernard's whole treatment of the fall can be summed up in this: that man lost his likeness to his Creator and Exemplar, but retained the image, ingrained in and inseparable from the very essence of his soul. To understand all that is implied by this is to possess the key to the whole mystical theology of St. Bernard... The whole tragedy of fallen man, from the point of view of his own spiritual condition and the proximate cause of all unhappiness is the constant self-contradiction generated within him by the confronting of the essential image of God in his soul with the lost likeness that has been unutterably disfigured by sin.

He goes on to say:

St. Bernard has really vindicated the fundamental goodness of human nature in terms as strong as have ever been used by any philosopher or theologian. And if the first step in the Cistercian ascent to God is for the monk to know himself we may reasonably say that, in some sense, the whole life of such a one will consist in being himself, or rather trying to return to the original simplicity, immortality and freedom which constitute his real self, in the image of God.

A few years later, in his introduction to the papal encyclical, Merton would state this same truth:

...the eighty-third sermon on the Canticle of Canticles, written shortly before Saint Bernard's death, and representing the highest development of his thought... Now the opening lines of this sermon, which Pope Pius quotes extensively, declare that every soul, no matter how burdened with sins, no matter how conscious of its exile from God, and no matter how close it may be to damnation and to despair, can nevertheless find in itself a reason for hope not only for pardon, not only for mercy, but even for perfect union with God in "the mystical marriage." The context of these lines shows that Saint Bernard was here developing his doctrine of the soul as the image of God, created for the most perfect union with Him.

What Frater Louis got hold of in his reading of Saint Bernard is the fact that the essential dignity of the human person lies not in something that is accidental to the person but in the person's very essence. We are essentially the image of God. And no matter what we do or how far we stray, we never lose that essential dignity. It belongs to us in our common shared humanity. Thus every human person deserves respect, no matter what be our race, colour, sex or sexual orientation, religion or lack of religion, because of our common shared participation in human nature which is the image of God. In this humanity we are one and it is our highest dignity.

Merton did not only insightfully discern the foundational texts of Saint Bernard and comment on them with clarity and preciseness. He incorporated them deeply into his own outlook on life and reality. He did this instinctively under the Holy Spirit because the grace of his vocation was precisely a sharing in the Cistercian charism. There was a working together here of nature and grace. Sometimes I think in our appreciation of Merton's wonderful humility (the basic Benedictine virtue) which made him so approachable, so much of an "ordinary Joe" – something he came to rejoice in – we fail to appreciate we have here a man of extraordinary genius. His facility in Medieval Latin enabled him to move quickly through the hundreds of columns of Migne's edition of Saint Bernard. He quickly grasped the central ideas. And he retained key texts in his memory, able to call them up and relate them with texts from very diverse parts of the Saint's corpus, drawing them together in a powerful synthesis.

Thomas Merton, the poet, had a great love for Saint John of the Cross. The Saint's mystical poetry spoke deeply to his soul. Yet the post-Tridentine, more rationalistic presentation in the Saint's treatises did not integrate easily with the holistic anthropological mysticism of Father Louis' Cistercian Father Bernard. Merton struggled with this. In a series of articles he sought to reconcile the two. In loyalty to his earlier love, he sought to write a synthesis of the teaching of John of the Cross. This labour led to Merton's only experience of writer's block. After a near nervous breakdown he did finish the volume in a very unsatisfactory way at least unsatisfactory to him – and resolved never to undertake this sort of task again. John of the Cross, the poet, remained with Merton till the end – Tom cites him in the last book he prepared for publication, *The Climate of Monastic Prayer* – but it was Bernard who grounded his theological outlook as he moved toward what is his own most masterful treatise in mystical theology and Christian anthropology, *The New Man*.

As important as was Bernard's influence on the formation of Merton's theological outlook, the Saint's influence on Merton's basic stance on life, on the life he chose to live, on the meaning of his life, is more fundamental. Shortly after his enlightening experience at Fourth and Walnut, Merton assembled what could appear to be a rather disparate collection of essays for publication as *Disputed Questions*. In the introduction Merton indicates what he sees as the uniting force: they all address "the relation of the person to the social organization." The last essay in this volume and perhaps the oldest – reflecting much of the piety of the young monk – is one on Saint Bernard: "Saint Bernard, Monk and Apostle." In this essay Merton enumerates and quickly lays aside Bernard's many achievements, not the least of which was peacemaking, and devotes most of the essay to underlining Bernard's pre-eminent contribution as a person who is a sacrament of God's love in this world. This ultimate statement of the book on the person's relation to the social institutions of this world

I believe expresses how Merton under the influence of Saint Bernard and sharing his vocation ultimately saw himself — and how most ultimately see him. Merton's life, presented in an autobiography which later caused him embarrassment, has spoken to millions because it is such a powerful sign and sacrament of God's love and action in this world, of the fact that the image of God, our true dignity, remains no matter how much it is covered over by duplicity, no matter how much our true freedom is chained by a false self. Bernard, by being who he was even more than by the teaching which he taught, enabled Merton to come to see who he was. Bernard stands at the beginning of Cistercian history as a sacrament of what all Cistercians should be for the Church and for the world whether solely through the hidden apostolate of prayer or through exceptional dynamic action. Father Louis of Gethsemani was, in this pattern of Bernard of Clairvaux, a Cistercian to the full.

We have all heard Dan Walsh's exclamation as he first read *The New Man*: "The New Man — the new Merton!" Not really new — rather the fullest and profoundest revelation of the Merton that twenty years of Cistercian living had been slowly and steadily forming by contact with the wisdom of the Cistercian Fathers and Mothers and by living the life they had lived. *The New Man* is the crowning expression of nearly a two decades of profound integration. He says nothing new in *The New Man* but he says it with a new power and grace for it now comes forth from a lived experience and not just hearsay from his Father Bernard. He can now say: I know what I have believed.

In the opening chapters of this book Merton dares, like his mentor Bernard, to reach into classic mythology to bring forth a fundamental human aspiration, one which, he clearly sees, can only be fulfilled and is fulfilled beyond all expectation in Christ Jesus. As he continued his exploration he brought forth key texts of Bernard's commentary on the Song of Songs showing that the fundamental malaise of the human spirit lies in its divine likeness in simplicity being cloaked over with duplicity — the false self.

As he comes to the heart of his teaching, Merton acknowledges that other Fathers interpret these key Scriptural texts of the image and likeness in different ways but he is following the thought of Saint Bernard. He sums up Bernard's thought in this brief paragraph:

> The human soul is still the image of God, and no matter how far it
> travels from Him into the regions of unreality, it never becomes so

completely unreal that its original destiny can cease to torment it with a need to return to itself in God, and become, once again, real.

He goes on:

> The inner recesses of our consciences where the image of God is branded in the very depths of our being ceaselessly remind us that we are born for a far higher freedom and for a far more spiritual fulfilment.

Or, as he puts it in *The Last of the Fathers*: "Liberty constitutes man in God's image...we fully realize our own identity by becoming perfectly free and therefore by loving God without limit."

The modern existential thinker who wants *lectio* that is fully in the spirit of Saint Bernard yet benefits from the subsequent development in human thought and Christian doctrine can find no better place to do it than in Thomas Merton and, most especially, in *The New Man*.

Through the years Merton constantly returned to this basic insight: the essential dignity of every human person, made in the very image of God, called to true freedom, enjoying a oneness with every other human person in sharing a common humanity. He expressed it again in an article he published just a few weeks before he died:

> This kind of maturity is exactly what the monastic life should produce. The monastic life is precisely this sort of freedom in the spirit, this liberation from the limits of all that is merely partial or fragmentary in a given culture. Monasticism calls for a breadth and universality of vision that sees everything in the light of One Truth, as St. Benedict beheld all creation embraced "in one ray of the sun." This too is suggested at the end of chapter seven of the Rule where St. Benedict speaks of the new identity, the new mode of being of the monk who no longer practices the various degrees of humility with concentrated and studied effort, but with dynamic spontaneity "in the Spirit." It is suggested also in the "degrees of truth" and the "degrees of love" in St. Bernard's tracts on humility and on the love of God.

A friend of mine once said that it seemed to him a good writer got one good insight and spent the rest of his life developing and illustrating it in diverse and varied ways. This is an interesting thesis that might be worth exploring. What is true is that the basic theme of the Cistercian Fathers, the restoration of the likeness and the return to God from the land of unlikeness, is basic in the writings of Father Louis. It is deeply explored, richly developed and set forth in so many varied ways that almost any pilgrim on the homeward

journey can identify with him and receive from him helpful guidance and companionship along the way. Consoling for us is the fact
that it took Merton years to significantly integrate this insight which
he got in the first days of his monastic conversion. When it finally
did become truly his insight, he became fully in touch with the
perduring wonder of every human person. From this flowed his
reverence for all, his openness to all, his universal compassion, his
deep social concern. Still looking to Bernard, Merton would write:

> The interior life is the life of the whole Church, of the Mystical Body of
> Christ, shared by all who are members of that Body. But the invisible
> and interior peace of the members among themselves and with their
> God is not separable, in the mind of Bernard, from an exterior and
> visible order which guarantees the effect of his salvific action upon
> souls... Bernard is a builder, a man at once of liberty and of order, a man
> who builds individual liberties into a universal order, that all may be
> more perfectly free.

We may well wonder: would there have been *The Seven Storey
Mountain* if the Franciscans had accepted Thomas Merton. Certainly
there would not have been a "Firewatch" or *The Sign of Jonas*. But
Merton may well have led the renewal of the eremitic among the
sons and daughters of Francis.

As all of us, Tom was shaped by many influences, by various
schools of thought and most significantly by his own life experience.
By God's design he was a Cistercian, spent the more significant half
of his life as a Cistercian, however much he kicked against the goad
at times. He received the Cistercian charism and was formed by the
Cistercian school, above all by the master of that school, Bernard of
Clairvaux. We have seen how his own description of the Cistercian
Fathers fits him to a 'T.' He entered upon a way of spirituality, of life,
that forsakes as much as possible what this world treasures with one
glaring exception: a love for authentic beauty, especially in
architecture, music and literature. The Cistercians created
magnificent buildings — Tom illustrated *The Spirit of Simplicity* with
fourteen pages of pictures of Cistercian monasteries and was very
active in the committee that recreated the church and cloisters at
Gethsemani.

The Cistercians filled these magnificent buildings with soul-
embracing chant — Merton served the community at Gethsemani as
a cantor through many years. And they set forth their mystical

experience in an unsurpassed poetic prose that explored what is deepest in the human, in the divine and in the marriage of the two. While Father Louis hardly stepped out of his monastic enclosure, like his Father, Saint Bernard, all the deep concerns of the Church and of the human family became his. He did not go out to lead mobs back to the gates of Gethsemani but every Christian monastery in the world has had candidates drawn to them by this monk's writings and example. And countless others, through his influence, while still following their own proper vocations, have been drawn to the essential values of the monastic way and have had their lives enriched by them. Both were exceptionally good letter writers. If this monk of Gethsemani does not wear the halo of the wonder-worker, there can be little doubt that he is a Cistercian, through and through, a true son of Saint Bernard and the other Fathers and Mothers of the ever-alive and fruitful Cistercian tradition.

It is remarkable how much movement has come from the nudge this monk gave to the Church and society some thirty and more years ago. If that momentum is not to lose its force we who eagerly celebrate the fact that we are in varying degrees moved by that nudge need to open ourselves to the sources that so empowered Father Louis. We need to give priority to our daily contemplative practice. We need to let the Spirit enlighten us through regular contact with the Sacred Scriptures and the spiritual masters of the ages, especially the Cistercian Fathers and Mothers. We need to be wide open to the wisdom of all other traditions through a truly dialogical spirit and practice.

To celebrate Father Louis without seeking to inculcate into our lives, into our ideas and into the world in which we live and labour, the values he so luminously and effectively professed and incarnated would be a charade.

I am sure Tom is here with us and he is thoroughly enjoying the whole scene, rollicking with laughter at times seeing how deadly serious we become over the details of his journey. As his Cistercian brother and friend, I would dare to say his one message to us would be: You guys can do so much more in all this than I — do it!

THOMAS MERTON
poet · monk · prophet

BONNIE THURSTON

PAUL M. PEARSON

CHRISTINE M. BOCHEN

SONIA PETISCO

"Epiphany and Eden:"
Human Love and the Love of God
in Thomas Merton's *Eighteen Poems*[1]

BONNIE THURSTON

Biographical Introduction

PERHAPS THE BEST KNOWN, and certainly the most 'notorious' aspect of Thomas Merton's biography is his relationship with the student nurse. Merton entered the hospital in Louisville, Kentucky on March 23, 1966 for a back operation which occurred on the 25th. During his hospital convalescence, the young woman attended Merton and, from all accounts, they fell deeply in love. From spring through the fall of 1966 Merton's relationship with 'M.,' his designation for the woman, dominates his journal and references to her continue into 1967.[2] The affair is treated extensively in the Michael Mott biography,[3] in the quirky but interesting work by John Howard Griffin, *Follow the Ecstasy: Thomas Merton, The Hermitage Years, 1965-1968*,[4] and is mentioned in most biographical studies of Merton written after 1985.

We know more than we need to know about Merton and M.. This paper does not cover that already much trampled ground. In fact, I confess that reading the journal that chronicles the relationship made me very uncomfortable. I did not like the Merton I met there. He is compulsive, selfish, and dishonest. I was shocked to read that during their affair Merton knew that M. had a fiancé in Viet Nam (LL, 89, whom he later refers to as 'the boy'! LL, 232), and I was annoyed that he consistently referred to his paramour as a 'girl,' a diminutive designation at best for a woman with whom he was in love. (See, for example, LL, 50-51, 77.) However, the importance to Merton of the relationship cannot be overestimated. As Michael Mott notes, Merton "loved greatly and was greatly loved. He was overwhelmed by the experience and it changed him forever." (SMTM, 438.) With characteristic good sense, William Shannon concludes that this was an episode in his life that showed his vulnerability and his humanness... What the experience showed him was that he could love and be loved. [5]

Merton, himself, quickly concluded that he would not keep "the M. business entirely out of sight." He continues, "I have always wanted to be completely open, both about my mistakes and about my effort to make sense out of my life. The affair with M. is an important part of it... "(LL, 234) And so through Merton's own writing and secondary scholarly works we do know a great deal about him and M.. In reflecting on the experience after the fact Merton thought that the "true feeling is no doubt in some of the poems." (LL, 234) And it is to the poems he wrote about the relationship that we now turn.

Literary Introduction

In addition to "A Midsummer Diary for M.," published in *Learning to Love*, Merton wrote at least eighteen poems for the young woman. All were written in 1966; by means of his journal many can be specifically dated. "He entrusted them to a friend, requesting that they be published after his death."[6] In 1985, New Directions sponsored the publication of a limited edition of 250 hand set copies, which made the poems available, but not widely accessible.[7]

Interestingly the work in the Merton poetic corpus that *Eighteen Poems* most resembles is, to my mind, 'Hagia Sophia,' which was published in the 1963 volume, *Emblems of a Season of Fury*. In 'Hagia Sophia,' wisdom is personified by the Blessed Virgin Mary and clearly is Merton's anima, the feminine principle. As the "feminine principle in the world"[8] she is the source of creativity, associated with God in creation, and a way to God.[9] As we shall see, the figure of the lover functions in a similar way in *Eighteen Poems*. In 'Hagia Sophia' the woman is an abstraction personified (wisdom); in *Eighteen Poems* the woman is real, fleshly, and incarnate rather than an abstract love, and yet the language and 'feel' of the two sets of poems is remarkably similar.

Although Merton himself noted on June 2, 1966 that he had "written some of my best poems about all this," (LL, 76), in my estimation, these are not Merton's best poems. They certainly convey the anguish of the writer, his yearning and frustration. In her 1954 dissertation on Merton's (then early) poetry, Susan M. Campbell remarked "that illuminations worthy of communication follow upon struggles valiantly endured and intelligently resolved..." She continues, "if a poet wishes to communicate the understanding and value of such an experience through poetry, he must do more than transfer the emotional tenseness of the struggle and the emotional release afforded by the illumination."[10] I am not certain that Merton accomplishes the 'more than.'

In Eighteen Poems there are many good, and a few truly arresting, lines. But the over-all technical achievement which one finds in many of the poems in The Strange Islands (1957), Emblems of a Season of Fury (1963), or even the experimental Cables to the Ace (1968), is lacking. There are notable exceptions. "Untitled Poem," "Two Songs for M." and "Six Night Letters" are very fine. As noted, most of the Eighteen Poems can be placed with great precision in their author's biographical context. But does this really illuminate them as poems, as 'made things,' as works of art? My suspicion is that what Robert Lowell wrote about Merton's first poetry holds for this later work: "the poet would appear to be more phenomenal than the poetry."[11] For some time the biographical circumstances will probably cloud our estimation of the poetry. What William Shannon said about "For M. in October" characterizes, I think, the whole volume. It "has a poignant stanza [I would say 'quality'] that embodies the helpless yearning for a love that could not be." [12]

If, then, one were to read Eighteen Poems as a New Critic (now an old form of criticism!), putting aside what she knows of the biographical setting of the poetry, what would be most striking about them? In terms of the poems standing alone as a volume, it is the conventionality of the set of controlling images that one finds. Love is described in terms of images of fire (see, for example, "Untitled Poem," "I Always Obey My Nurse," "The Harmonies of Excess," "Louisville Airport"), of the moon ("Evening: Long Distance Call," "Six Night Letters," "For M. in October"), in terms of waking and dreaming ("Aubade on a Cloudy Morning," "Certain Proverbs Arise Out of Dreams"), and of spring and growth ("May Song," "The Harmonies of Excess"). There are a great many expressions of the lovers' oneness and need for each other: "We are two half-people wandering/In two lost worlds" ("Evening: Long Distance Call"); "You are myself" (VI of "Six Night Letters"); "If we could come together like two parts/Of one love song/Two chords going hand in hand" ("For M. in October"); "Our common need/Which is our common presence" ("For M. on a Cold Grey Morning"). I wouldn't go so far as to say these images are clichéd, but they are certainly 'familiar' in love poetry.

In terms of literary history, the family resemblance of these poems to the work of the Metaphysical poets of the seventeenth century is striking. Many scholars who have commented on Merton's poetry have drawn comparisons between Metaphysical Poetry and Merton's work.[13] In its day, Metaphysical poetry represented a reaction against the overly formal conventions of the Petrarchan conceit. The Eighteen Poems are all free verse and many represent experimental forms like those Merton uses in Cables to the Ace and the unfinished work, The Geography of Lograire. Metaphysical poetry moved "toward psychological analysis of the emotions of love and religion;" it represented "a technique intended to express honestly, if unconventionally, the poet's sense of the complexities and contradictions of life. The poetry is intellectual, analytical, psychological, disillusioning, bold; absorbed in thoughts of...physical love, religious devotion."[14] This description of Metaphysical poetry might also be used to characterize the Eighteen Poems, and it brings me, finally, to the issue I find most interesting in the volume, the relationship between human and Divine love, one of the great themes of the Metaphysicals.

Human Love and the Love of God in Eighteen Poems

The tradition of poets who have related human and divine love reaches back into antiquity. For example, the Biblical "Song of Songs" is a paean to sexual love which St. Bernard of Clairvaux later allegorized to express the love of humanity for God (and, of course, his own poems are frequently love lyrics to God). St. Teresa of Avila and St. John of the Cross both wrote what is essentially love poetry to God. Much Metaphysical Poetry conflates the love of the beloved with that of God. (When I taught poetry to undergraduate university students, they were often shocked to learn that John Donne did not write the "love poetry" as a young man and the "religious poetry" as an old divine!) And in the Sufi tradition with which Merton was deeply involved in the mid-1960s,[15] especially in the work of Rumi and Rabia, love of God is expressed in very incarnational language, indeed.

To revert for a moment to biography, in journal entries which appear during the time the poems were being written Merton is quite explicit about the relationship between his love for God and for M.. On July 22, 1966, he writes:

> ...I thought of God's love for her and mine. I can see absolutely no reason why my love for her and for Christ should necessarily be separated and opposed, provided I do not go loving her in some way opposed to His will. But if I love her purely and unselfishly...then my love for her is part of my love for Him, part of my offering of myself to God. (LL, 99)

Again, on September 4, 1966 Merton muses

> ...I could not help questioning the idea that the love of a human being *necessarily* comes in conflict with the perfect love of God... the affection I have for her — with the explicit *sacrifice* of sex and of erotic satisfaction seems to me not to conflict with God's love, but to be in harmony with it. (LL, 122)

However imperfectly he may or may not have accomplished this 'sacrifice,' it is clear that, for Merton human and Divine love were intrinsically related in his experience of M. In "May Song," Merton associates M.'s body with God's love: "Lend me for God's love/Your lifeboat/Your saving body." In "Aubade on a Cloudy Morning" M.'s presence is love personified with a capital 'L': "And your presence/The very necessary presence/And even the person of Love/Has been thank God granted us again." There are other incidental equations of human and divine love among the poems, but in the volume as a whole that relationship appears in two primary guises: when M. appears as Merton's Beatrice, an epiphany pointing him to a deeper understanding of Love and of God, and when their relationship is compared to the recovery of Eden, the recreation of Paradise. It is, in fact, the Genesis/Eden imagery which I think unifies *Eighteen Poems*.

While Merton never explicitly calls M. "Beatrice," it is clear that she functions as such, as the wise woman who points Merton toward a more profound understanding of love and of God. (In this regard, she functions like wisdom in 'Hagia Sophia.') In "I Always Obey my Nurse" (written May 8, 1966), the whole poem turns on the "Beatrice conceit" as the nurse is the one who keeps the fire of love "Deep in her wounded breast." It is she "Who in her grey eyes and her mortal breast/Holds an immortal love." Merton is the patient who wants "to get well" and who learns from the nurse that "No one ever got born/All by himself: It takes more than one." Similarly in the poem "Certain Proverbs Arise Out of Dreams" (written the week of May 20, 1966 and whose title is almost certainly a pun on Merton's own experience[16]) the speaker is a dreamer led by the vision of his beloved: "...the dreamer/knows that without his Beloved he is lost" and confesses "...In the night when nothing can be seen I turn/to my Beloved and her voice is my security." He believes that "...God created [the Beloved] to be in the center of my being?/You are utterly holy to me, you have become a/focus of inaccessible light." The dreamer awakes "with the knowledge of my whole meaning,/which is you." Without the Beloved, light is inaccessible to the poem's speaker; she gives him knowledge of his meaning, which is found in relationship with her. In "Cancer Blues" (written July 29, 1966) she "knows how to heal" and "She grows another day more perfect and wise." This Beatrice figure is perhaps most clear in "Six Night Letters" in which she comes "Bringing the truth I need"(I). In love's "school" her "gentle love/Still follows me with patient lessons"(IV).

Merton was quite explicit about the fact that this was how M. functioned in his life. On May 9, 1966 he wrote, "...I realize that the deepest capacities for human love in me have never been tapped... Responding to her has opened up the depths of my life in ways I can't begin to understand or analyze now." (LL, 54) And again on June 22, 1966

> I cannot regard this as "just an episode." It is a profound event in my life and one which will have entered deeply into my heart to alter and transform my whole climate of thought and experience: for in her I now realize I had found something, someone that I had been looking for all my life. (LL, 328)

That 'something,' I submit, was the simple, total self-giving that is rare but possible in human love, and that mirrors in the human arena God's way of loving. M. pointed the way for Merton to understand love, that defining Christian virtue, in new and deeper ways than he had before. Not surprisingly, such an experience is likened in the poems to a return to Eden.

In the journals, Merton used 'Eden language' to describe experiences with M.[17] In the journal entry for September 4, 1966, Merton is reflecting on what he calls "my affair," and in recalling particular days describes them as "miracles of innocence and spontaneity. Paradise Feasts!" (LL, 124) Two months later, on November 4, 1966, after reading Milton's "Paradise Lost" he notes, "M. and I are so much, in so many ways, Eve and Adam." (LL, 157) Although on June 1, 1967 Merton speaks disparagingly of "the most naive myths about Adam and Eve" (LL, 242), in fact, reflections of such 'myths' permeate *Eighteen Poems*. Seven of the poems use the language and imagery of Genesis/Eden/creation: "Untitled Poem," "I Always Obey my Nurse," "Louisville Airport," "May Song," "Certain Proverbs Arise Out of Dreams", "A Long Call is Made Out of Wheels," and two of the "Six Night Letters."

In some of these poems the Eden allusion is incidental. In "A Long Call is Made Out of Wheels" anywhere the lovers find themselves "Is still the edge of Eden." Similarly in "Untitled Poem" Eden is used in a geographical sense as the speaker notes that "In a stone wall Eden/An unknown flower loves me more" and because of the lovers separation from each other "Paradise weeps in us/And we wander further away." It is in "Certain Proverbs Arise Out of Dreams" (see note 16 below) that the lovers' relationship is understood as a new Genesis. Merton writes "...Together we create the light of this one day for/each other. This is love's Genesis, always beginning and/ never ending. We are at all times the first day of creation." The lovers become light for each other. They are, "at all times the first day of creation," eternally innocent, eternally the day when God created light. They are the origin of love ("love's Genesis") which is, itself, eternal ("always beginning and/never ending") The lovers, in short, are associated with Biblical attributes of God: creativity, light, immortality, love. They are in the words of poem III of "Six Night Letters," "(That ancient and first love that was new/In the unheard of beginning)."

Both "Louisville Airport" and poem II of "Six Night Letters" are explicitly built around the description of their love as an image of God's original creation. In "Louisville Airport," God re-makes the original creation in the lover's relationship.

> We with the gentle liturgy
> Of shy children have permitted God
> To make again His first world
> Here on the foolish grass
> After the spring rain has dried
> And all the loneliness

Is for a moment lost in this simple
Liturgy of children permitting God
To make again that love
Which is His alone
. . .

This is God's own love He makes in us
As all the foolish rich fly down
Onto this paradise of grass
Where the world first began
Where God began
To make His love in man and woman
For the first time

The lovers are allowing God to re-make Divine love in them. But
it is also clear from the lines "Where God began/To make His love in
man and woman/For the first time" that Merton understood God
originally to have placed divine love in the love of man and woman
for each other. His particular relationship with M. is a recreation of
the original love which God gave to man and woman; it recreates the
relational matrix that God intended for human beings. The poem
continues

We with the tender liturgy
And tears
Of the newborn
Celebrate the first creation
Of solemn love
Now for the first time forever
Made by God in these
Four wet eyes and cool lips
And worshipping hands
When one voiceless beginning
Of splendid fire
Rises out of the heart
And the evening becomes One Flame
Which all the prophets
Accurately foresaw
Would make things plain
And create the whole world
Over again

There is only this one love
Which is now our world
Our foolish grass
Celebrated by all the poets

Since the first beginning
Of any song.

It is not only their love which re-creates God's original love. All such love is, in fact, part of the "one love" "Since the first beginning." Passionate human love approximates, in the human lovers, God's original creation of love from Love.

In poem II of "Six Night Letters" the Eden imagery is most clear as Merton describes himself and his lover as Adam and Eve. The poem opens with a striking image of mutuality:

This is the morning when God
Takes you out of my side
To be my companion
Glory and worship

O my divided rib
It is good to be willing
To be taken apart
To come together

The terrible paradox here expressed is that man and woman must be separated in order to enable the two, as separate persons, to come together again and, thereby, to create new life. The poem continues

We bring glad life
To all white-waving fields
To our handsome earth
And we go worshipping together
All over the world's heaven

Their life of love is worship for, in the terms of the poem, to love is to worship God. The lovers are like the first created human beings. Their love brings life to the created world, and, in fact, makes of earth heaven. It is through this very human love, that divine love is known. The poem expresses beautifully what Merton wrote to Victor Hammer on May 14, 1959, that the "'masculine – feminine' relationship is basic in all reality — simply because all reality mirrors the reality of God."[18]

Reflecting on material that Merton wrote for M. between May 19 and 26, 1966, Michael Mott reports that Merton said "each of them was on the threshold of a love hidden even from them. They had the chance of creating a new paradise, one that was still only potential, but which God had reserved for them alone." (SMTM, 453) The Eighteen Poems suggest that, in fact, their human love did, indeed, create a "new paradise," an Eden realized not only by them alone, but by all lovers, by all who would open the experience of human love to the presence of God whose creative essence is Love.

Conclusion

As a poet, Merton's insights about the relationship of human and divine love are hardly new or novel. Probably all lovers feel themselves and their relationship to be unique, that they are specially graced. And so they are, for the innocent wonder of human love was created by God and intended for human delight. In the *Eighteen Poems*, human love and the love of God come together in moments of Epiphany and re-creations of Eden. The human beloved becomes the incarnate epiphany, the manifestation of a heretofore unknown love rooted in God Who Is Love. The experience of human love recreates the original relationship between man and woman in Eden, a relationship that is perfect, "unfallen," open, creative, spontaneous. And in so experiencing human love, divine love is known.

In her study of his poetry, *Words and Silence*, Sr. Thérèse Lentfoehr noted that Merton's central vision was "the God-awareness at the center of one's being...this was his essential theme..."[19] I think Sr. Thérèse was exactly correct. Although the *Eighteen Poems* were written to celebrate human, sexual love, they are filled with "God-awareness." I may not particularly like how Merton apparently conducted his human love affair, but I very much approve of how he understood it, in all its pain and partiality, as both gift of God and path to God. That understanding as it is reflected in the *Eighteen Poems* bespeaks the truth of the writer of 1 John who said "...love is of God, and he who loves is born of God and knows God." "...if we love one another, God abides in us and his love is perfected in us." (1 John 4: 7, 12 RSV)

In an article entitled 'As Man to Man' published in 1969 in *Cistercian Studies*, Merton wrote,

> ...it is the love of my lover, my brother or my child that sees God in me, makes God credible to myself in me. And it is my love for my lover, my child, my brother, that enables me to show God to him or her in himself or herself. Love is the epiphany of God in our poverty.[20]

It is my suspicion that Merton learned this, not as 'man to man,' but as 'man with woman' and, although in frustration and fragmentary fashion, he celebrated the insight in the eighteen poems he wrote for M.. I am glad he had the experience of her, and I am glad we have the experience of the poems.

Notes and References

1. I should like to offer this paper as a small gesture of gratitude to William Shannon whose great generosity as a friend is exemplified by the gift he made me of a copy of *Eighteen Poems*. Bill knew I had a special interest in Merton's poetry because I wrote my doctoral dissertation on that subject and thought I should have the "complete works."
2. Christine M. Bochen (ed.), *Learning to Love: The Journals of Thomas Merton 1966-1967* (San Francisco:HarperSanFrancisco, 1997). Hereafter in the text as LL.
3. Michael Mott, *The Seven Mountains of Thomas Merton* (Boston: Houghton Mifflin Co.1984). See especially pp.434-468. Hereafter in the text as SMTM.
4. John Howard Griffin, *Follow the Ecstasy: Thomas Merton. The Hermitage Years 1965-1968* (Published by the Estate of John Howard Griffin under the imprint JHG Editions/Latitudes Press, 1983).
5. William H. Shannon, *The Silent Lamp: The Thomas Merton Story* (New York: Crossroad,1992) p.200
6. Thomas Merton, *Eighteen Poems* (New York: New Directions, 1985), title page. The pages of the limited edition are not numbered. I have referred to poems by title only in the text of this paper since there seemed no other way to reference the edition.
7. To my knowledge, only three of these poems appear in *The Collected Poems* (New York: New Directions, 1977): "With the World in My Blood Stream" (CP p.615), "The Harmonies of Excess" as part of *Cables to the Ace* (CP p.447); and "Never Call a Babysitter in a Thunderstorm" (CP p.801).
8. Thomas Merton, *Collected Poems* (New York: New Directions, 1977) p.369. (hereafter in the text as CP.)
9. For my thoughts on wisdom in Merton's thought see "'The Tradition of Wisdom and Spirit': Wisdom in Thomas Merton's Mature Thought," *The Merton Seasonal* 20/1 (1995) pp.5-8
10. Susan M. Campbell, *The Poetry of Thomas Merton: A Study in Theory. Influences. and Form*. Doctoral Dissertation. Stanford University, 1954. MS pp. I 90-191.
11. Robert Lowell, "The Verses of Thomas Merton," *Commonweal* (June 22, 1945) p.240
12. Shannon, op.cit., p. 201
13. See, for example, A.M. Allchin, "The Cloud of Witnesses: A Common Theme in Henry Vaughan and Thomas Merton," *Cistercian Studies* 11/2 (1976) pp. 124-136; Sr. Bridget Marie "Merton and the Metaphysicals", *Delta Epsilon Sigma Bulletin* 16/4(1971) pp.128-140; Susan Campbell (see note 6); Sr. Rosemarie Julie, "Influences Shaping the Poetic Imagery of Merton", *Renascence* 9/4 (1957) pp.188-197, 222; Bonnie Bowman [Thurston], *Flowers of Contemplation: The Later Poetry of Thomas Merton*, Doctoral Dissertation, University of Virginia. 1979.
14. C. Hugh Holman, *A Handbook to Literature* Third Edition (Indianapolis: Odyssey Press,1976) p.316

15. References to Islam and Sufism occur in the 1966 journal, most importantly a discussion of the "momentous visit of Sidi Abdesalam, from Algeria". (LL, p.152) For discussions of Merton's interest in Islam see Sidney Griffith. "Thomas Merton, Louis Massignon, and the Challenge of Islam," *The Merton Annual* 3 (1990) pp.151-172; Herbert Mason, "Merton and Massignon," *Muslim World* 59 (1969) pp. 317-18; Bonnie Thurston, "Thomas Merton's Interest in Islam: The Example of Dhikr" *American Benedictine Review* 46 (1994) pp. 131-141; Burton Thurston, "Merton's Reflections on Sufism," *The Merton Seasonal* 15 (1990) pp. 4-7; and the very excellent work of Erlinda G. Paguio of the University of Louisville.

16. In a letter dated October 23, 1958, Merton wrote to Boris Pasternak of a "very young Jewish girl" of whom he dreamed. The girl's name was "Proverb," which itself suggests the Wisdom traditions of scripture. "Proverb" became an important symbol for Merton, one to which he made frequent reference. For example on November 9, 1964 he wrote, 'Last night I had a haunting dream of a Chinese princess... ("Proverb" again.) This lovely and familiar and archetypal person... She comes to me in various mysterious ways in my dreams... I felt deeply the sense of her understanding, knowing and loving me, in my depths..." (*A Vow of Conversation: Journals 1964-1965* New York: Farrar, Straus, Giroux, 1988, p. 101). See SMTM pp. 361-364 for a discussion of the image. Robert Waldron in his article "Merton's Dreams: A Jungian Analysis" (*Merton Seasonal* 16/4, 1991, pp.1-23) makes much of "Proverb."

17. For a more general discussion of Merton's use of Genesis see Brent Short, "The Hidden Paradise: Thomas Merton and the Wisdom of Genesis," *The Merton Seasonal* 20/1 (1995) pp.10-14

18. I am quoting from the manuscript edition of the letter which I read at the Thomas Merton Studies Center at Bellarmine College, Louisville, Kentucky.

19. Sr. Thérèse Lentfoehr, *Words and Silence: On the Poetry of Thomas Merton* (New York: New Directions, 1979) p. 142

20. Thomas Merton, "As Man to Man," *Cistercian Studies* 4 (1969) pp. 93-94

The Geography of Lograire:
Thomas Merton's
Final Prophetic Vision

PAUL M. PEARSON

IN HIS INTRODUCTION TO *A Thomas Merton Reader*, Merton commented on some of the choices he had made in his life suggesting that, although he chose to be a monk he did not choose to be a writer, "I was born one and will most probably die as one," he wrote. Writing was in his genes.[1] He himself wrote of his first literary attempts in his autobiography, and documents discovered by Robert Daggy and myself in 1993 testify to the truth of his description.[2] Central to Merton's vocation as a writer was his use of the poetic genre. Before his entry to Gethsemani in 1941, he was sending copies of his poems to various magazines and, on entering Gethsemani, his abbot encouraged him to continue writing. In 1944 his first published book was a collection of poems — Thirty Poems, published by New Directions.

Surprisingly little has been written about Merton's poetry and even less has been published. A groundbreaking book was George Woodcock's biography, *Thomas Merton: Monk and Poet*[3] where he suggested that Merton's poetry could be divided into two major categories — "poetry of the choir" and "poetry of the desert."[4] This division has not really been challenged, though other categories have been added most notably "poetry of the forest" and "poetry of paradise consciousness" — both added by George Kilcourse.[5] Between them, these four categories cover most of Merton's poetic output, the major exception being some of Merton's later poetry written as "anti-poetry."[6] Merton wrote two complete books of poetry in this style, *Cables to the Ace* and *The Geography of Lograire*, as well as other poems included in Emblems of a Season of Fury and in his Collected Poems.

George Woodcock virtually ignored Merton's anti-poetry, suggesting it was a kind of aberration and that the final book of poetry he was working on, Sensation Time at the Home, was a return to his more acceptable poetic style with "the old quiet Merton of the poems of the desert...asserting his survival."[7] Woodcock's view is understandable as some of Merton's later poetry is difficult to understand, but it is not the view Merton himself took of that poetry. This paper will concentrate mainly on Merton's final poetic work The Geography of Lograire, and will attempt three things: to place it within the context of Merton's poetic output; to tease out some of its meaning; and finally, to make an assessment of its importance.

Writing for a new Geography — the development of Merton's poetry

In the mid-sixties, as Merton was overseeing the setting up of his Legacy Trust and the Merton Room at Bellarmine College, the preservation of his work was very much on his mind. He had already begun sketching out passages for The Geography of Lograire and he was "taking greater care than ever that tapes and drafts of the new poem should be preserved in case he died before the work was complete."[8] Merton wrote to his friend 'Ping' Ferry telling him that "a publishable text, even though imperfect" of Lograire could be made from the tapes[9] "if I drop dead or something" before completing it.[10] Before leaving Gethsemani in the late summer of 1968, Merton had sent a copy of Lograire to James Laughlin of New Directions describing it as "a purely tentative first draft of a longer work in progress...a beginning of patterns, the first opening up of a dream,"[11] a "first section" which "could stand by itself."[12]

In Merton's journal for October 2nd, 1967, after some comments on the Merton Room at Bellarmine College, he went on to speak of Lograire in a quote which shows the importance of it to him and to his autobiographical work. He wrote:

> Writing this is most fun for me now, because in it I think I have finally got away from self-consciousness and introversion. It may be my final liberation from all diaries. Maybe that is my one remaining task.[13]

But even as Merton wrote this he continued to write in his private journal, as he would do right up until his death, and to write more conventional poetry as seen in "Sensation Time at the Home" and his

"Uncollected Poems."[14] Like *Cables* which preceded it, *Lograire*, described by Merton at one point as "an apocalypse of our age,"[15] is an anti-poem based on Merton's diverse reading as well as some of his own personal experiences. Its vision, though, is far broader. *Lograire*, like *Cables*, is a mosaic of "poems and dreams" which Merton says is a mixture of "my own experience with what is almost everybody else's." [16]

Anthony Padovano has described *The Geography of Lograire* as "simply astonishing, the language stunning, the imagery innovative and probing" adding, it contains "all of Thomas Merton."[17] He also sums up very succinctly the theme of this enormously complex poem describing it as "the history of a human family tragically torn asunder but pathetically persistent in its dream for harmony."[18] This is a good description as, in *Lograire*, Merton, through the use of the geographical points of the compass, encompasses the whole world – North, South, East and West. Conflict is found throughout the poem. In the North and South cantos it is racial conflict, whereas in the East and West cantos it is cultural conflict. The poem reflects the extent of Merton's reading and the broadness of his vision as he encompasses various cultures, races, ages, religions, in fact the whole world, in a great vision of compassion. His growing compassion and the broadness of his vision are reflected in a journal entry for 10th July, 1964 in which Merton wrote:

Some conclusions: literature, contemplation, solitude, Latin America — Asia, Zen, Islam, etc. All these things combine in my life. It would be madness to make a 'monasticism' by simply excluding them. I would be less a monk. Others have their own way, I have mine."[19]

In *Cables to the Ace* Merton had been concerned about the alienation of the individual and the breakdown of communication between the individual and God, and between the individual and others, leading ultimately to a breakdown in community and communion. Merton broadens this theme in *Lograire* pointing towards the oneness of all humankind. Merton's geography in this poem points to the underlying unity of all people which from the very beginning of history has failed. In *Lograire* the voice of God is to be heard in the voice of the stranger whose wounds "turn out to be my own,"[20] a theme Merton had stressed at the end of his essay "From Pilgrimage to Crusade"[21] included in his 1967 collection *Mystics and Zen Masters*.

Exploring and Surveying Lograire

At this point in this paper I think it will be worthwhile to sketch, all too briefly, the basic structure and movement of the poem.[22]

The poem is made up of a short prologue, "The Endless Inscription," and four cantos entitled South, North, East and West respectively. Throughout the poem, journey is an important theme. As Merton covers the four corners of the globe he is constantly travelling and travelling in a great variety of ways — by river, sea, foot, car, train and aeroplane. In the prologue, beginning in a boat, Merton recalls some of the influences which have been acting upon him including his ancestors from Wales. The prologue touches on his own search for roots, both his Celtic roots in Wales, his dead parents and his own youth. It then moves on to cover many of the themes of the whole poem — the American South, the slave trade, Cain and Abel, Abraham, racial violence, Africa, the Spanish conquests and points to the Saviour who, ultimately, "Buys Mars his last war,"[23] thus eventually restoring unity.

The South canto is set in three areas: the American South, Africa and Mexico. The theme is of brotherhood which has been violated by a culture riddled with racism. In part three of this canto entitled "Hymns of Lograire," Merton uses quotes from hymns and biblical texts as examples of the way Christianity in the past used such texts to justify slavery. In part four "Miami you are about to be surprised," Merton points to the decay underneath the surface of this glittering city. George Kilcourse has suggested that this section of the poem expresses Merton's "express design for Lograire"[24] as Merton challenges his reader to confront their false self. In this challenge, the author

> ... will try to help you decode
> Your own scrambled message
> Teach you your own way, [25]

and Merton warns his reader, using capitalised text to stress the warning, that:

> IF YOU HAVE HEART FAILURE WHILE READING THIS THE POET IS
> NOT RESPONSIBLE [26]

adding that his warning, in anti-poetry, will be like being warned "by a gourmet with a mouthful of seaweed."[27]

In parts five to seven of the South canto which deal with Africa, Merton begins with a "Thonga Lament" which is a plea for unity:

> Let us eat together in peace
> Let us not disagree
> That I and my children
> May live long here outside.[28]

These cantos also look at the way missionaries have treated native peoples and their religions, showing Merton's compassion for those native religions. This is a theme that features in the remainder of the South canto (parts eight to eleven) as Merton looks at the flower festivals and feasts of the Mayan Indians and their destruction by Christian missionaries:

> With brimming tears
> We mourn our lost writings
> The burned books
> The burned men
> The flaming harvests
> Holy maize destroyed
> Teachings of heaven and earth
> Destroyed.[29]

The destruction of the South canto is reflected in Merton's final entry when he refers to "a banshee howl"[30] which in "Celtic lore...is said to be heard when death visits the house."[31] For Merton the howl of the banshee is "the death cry heard throughout"[32] *Lograire* and it is the sound he asks his readers to hear and to recognise in themselves.

Merton himself undertakes the personal exploration he has asked his reader to undertake in the North canto. In this canto, the most personal of the four, Merton speaks of his own inner life and journey and takes a journey back in memory:

> Alone
> Around the formerly known
> Places.[33]

Much of the early part of this canto is set in New York in areas Merton knew during his youth and later in his years at Columbia. Funnels and tunnels feature throughout this canto as Merton explores down into his own depths. Merton refers to his Mother's cremation:

> Woolforth budding up in the light. Look up to it from tunnels. Top the
> five and ten funnel smoking a little lightly up.
> Brooklyn river sing my orange song: rickety bridge to the funeral
> parlor.

Life and death are even.
My Lady Mum is all alive in Homer. May might be in love poems or
others. Quick into another tunnel.[34]

This canto also contains references to his father, Owen Merton,
and to his brother, John-Paul, whose death is recorded as "Icarus
falls."[35] Another theme that emerges is that of the feminine and
Merton makes reference to Margie describing how "I go run for the
vanished nurse in the subway tunnels of every night."[36] As the first
part of the North canto comes to an end Merton can say, reflecting
from his own experience, that: "Geography is in trouble all over
Lograire."[37]

In the third part of the North canto, Merton moves on to the
theme of religious persecution as he writes about a sect called the
Ranters, a fanatical sect found in seventeenth century England.
The Ranters, who were antinomian, spiritualistic and pantheistic,
represent for Merton all the sects and dissenters who have been
persecuted down through the ages:

> They teach that there is neither heaven nor hell
> But what is in man.
>
> They do not apprehend any wrath
> To be in God.
>
> I saw a letter that one of them writ to a friend of his
> And at the bottom of the letter he writ thus:
> 'From Heaven and Hell or from Deptford
> In the first yeare of my reconciliation to my Selfe.'
>
> Then God does not hate? Not even sin?
> So heaven and hell are in Deptford, Woolwich, Battersea and Lambeth?
>
> Burn him through the tongue![38]

The final part of the North canto, called "Kane Relief
Expedition"[39] contains an ominous silence which reflects its setting
in the Arctic. In the austere beauty of the Arctic white men are
defeated by their own lust and greed in a region which they cannot
tame. They still manage to bring death to the region before they are
defeated as seen in stanza eight:

> Pond's Bay
>
> Rookery of loons

'Greatest sight of bird doings'
Cliffs terraced notched every projection
Covered

Thousands
Wheeling over us in moon-
Light so tame
You could knock them down with an oar

Deafening.

'We entered a cave at the foot of the cliff and found it
filled with young loons and gulls.'

So we shot 500 weighing 1172 lbs.[40]

After having been the hunter, the white man now becomes the victim as, in the next stanza, their ship is destroyed by an iceberg in a midnight gale. Kane, for Merton, "typifies Western man fleeing from himself, from self-knowledge, subduing the earth before he subdues himself."[41]

In the East canto Merton moves on to look at cultural conflict, the way in which people are violent with one another because of different traditions and values. The first part of this canto, "East with Ibn Battuta," is based on an account of a Muslim from Morocco travelling in Asia and Africa in the fourteenth century. In this section Merton sees some of the problems of the East and his attitude is of a more refined critical approach to the East than is found in some of his prose of the sixties. The second part of this canto "East with Malinowski" is based on a journal about the South Sea Islands in which Malinowski violates a culture by his own vulgar behaviour and then presumes to criticise that culture for its vulgarity.

The remaining sections of the East canto are concerned with Cargo Cults. These cults were a means for the natives of handling cultural change brought by white men. Having seen the way supplies arrived by sea and air for the white man, the natives tried to enchant their deities so they would also receive cargo and the power that went with it for the white man. Merton had developed a great interest in Cargo Cults and wrote about them in an essay in his book Love and Living[42] which was published after his death. The stories he included in this canto show how deeply the natives psyche had been

influenced by the white man, so much so that non-violent people
resorted to violence in a last desperate effort to become white, or at
least to learn the white man's secrets about cargo:

Ghost wind come O Brother
Sell me the shivering
For a little piece of paper
Sell me the shivering
For a little piece of Whiteman Times
To roll my cigarette
To blow my Whiteman smoke
In Ghostwind good feeling
O sell me the shivering brother
Give me a ticket to the happy dark
Trade me a houseful of rifles
For a new white skin
In Dark Ghost Wind
Sell me the shivering, Brother,
For Whiteman good times! [43]

The final canto, West, begins at O'Hare airport, Chicago, an
airport Merton had passed through early in 1968 on his way to
California. It is concerned with illusion and with the failure of
humans to communicate. Entitled "Day Six O'Hare Telephane" the
first section looks at the artificiality of human communication which
is implied in its title with the word "Telephane"— a mixture of
telephone and cellophane. The reference to Day Six also points to the
failure in communication going right back to the creation. In one
stanza Merton makes reference to the way humanity is united by the
food that we eat – the wheat of the prairies used to make a host,
"Christ-wheat," could as easily be "squares of Buddha-Rice" or
"Shiva-cakes"– and he concludes the stanza by pointing out that
humanity is also united in the bringing of destruction:

"I am one same burned Indian
Purple of my rivers is the same shed blood
All is flooded
All is my Vietnam charred
Charred by my co-stars
The flying generals. [44]

The second part of the West canto then goes on to look at some of
the symbols of the American myth-dream.

Finally, the last two sections are concerned with the Ghost Dances
of the American native peoples. These dances were messianic and

apocalyptic rituals which anticipated a time when the Indian's dead would return and the white man would disappear. Gradually, through the influence of the white man and his fears, these dances lost their true significance:

> Annie Peterson said Coquille Charlie carried the dance around only to make money. He did not say the dead would return or tell what would happen to the whites. Nobody had any visions at Charlie's dance.

> After a while the dreaming stopped and the Dream Dance turned into a Feather Dance. It was just a fun dance. It was mostly a white man's show. [45]

The testimony of Lograire

The scope of *The Geography of Lograire* is vast. It reflects the diversity of Merton's reading and interests as he incorporates mythic materials from various cultures, historical accounts, anthropological records of expeditions alongside his own autobiographical experience. All the interests of Merton's later years are here and all his own history, thus justifying Padovano's remark that "all of Thomas Merton"[46] is in *Lograire*. In the "Queens Tunnel" section of the North canto Merton writes, once again, his autobiography, only this time he writes it in poetry. [47] *Lograire* also reveals Merton's concerns and the issues he was dealing with at this stage of his life. In his author's note he describes "Queens Tunnel" as the "most personally subjective part" of *Lograire* calling this section a "meditation on Eros and Thanatos,"[48] on love and death. Merton then goes on to say that the South, East and West cantos "play out in more universal and primitive myth-dream terms the same struggle of love and death," enacting "the common participation of the living and the dead in the work of constructing a world and a viable culture."[49] This is the core of the poem.

These themes of love and death run through each section of *Lograire* and were occupying Merton's attention in the final three years of his life. As he came to terms with his own capacity to love and to be loved so he also came to face up to death, especially with his declining health, to live with the fact of death and the questions it raised, and, ultimately, "to go beyond death even in this life, to go beyond the dichotomy of life and death and to be, therefore, a witness to life."[50] In *Lograire* Merton witnesses to life by his stress on the oneness of all existence and the possibilities for that oneness to be restored, pointing to the place where that restoration can take place. Unlike other writers of epic poetry, "Merton does not look to the past for a solution,"[51] nor does he look to another place, for instance the East. Lograire ends not in the East but in the West.[52] In looking for a solution, Merton does not turn to God either, he "rejects any solution to the problem of values that is not grounded in the existential confrontation and suffering of social reality,"[53] but points instead to "the impinging realities of the actual world as the place in which men and women must work out (or fail to work out) their social as well as their personal salvation."[54]

Poetry has been described as the "barometer of the soul," implying that frequently it will reflect changes which are not otherwise apparent as the writer is free of the restrictions placed by other literary genres. Merton's poetry changed dramatically from his early "poetry of the choir" through his "poetry of the desert" to his final anti-poetry. These changes reflected both his own development as a monk and writer as well as developments in the world. Anti-poetry provided Merton with a method of writing for a post-Christian world. Through the use of irony and parody, he could communicate with the reader in a very different way than would have been possible with the more conventional forms of poetry he had used previously. The pages of Lograire cannot be read literally, they need to be read in a similar way to scriptural parables. By writing in this way Merton speaks his message to a new generation and the message he speaks is as relevant to our day as when he wrote it, if not more so.

Let me illustrate this briefly by highlighting Merton's writing in the final canto of Lograire about the artificiality of communication. Since Merton wrote it, communication has developed dramatically through advances in computer technology and space exploration barely dreamed of in his lifetime – satellite communication, e-mail, the internet – but where have our advances in communication taken us? In a journal entry from 1965 Merton reflected thus on the advances of his own day:

> "Wives of astronauts talk by radio with their husbands in outer space; a priest of St. Meinrad's in Peru can call Jim Wygal and talk to him on the phone he has in his car, while he is driving around Louisville. And what do they have to say? 'Hi! It's a nice day! Hope you are feeling

good, I am feeling good, the kids are feeling good, the dog is feeling good, etc., etc." [55]

In *Lograire* Merton presents his own view of the world and of the route humanity needs to follow to find salvation. In looking at the myth-dreams of various groups and cultures, his own personal myth-dream and the North American myth-dream, Merton paints a picture of the white man from the point of view of different cultures and of the way the individual's myth-dream or the Western myth-dream "denies the myth-dream of other cultures." [56] By breaking through the alienation caused by such cultures human unity can once again be restored in overcoming these myth-dreams.

As with *Cables*, Merton's choice of title for this book is important as it assists in conveying his meaning. At a picnic held at Gethsemani in November 1967, Sister Thérèse Lentfoehr, who had always taken a keen interest in Merton's poetry, asked Merton the significance of the name "Lograire" in the title of this work. Merton replied that "Lograire" came from the real name of the French poet François Villon which was François des Loges and "from this surname (really the name of a place)... he had "created" his own country of "Lograire." [57] "Loges" itself designated "huts or cabins used by woodcutters and foresters" [58] and Lentfoehr connects this reference with the role Merton had at Gethsemani for a while of forester as well as a reference "perhaps more importantly to his own hermitage on a wooded rise" [59] at Gethsemani. In Merton's "working notebook which contains the greater part" [60] of *Lograire* Lentfoehr has pointed out that the title of the poem does not appear until page thirty-five after a French quotation from François René Chateaubriand which she translates as:

> Each man carries within him a world made up of all that he has seen and loved, and to which he continually returns, even though he travels and appears to live in a foreign world. [61]

This is an apposite quotation for Merton to use as an introduction or epigram for *Lograire* and clearly brings together the geography of the outer and inner worlds which is *The Geography of Lograire*. [62]

The meaning of Merton's title for *Lograire* seems to be that it is his view, the geography he sees from his hermitage, a geography which had grown and expanded through his writings from being "enclosed in the four walls of my new freedom" [63] at the end of *The*

Seven Storey Mountain to a geography in Lograire which now covered all four corners of the globe and which also transcended all time. In The Geography of Lograire Merton went out to the whole world attempting to overcome the breakdown in communication which he saw as having destroyed real relationships and true community. Having discovered a deep sense of his own stability Merton had discovered a new geography, a geography he had expressed clearly in his introduction to an Argentinian edition of his complete works written in the late fifties:

> In the silence of the countryside and the forest, in the cloistered solitude of my monastery, I have discovered the whole Western Hemisphere. Here I have been able, through the grace of God, to explore the New World, without travelling from city to city, without flying over the Andes or the Amazon, stopping one day here, two there, and then continuing on. Perhaps if I had travelled in this manner, I should have seen nothing [64]

By the late sixties Merton's new geography had extended far beyond the Western Hemisphere to cover North, South, East and West in The Geography of Lograire.

Notes and References

1. Thomas P. McDonnell, Ed. A Thomas Merton Reader (New York: Image Books 1974)
2. Robert F. Daggy, "Discoveries & Rediscoveries Twenty-Five Years After Thomas Merton's Death," The Merton Seasonal 19 (Winter 1994): pp. 2-3
3. George Woodcock, Thomas Merton, Monk and Poet: A Critical Study, (Edinburgh: Canongate 1978)
4. The poems that Woodcock calls the poems of the choir are largely contained in the first four volumes of Merton's poetry – Thirty Poems, A Man in the Divided Sea, Figures for an Apocalypse and The Tears of the Blind Lions. These poems belong to the "cenobitic side of Merton's monastic life" (p.51) and seem to be ruled by "the ecstatic expansiveness of the Psalms" (p.61) similar to canticles at times. The majority of the poems of the choir were written in the forties with very few of this kind being written in the fifties and none appearing in the "sharply different books of verse" that began with the anti-poem "Original Child Bomb" in 1962. The poems of the desert are "a relatively small group of quite distinctive works which are characterised by spareness, control, short quiet lines, a laconic manner that bows towards silence." (p.75) The poems of the desert are poems of inner silence and reflect Merton's growing desire for solitude and the desert and are mostly found in The Strange Islands and Emblems of a Season of Fury.

5. George Kilcourse, *Ace of Freedoms:Thomas Merton's Christ*, (Notre Dame, Indiana: University of Notre Dame Press, 1993)

6. The chief influence on Merton in this style of writing was the Latin Ameri-can poet Nicanor Parra. Merton first used this style in some of his poems in *Emblems Of a Season of Fury* where he quoted large sections from newspapers and other books. With the major developments in media and communication in this century and with the growing problem of language and its meaning, Merton felt it was no longer necessary to use poetic language to get his message across, instead he felt it was sufficient to feed back "garbled newscast as antipoetry" which could "confront and shock readers." (Kilcourse, p.157)

7. Woodcock, p.182

8. Michael Mott, *The Seven Mountains of Thomas Merton* (London: Sheldon Press, 1986) p.500

9. The tapes of Merton reading sections of *Lograire* aloud are currently stored at the Merton Studies Center of Bellarmine College, Louisville.

10. Thomas Merton, *The Hidden Ground of Love*, Ed. William H. Shannon (New York: Farrar, Straus, Giroux, 1985) p.235. (Abbreviated to HGL.)

11. Merton, Thomas. *The Geography of Lograire* (New York: New Directions, 1969) p.1. (Abbreviated to GL) In references made to this poem in the text it will be referred to as *Lograire*.

12. Ibid., p.139

13. Ibid.

14. Both of these collections of poetry are included in *The Complete Poems*, though Merton had sent "Sensation Time" to his publisher as a complete manuscript obviously intending for it to be published as a book in its own right.

15. Thomas Merton, *The Courage for Truth*, Ed. Christine M. Bochen (New York: Farrar, Straus, Giroux, 1993) p.108. (Abbreviated to CT.)

16. GL, p.1

17. Anthony Padovano, *The Human Journey, Thomas Merton: Symbol of a Century* (Garden City, New York: Image Books, 1984) p.136, (Abbreviated to Padovano.)

18. Ibid., p.165

19. Thomas Merton, *Dancing in the Water of Life: Seeking Peace in the Hermitage*, Ed. Robert E. Daggy. (San Francisco: HarperSanFrancisco, 1997) p.125. (Abbrevi-ated to *Dancing*.)

20. HGL. p.155

21. Thomas Merton, *Mystics and Zen Masters*. (New York: The Noonday Press, 1988): pp. 91-112. In this essay Merton spoke of finding "*ourselves in the aborigine who most differs from ourselves*" and said: "our pilgrimage to the Holy Sepulchre is our pilgrimage to the stranger who is Christ our fellow-pilgrim and our brother." p.112

22. *Lograire* is a highly complex poem and it is not possible in this present work to deal adequately with all its themes, but the themes I have chosen to examine are from those highlighted by the small group of scholars who have so far undertaken any detailed work on this poem. They are, I believe, major themes and themes related to this current work, but, it is not to be denied, there are many other themes in *Lograire* as well.

23. GL., p.6

24. Kilcourse, p.186

25. GL., p.18
26. Ibid., p.17
27. Ibid., p.18
28. Ibid., p.19
29. Ibid., p.36
30. Ibid., p.38
31. Virginia F. Randall, "Contrapuntal Irony and Theme in Thomas Merton's *The Geography of Lograire.* " *Renascence*, Vol.28, (Summer, 1976) No.4, p.196. (Abbreviated to Randall.)
32. Ibid.
33. GL., p.41
34. Ibid., p.43. When Merton returned to New York in 1964 to meet with D.T. Suzuki, he made reference in his journal to Elmhurst, the place associated with the cremations of his mother and his grandparents. On 20th June 1964 he wrote in his journal: " So much recognition, everywhere, right down to the two big gas tanks in Elmhurst, landmarks of all the family funerals from mother to Aunt Elizabeth, to Pop's and Bonnemaman's!" *Dancing.*, pp.115-6
35. GL, p.56
36. Ibid., p.52
37. Ibid., p.60
38. Ibid., p.68
39. This section is based on Dr. James Law's journals and as Randall has pointed out is a clever play on words by Merton. Firstly, there is the extraordinary similarity of the name Kane with Cain from the Hebrew Scriptures. Then, secondly, the play on words continues as "Laws extends the irony – the righteous are always trying to save Cain, one way or another." Randall, p.198
40. GL., pp.76/7
41. James York Glimm, "Thomas Merton's Last Poem: *The Geography of Lograire.*" *Renascence*, Vol.26. (Winter, 1974), p.99
42. Thomas Merton, *Love and Living.* Edited by Naomi Burton Stone and Brother Patrick Hart (London: Sheldon Press, 1979) pp.80-94
43. GL., p.116
44. Ibid., p.123
45. Ibid., p.137
46. Padovano., p.136
47. In a letter to the poet Alfonso Cortes, Merton had described the writing of an autobiography using poetry as "a very beautiful" form of writing. CT., p.178
48. GL., p.1
49. Ibid., p.2
50. Thomas Merton, *The Asian Journal of Thomas Merton*, Edited by Naomi Burton and others, (London: Sheldon Press, 1974) p.306
51. Walter Sutton, "Thomas Merton and the American Epic Tradition: The Last Poems," *Contemporary Literature* 14 (Winter 1973) p.56, (Abbreviated to Sutton.)
52. The final two entries are chronologically in the wrong order, but spatially their order points to the West with entry three taking place East of the Rockies and entry four West of the Rockies.
53. Sutton., p.56
54. Ibid., p.57

55. Dancing, p.254
56. Kramer, p.137
57. GL., p.141
58. Ibid.
59. Ibid.
60. Lentfoehr, p.116
61. Ibid., p.152, Footnote 7
62. Mott has suggested that the "geography" of Merton's title originated in Merton's reading of The Voyage of St.Brendan in the summer of 1964. After reading The Voyage Merton toyed with its meaning in his journal asking: "Is the geography of the journey a liturgical mandala? I have to check back on the significance of directions. North is liturgical hell here too and the promised land is West, except that in reference to the paradise of the birds, it is East, which is more liturgical." Thomas Merton, A Vow of Conversation (Basingstoke, Hants: Lamp Press. 1988) p.66
63. Thomas Merton, The Seven Storey Mountain, (London: Sheldon Press, 1975) p. 372
64. Thomas Merton, Reflections on My Work, Ed. Robert E. Daggy (London: Fount Paperbacks, 1989) p.48

Speaking of Contemplation:
a Matter of Metaphor

CHRISTINE M. BOCHEN

Preface

I HAVE BEEN TEACHING a course on Thomas Merton to college students for more than a decade. That has been a privilege, a joy and a challenge. Taking my cue from Merton's own title for a collection of essays in which he grappled with urgent social issues in the light of his Christian faith, I recently renamed the course "Faith and Violence." Beginning with *The Seven Storey Mountain*, published 50 years ago, and selections from his early journals, we immerse ourselves in Merton's story.

At first glance, the gulf between his world and ours seems too wide to cross. So we focus on the externals of his journey —"from Prades to Bermuda to St. Antonin to Oakham to London to Cambridge to Rome to New York to Columbia to Corpus Christi to St. Bonaventure to the Cistercian Abbey of the poor men who labor in Gethsemani."[1] We explore the monastic world Merton entered when he became a Trappist, touching on the wisdom of the desert fathers (and mothers) as well as the Rule of St. Benedict and the way it frames a monk's day with a balance of prayer, work and study. Though the exterior aspects of Merton's way of life – in the monastery and in the hermitage – are new to my students, his way of life is not entirely inaccessible to them. Nor is his stand as a social critic. Reading a selection of letters, poems, and essays written in the early sixties, my students applaud his urgent resolve to speak against all that stands in the way of peace.[2] Most identify easily with Merton's opposition to war and racism. Remarking that he could have been writing today, they are struck by the timeliness of his message, his passion for peace, and his witness to non-violence.

But when we probe more closely Merton's inner journey and read his writings on contemplation, my students struggle to grasp his meaning. On first reading, what Merton has to say about contemplation seems to elude them and *New Seeds of Contemplation* mystifies them. So I focus their attention on how Merton speaks of contemplation – namely the metaphors he uses – as a way of getting at what he is saying. As we decode Merton's message, our understanding is enriched.

What is Contemplation?

Thomas Merton uses the multivalent term to name a practice of silent, wordless prayer; to describe a way of life, inside and outside the monastery; and, most important, to express the direct experience of God's presence. The three meanings are interrelated. The practice of contemplative prayer opens persons to the discovery of God's presence within them. Life lived in the awareness of God's presence – whether it be in the monastery or outside it – is "contemplative life."

Contemplation – in all these three senses – is central to Merton's thought because it is central to his experience. The fervent young monk enthusiastically embraced the life of a contemplative. He learned about that life by studying it and living it. He persevered in contemplative prayer. As he matured, he discovered that a contemplative way of life is open to all. Merton's inner journey informed what he had to say about contemplation to his readers. And he invited his readers to join him on the journey — not necessarily by following him into the monastery but by joining him on the journey of the heart. Beginning with *What Is Contemplation?* and *Seeds of Contemplation*, published in the late forties, continuing through the fifties with *The Inner Experience* and the sixties with *New Seeds of Contemplation*, *The New Man* and *The Climate of Monastic Prayer* as well as numerous essays and prefaces, Merton made contemplation a reality his readers might not only learn about but actually experience and nourish in their own lives as he had in his own.[3] He began by breaking open the wisdom of patristic, monastic, and mystical writers, translating their insights for contemporary readers and, then, added his own, searching for fresh and effective ways to speak about contemplation. At first, he wrote for a Catholic audience; eventually he addressed religiously and culturally diverse readers worldwide.

A number of Merton scholars, including Donald Grayston and William H. Shannon, have shown the development of Merton's thinking on contemplation by documenting the development of his understanding as he wrote and rewrote — refining, expanding and deepening his ideas along the way.[4] They have shown how Merton's ideas about contemplation grew under the influence of his own prayer life and his exposure to new perspectives such as Christian personalism, Zen Buddhism, and his deepening engagement with social issues. Their work and that of many other Merton scholars set the groundwork for my approach and the context for this paper.

The purpose of this paper is to explore how Merton spoke of contemplation, paying particular attention to some of the metaphors he used: diving deep, waking up, and being born again. Growing out of his own experience, these metaphors enabled Merton to express what the experience of God was like and to articulate "contemplation" itself as a metaphor for the Christian life, fully lived. Merton's metaphors invite readers (including my undergraduates) to glimpse the mystery of God's presence within themselves and others and to live aware of God's presence in the ordinariness of daily life.

A Word on Metaphor

Speaking of God and our relationship to God is a daunting task. Speech about the holy strains language and reveals the poverty of our words. That is why many Christian spiritual masters embraced the apophatic way, the way of silence. A sense of the inadequacy of words to express the divine is apparent across the world's religions as well. Recall how Hindus modify their speech about the divine with the phrase "neti, neti"—"not this, not that." Note how Muslims attest to the poverty of language as they chant the names of Allah in a litany of affirmations celebrating Allah's attributes, ninety-nine, until in silence they acknowledge the one-hundredth name that can only be spoken in the silence of the heart. It is clear that Merton shared with his brothers and sisters in the world's religions the realization that words cannot adequately express deepest Reality. Contemplation, as the experience of that Reality, is a knowledge too deep to be grasped in images, in words or even in clear concepts. It can be suggested by words, by symbols, but in the very moment of trying to understand what it knows the contemplative mind takes back what it has said, and denies what it has affirmed.[5]

The true language of contemplation is the language of silence. While Merton knew that words could never adequately convey the experience of deepest Reality, he celebrated the power of human language to express something of that Reality. He recognized that metaphoric language best expresses the Mystery that is God and our relationship to God. Metaphors do not define, limit or exhaust the realities they describe. Metaphors do suggest, hint at, evoke, and intimate. They speak to head and heart. They stir the imagination, which is an essential ingredient in spirituality. Imagination "has the creative task of making symbols, joining things together in such a way that they throw light new light on each other and on everything around them."[6] Writing about contemplation for two decades, Merton gave free rein to his imagination as he invented fresh metaphors and recast familiar metaphors to reach a growing circle of readers to express what he knew well: contemplation. Merton readers must do likewise, reading imaginatively and allowing Merton's words to stir their imaginations and touch their hearts. Readers with a penchant for the concrete and literal may at first resist Merton's metaphorical language. But working with Merton's metaphors is a way to "break open" his writing even on this most elusive of subjects. Nevertheless, Merton's readers need to be mindful that metaphors remain just that: metaphors. "One may isolate the reality in a symbol, but then one must remember that it is not the symbol and the symbol itself is incapable of communicating the full reality."[7]

Diving Deep Within

An early metaphor for contemplation is found in the closing pages of The Sign of Jonas. Fittingly, given the controlling image of the book, Merton elaborates a nautical metaphor as he reflects on his experience of prayer on Shrove Tuesday, February 26, 1952:

> The blue elm tree near at hand and the light blue hills in the distance: the red bare clay where I am supposed to plant some shade trees: these are before me as I sit in the sun for a free half hour between direction and work. Tomorrow is Ash Wednesday and today, as I sit in the sun, big blue and purple fish swim past me in the darkness of my empty mind, this sea which opens within me as soon as I close my eyes. Delightful darkness, delightful sun, shining on a world which, for all I care, has already ended.

> It does not occur to me to wonder whether we will ever transplant the young maples from the wood, yonder, to this bare leveled patch – the place where the old horsebarn once stood. It does not occur to me to

wonder how everything here came to be transformed. I sit on a cedar log half chewed by some novice's blunt axe, and do not reflect on the plans I have made for this place of prayer, because they do not matter. They will happen when they will happen. The hills are as pure as jade in the distance. God is in His transparent world, but He is too sacred to be mentioned, too holy to be observed. I sit in silence. The big fish are purple in my sea. [8]

In the paragraphs that follow Merton amplifies the experience with a reflection which he introduces with the phrase: "Different levels of depth."

Merton describes three levels. The first is "the slightly troubled surface of the sea" where people pass each other like liners. This is the level of action and plans. "I speak to the scholastics. I make resolutions to speak less wildly, to say fewer things that surprise myself and them." This is where the "ego self" lives and moves. Real enough in one sense, this first level is just the surface. Diving below the surface into the darkness, he sees "big blue, purple, green, and gray fish swim by." The darkness is beautiful and peaceful; it is a watercavern, a cave in which he easily lives. Eyes closed, he enjoys a second level of consciousness; it is a place of natural prayer: restful, comfortable, peaceful, "almost slumber." It is about this level that Merton thinks God intends him to write even though this is the realm of silence not speech. He notes that while the Desert Fathers talked about purity of heart, obedience, solitude, and God, "the wiser of them talked very little about anything." [9]

Diving deeper still Merton discovers "positive life swimming in the rich darkness, which is no longer thick like water but pure, like air. Starlight and you do not know where it is coming from. Moonlight is in this prayer, stillness, waiting for the Redeemer." Darkness becomes light. "Everything is charged with intelligence, though all is night." It is a level beyond speculation where everything is Spirit. "Here God is adored." Here God is and is not. "Everything and Nothing. Not light, not dark, not high not low, not this side not that side." [10] Paradox turns into negation. In the deep, all is transformed and duality is transcended — even in metaphor.

The deep sea opens to the sky. From the "holy cellar" of mortal existence, one glimpses the sky: "It is a strange awakening to find the sky within you and beneath you and above you and all around you..."[11] This passage echoes lines found in a poem Merton wrote in the forties, entitled, "A Psalm":

> When psalms surprise me with their music
> And antiphons turn to rum
> The Spirit sings: the bottom drops out of my soul
>
> And from the center of my cellar, Love, louder than thunder
> Opens a heaven of naked air.[12]

Like the passage in The Sign of Jonas, this poem recounts a personal experience in prayer. This is what the experience is like.

As a metaphor for contemplation, "diving deep within" is vivid, colorful, compelling. Speaking of diving deep within, Merton calls attention to our capacity for deep consciousness, for exploring reality beneath the surface, for tapping into the "deep self within." Contemplation involves experiencing a new level of consciousness and the contemplative life, living beneath the surface of life in touch with the depths. The contemplative life is the life of the deep self — alive and swimming beneath the surface. But, as Merton gradually realized, one surfaces from the depths to return to the first level – the level of action – buoyed up by the experience of the deep.[13] Aware of the deep, one does not deny the significance of the ordinary; rather one discovers that the ordinary is transformed. This dynamic characterizes the spiritual life: it is a movement of withdrawal and return. Having experienced life beneath the surface, one returns to the surface able to see with clarity and to act with courage. That was Merton's personal experience: having known God's loving presence in prayer, he returned to the world he thought he had left behind when he entered the monastery and became a witness to freedom. Thomas Merton discovered that God intended him to write about the first level after all.

Waking Up, Becoming Aware

New Seeds of Contemplation is full of metaphors. Contemplation is "being touched by God," a response in which we become God's echo, a gift of God who "completes the hidden and mysterious work of creation in us."[14] Merton likens contemplation to "a journey through the wilderness," a journey from the "region of unlikeness" to "our own land."[15] Contemplation is "Love Living in Freedom."[16] It is an invitation to join in the "General Dance."[17] Among all these provocative metaphors, one stands out. Contemplation is waking up and becoming aware. Contemplation "awakens us to a new level of awareness."[18] This metaphor, threaded through two decades of writing, becomes especially prominent in New Seeds, as Merton sets his understanding of contemplation within the framework of his understanding of the human self. Merton's distinction between the false self (external, exterior, superficial, illusory) and true self (real, interior, hidden, deep) enables him to speak of the true self as the center, the point or spark of God in us and so to speak of contemplation as the awakening of the true self. Awakening is a matter of realizing who we are, who we have always been.

"Awake!" The imperative is direct and familiar. We all "wake up"— each in our own way, whether roused by an inner clock or summoned by bell or buzzer. Some bound up without a moment's hesitation while others linger abed, toying with snooze alarms and bargaining for just a few more minutes. Once up, some of us are wide awake while others stumble about half asleep until we drink that first cup of coffee or tea. But there is more to waking up then getting upright and mobile. Being awake is a matter of being aware, of being attentive and mindful to the present moment and resisting to distractions, daydreams, and illusions. Spiritually speaking, there is a level of consciousness beyond the ordinary states of wakefulness, sleep, and dream. "Waking up and becoming aware" is a natural way of speaking of the spiritual life. The Buddha is the one who woke up. His awakening becomes an invitation to follow his example. Jesus instructs his disciples to be vigilant and stay awake and the early Christian hymn, possibly from a baptismal liturgy, which St. Paul cites in his letter to the community of Christians at Ephesus (Ephesians 5:14), urges wakefulness:

"Awake, O sleeper,
and rise from the dead,
and Christ will give you light."

In the Prologue to his Rule, St. Benedict quotes St. Paul's directive to Christians in Rome: "Let us get up then, at long last, for the Scriptures rouse us when they say: It is high time for us to arise from sleep (Romans 13:11).[19]

The awakening of which Merton speaks is threefold: we awaken to our inner selves, we awaken to God's presence within us, and we awaken to our unity with others. Contemplation is an experience of heightened consciousness, encounter and communion. Our inner self is who we are — who we really are. It is not just a part of our being, "like a motor in a car." It is our entire substantial reality itself, on its highest and most personal and most existential level. It is like life, and it is life... It is the life by which everything in us lives and moves... If it is awakened...it becomes a living awareness of itself: and this awareness is not so much something that we ourselves have, as something that we are. It is a new and indefinable quality of our living being.[20]

The inner self is "the true indestructible and immortal person, the true 'I' who answers to a new and secret name" known only to oneself and to God.[21] Contemplation, Merton writes, is "life itself, fully awake, fully active, fully aware that it is alive."[22] Contemplation is the awareness of our very being as "a free gift of love."[23] Awakened, we are alive to "an interior dimension of depth and awareness."[24] It is God who awakens in us this awareness that "Creating Spirit (Creatus Spiritus) dwells in us, and we in Him."[25]

Awakening to the inner self, we discover God within, or rather we allow God to discover us. We discover God, not as an object external to us, but as the very ground of our being — the Hidden Ground of Love. "We awaken not only to a realization of the immensity and majesty of God "out there" as King and Ruler of the universe (which He is) but also a more intimate and more wonderful perception of Him as directly and personally present in our own being..."[26]

We do not merely know about God; we actually know God dwelling in us in Love. "Contemplation is the awareness and realization, even in some sense, the experience, of what each Christian obviously believes: 'It is no longer I that live but Christ that lives in me.'" Contemplation is "awakening, enlightenment and the most amazing intuitive grasp by which love gains certitude of God's creative and dynamic intervention in our daily life."[27] Awakening to God within, we awaken to our unity with others in God with whom we are one in that "Hidden Ground of Love."[28] Merton invoked that Love as he invited all those present to join him in prayer at the First Spiritual Summit Conference in Calcutta in October 1968. He asked them to be "aware of the love that unites us, the love that unites us in spite of real differences, real emotional friction" and to remember that "things that are on the surface are nothing, what is deep is Real. We are creatures of love."[29] Earlier, in an informal talk, he insisted that "communication on the deepest level is possible." Such communication is actually "communion":

> It is wordless...beyond words...beyond speech...beyond concept. Not that we discover a new unity. We discover an older unity...we are already one. But we imagine that we are not. And what we have to recover is our original unity. What we have to be is what we are.[30]

Waking up to our selves, to God and to others is an experience — a breakthrough. But the metaphor lends itself to describing more than a discrete experience: it names a contemplative way of life, a way of living that nurtures wakefulness and awareness, a life enriched by many moments of awakening.[31] Though this way of living is certainly exemplified by monks, the values that inform the life of a monk are open to all who seek God. Contemplation has a place in the world of action. Writing to college students, Merton described the contemplative life as "a special dimension of inner discipline and experience, a certain integrity and fullness of personal development" which, though "not compatible with a purely external, alienated, busy-busy existence," certainly is essential to living a life committed of service to others.[32]

Being Born Again

Another image that Merton uses to express the discovery of our true identity in God is that of being born again. Merton's use of this metaphor is an example of his speaking of contemplation, without actually using the term, to a new audience in the "Preface to the Japanese Edition to The New Man," written in October 1967.[33] The New Man, published in 1961, reads as a companion to New Seeds of Contemplation, published in the same year. The "new man" and the "new woman" realize the image of God within as the "highest peak of self-realization."[34] They experience an "inner awakening." (Note how frequently Merton employs one metaphor to explicate another.) They recover their true identity. "The recognition of our true self, in the divine image, is...a recognition of the fact that we are known and loved by God."[35] Christ lives in the "new man" and the "new woman." They experience "the great existential awakening of Easter morning."[36]

Merton reads the imperative uttered by Jesus in the context of the world's religion – eastern and western – noting that "spiritual rebirth" is an aspiration shared by Buddhism, Hinduism, Judaism,

Islam, and Christianity. "There is in us an instinct for newness, for renewal, for a liberation of creative power. We seek to awaken in ourselves a force which really changes our lives from within." That change is actually "a recovery of that which is deepest, most original, most personal in ourselves. To be born again is not to become somebody else, but to become ourselves." This rebirth, Merton insists, is not accomplished through psychoanalysis or psychiatry; nor is it achieved through identification with mass movements; it is "a spiritual and religious transformation."[37]

Though rebirth begins with sacramental baptism − "birth by water" − which occurs once, the birth in the Spirit which baptism initiates happens many times as one "passes through successive stages of spiritual development." This is the rebirth of which Jesus spoke to Nicodemus: "not a single event but a continuous dynamic of inner renewal."[38] Being born again is essential to Christianity.

True Christianity is growth in the life of the Spirit, a deepening of the new life, a continuous rebirth, in which the exterior and superficial life of the ego-self is discarded like an old snake skin and the mysterious, invisible self of the Spirit becomes more present and more active. The true Christian rebirth is a renewed transformation, a "passover" in which man is progressively liberated from selfishness and not only grows in love but in some sense "becomes love." The perfection of the new birth is reached where there is no more selfishness, there is only love.[39]

Expressed differently, in what Merton calls the "the language of the mystics,"

> there is no more ego-self, there is only Christ; self no longer acts, only the Spirit acts in pure love. The perfect illumination is then the illumination of Love shining by itself. To become completely transparent and allow Love to shine by itself, is the maturity of the "New Man."[40]

Speaking of contemplation, without naming it, Merton nevertheless expresses what is at the core of contemplation and the contemplative life. Rebirth is the heart of the matter. The essence of Jesus Christ's invitation remains clear: Jesus challenges us to become new men and new women by recovering "the interior, the silent, the contemplative, the hidden wisdom" which calls us to move beyond activism to listening in the silence of our hearts to the inner urgings of the Spirit.

In spring 1968, Merton rewrote and enlarged the "Preface to the Japanese Edition of the New Man" and entitled the resulting essay, "Rebirth and the New Man in Christianity."[41]   In it, he speaks of "new being" and "new creation" – reflecting the influence of Pauline and Johannine theologies – and of metanoia — the change of heart in which persons are recreated. Metanoia, Merton wrote in The New Man, happens when one "comes into intimate spiritual contact with God" and is changed "from within." Metanoia "reorients our whole being." We realize that we are "quite different from our normal empirical selves" and conscious that "this new mode of being is truly more 'normal' than our ordinary nature." Being "out of ourselves" and oriented toward God and in God's self and in others is "natural" to us. "We find ourselves to be most truly human when we are raised to the level of the divine." This change of heart is a gift that "brings us back to the paradisial state for which we were originally created."[42]

Merton's use of the metaphor of being born again evokes his own spiritual journey. Recall the well known opening lines of The Seven Storey Mountain:

> On the last day of January 1915, under the sign of the Water Bearer, in a year of a great war, and down in the shadow of some French mountains on the borders of Spain, I came into the world. Free by nature, in the image of God, I was nevertheless the prisoner of my own violence and my own selfishness, in the image of the world into which I was born. That world was the picture of Hell, full of men like myself, loving God and yet hating Him; born to love Him, living instead in fear and hopeless self-contradictory hungers.[43]

Alienation – from self, God, and others – characterized his first birth and a world in the throes of war became a symbol of violence he saw in himself. He was enslaved, unfree and longing for liberation, for rebirth. And when he wrote the following, he was expressing autobiography as well as theology:

> To be born of flesh is to be born into human race and to our society, with its fighting, its hatreds, its loves, its passions, its struggles, its appetites. To be born of the spirit is to be born into God (or the Kingdom of God) beyond hatred, beyond struggle, in peace, love, joy, self-effacement, service, gentleness, humility, strength.[44]

He saw his initiation into the Catholic Church as a new beginning. Entering Gethsemani marked another beginning. But these were only beginnings. As a Cistercian monk, Merton committed himself to the practice of *conversio morum*. Conversion became, for him, a way of life. Conversion is a dimension of contemplative life: one is born again and again and the birth of God within signals a new existence, open to depth, silence, and attention to the voice of the Spirit.

Words and Practices

For Merton, writing about contemplation was not a theoretical exercise. His words reflect his own experience and practice. If all we do is write, read, and talk about contemplation, we miss the point of what Merton has to share with us. Contemplation is not about words; it is about experience and practice or, in Merton's words, contemplation is both "gift" and "art."[45] The gift is the pure awareness of God. The art is living in such a way that we are open to experience God's presence. Contemplation names the experience; contemplative prayer and contemplative living name the practice. While each of the metaphors discussed above – diving deep, waking up and becoming aware, and being born again – expresses something of what the experience is like, each metaphor also invites practice. Practicing "the art" of contemplation includes nurturing interiority, listening to God's Word in scripture and in the heart, praying with and without words, reaching out with compassion in justice — always responsive to the "creating Spirit" within.

Reading Merton is an invitation to consider how contemplation can become a reality. Giving witness to his experience of God's presence in the ordinariness of his life, Merton invites his readers to look into their own hearts and lives and to discover God already there.

Notes and References

1. Thomas Merton, *The Seven Storey Mountain* (Harcourt, Brace & Co. 1948), p.412
2. Thomas Merton, *The Hidden Ground of Love*, edited by William H. Shannon (New York: Farrar Straus & Giroux, 1985); Thomas Merton, *Passion for Peace. The Social Essays*, edited by William H. Shannon (New York: Crossroad, 1995); Thomas Merton, *The Collected Poems* (New York: New Directions, 1977).
3. Thomas Merton, What Is Contemplation? (Springfield, IL: Templegate Publishers, 1950); *Seeds of Contemplation* (New York: New Directions, 1949; revised edition, December, 1949); *The Inner Experience*, unpublished, 1959; *The New Man*

(New York: Farrar Straus & Giroux, 1961); *New Seeds of Contemplation* (New York: New Directions, 1962); *The Climate of Monastic Prayer* (Kalamazoo, MI: Cistercian Publications, 1969); also published as *Contemplative Prayer* (New York: Herder and Herder, 1969). For excerpts from *The Inner Experience*, see William H. Shannon, *Thomas Merton's Dark Path* (New York: Farrar Straus Giroux, 1981; revised 1987); also see *Cistercian Studies*, 18 & 19 (1983, 1984).

4. Donald Grayston, *Thomas Merton: The Development of a Spiritual Theologian* (New York: Edwin Mellen Press, 1985); Shannon, *Thomas Merton's Dark Path*.

5. Merton, *New Seeds of Contemplation*, p. 1

6. Thomas Merton, "Is the Contemplative Life Finished?" in *Contemplation in a World of Action* (New York: Doubleday, 1971), p.345. In this essay, constituted of notes from taped conferences, Merton acknowledges the importance of imagination in prayer and in the reading of scripture.

7. Thomas Merton, "The Inner Experience: Prospects and Conclusions (VIII)," *Cistercian Studies*, 19:4 (1984), p.343

8. Thomas Merton, *The Sign of Jonas* (New York: Harcourt Brace Jovanovich, 1953), p.338. See also Thomas Merton, *Entering the Silence. The Journals of Thomas Merton, Volume Two 1941-1952*, edited by Jonathan Montaldo (San Francisco: HarperSanFrancisco, 1996), p.467

9. Merton, *The Sign of Jonas*, pp. 338, 339

10. Ibid., pp.339, 340

11. Ibid., p.340

12. Thomas Merton, "A Psalm," reprinted in *Collected Poems* (New York: New Directions, 1977), pp.220-221. The poem was first published in *The Tears of Blind Lions* (NY: New Directions, 1949).

13. I am reminded of the striking title of Carol P. Christ's book on women's spirituality, *Diving Deep and Surfacing: Women Writers on Spiritual Quest* (Boston: Beacon Press, 1980).

14. Merton, *New Seeds of Contemplation*, p.3

15. Ibid., pp.280-281

16. Ibid., p.283

17. This is the title of last chapter of *New Seeds of Contemplation*.

18. Ibid., p.226. Compare with: contemplation "awakens us to a new world." Merton, *Seeds of Contemplation*, p.145

19. *The Rule of St. Benedict in English*, edited by Timothy Fry, OSB (Collegeville, MN: The Liturgical Press, 1982).

20. Merton, *The Inner Experience* as excerpted in *Thomas Merton: Spiritual Master*, edited by Lawrence S. Cunningham (New York: Paulist, 1992), pp.297-298

21. Merton, *New Seeds of Contemplation*, p.297

22. Ibid., p.1

23. Ibid., p.3

24. Thomas Merton, *Witness to Freedom: Letters in Times of Crisis*, edited by William H. Shannon (New York: Farrar Straus & Giroux, 1994), p.329

25. Merton, *New Seeds of Contemplation*, p.5

26. Merton, *Contemplation in a World of Action*, p.175

27. Merton, *New Seeds of Contemplation*, p.5

28. See Merton to Amiya Chakravarty, April 13, 1967 in *The Hidden Ground of Love*, p.115

29. Thomas Merton, *The Asian Journal*, edited by Naomi Burton, Brother Patrick Hart and James Laughlin (New York: New Directions, 1973), p.318

30. Ibid., p.308

31. Note how the Rule of Benedict functions as a guide for Christian living. The values central to the rule may be embraced and practiced by all Christians: listening, working attentively, and praying always. See the writings of Esther de Waal and Joan Chittister.

32. Merton's "Contemplation in a World of Action," written in April 1968, was first published in the *Bloomin' Newman*, a student publication at the University of Louisville. It is reprinted in *Contemplation in a World of Action* (New York: Doubleday, 1971), p.157

33. Thomas Merton, "Preface to the Japanese Edition of The New Man." in *"Honorable Reader" Reflections on My Work*, edited by Robert E. Daggy (New York: Crossroad, 1989), pp.127-136

34. Merton, *The New Man*, p.63

35. Ibid., p.124

36. Ibid., p.240

37. Merton, "Preface to the Japanese Edition of *The New Man*, " p.131

38. Ibid., p.133

39. Ibid., p.134

40. Ibid.

41. Thomas Merton, "Rebirth and the New Man in Christianity" in *Love and Living*, edited by Naomi Burton Stone and Brother Patrick Hart (New York: Harcourt Brace Jovanovich, 1979), pp.192-202

42. Merton, *The New Man*, pp.125-126

43. Thomas Merton, *The Seven Storey Mountain* (New York: Harcourt Brace & Co., 1948), p.9

44. Merton, "Rebirth and the New Man in Christianity," p.198.45. See Thomas Merton, "Contemplation and Dialogue" in *Mystics and Zen Masters* (NY: Dell, 1967), pp.203-204

Recovering Our Innocence: the Influence of William Blake on the Poetry of Thomas Merton

Sonia Petisco

M Y PAPER IS GOING to focus on the fruitful dialogue between Thomas Merton (1915-1968) and William Blake (1757-1827), a dialogue between two interesting modern poets and thinkers who did not meet in time but in whom we find a connection of sensibilities, concepts, ways of expression and feelings. Both authors built one of the most solid paths of Modernity and tried to give a new shape to experience based on an emergent solidarity which will only flourish if we leave our individualism behind and develop our awareness of the cosmic unity, of the fact that we are ONE in the Spirit of God.

Religious transfiguration of reality

The poetry of Blake and Merton cannot be separated from their mystical experience.[1] In both authors, poetry is identified with religion, understanding by religion the experience of the transcendency. They consider the poet as the intermediary between the individual soul and that soul which Renaissance man called the soul of the world or *anima mundi*. Through their aesthetic look, they wanted to go beyond the surface, beyond "the epidermis" in order to experience the sacredness of nature.

A good example of this religious transfiguration of reality can be found in Blake's book *America, a Prophecy*, where he wrote this beautiful and meaningful line which immediately reminds us of the sacred character of the whole Creation. It says: "For everything that lives is holy, life delights in life."[2] Merton also thought that everything we see in reality is an allegory of the immensity and love of God as we can realize in his poem "Stranger":

When no one listens
To the quiet trees

When no one notices
The sun in the pool

When no one feels
The first drop of rain
or sees the last star

Or hails the first morning
of a giant world
where peace begins
and rages end:

One bird sits still
watching the work of God:
One turning leaf
Two falling blossoms,
Ten Circles upon the pond...[3]

Merton considered that everything that exists discloses something of its Maker and that Grace was everywhere, in the quiet trees, in the first drop of rain or the last star, hidden but ready to emerge for the eyes of those who want to see and the ears of those who wish to listen.

The reading of William Blake's poetry was going to influence Merton's sapiential and transcendental vision of reality, his conception of life, art and poetry, his search for totality and unity, and his interest in the East and Zen. In his autobiography *The Seven Storey Mountain*, he acknowledges the importance of Blake in his life:

> I think my love for William Blake had something in it of God's grace. It
> is a love that has never died, and which has entered very deeply into the
> development of my life.

Merton had heard about Blake since his childhood, when his father, Owen Merton, read to him the *Songs of Innocence*. Later on, he himself read Blake as a schoolboy at Oakham and in 1938, after finishing his degree in Columbia University, he decided to write his master's thesis on "Nature and Art in William Blake: an Essay in Interpretation." Moreover, it is possible that Blake, together with Gerard Manley Hopkins, influenced Merton's conversion to Catholicism and also his profound intuition of the inner God dwelling within us.

Both Blake and Merton had read St. Augustine[4] and Meister Eckhart and learnt from them that God flourishes in man's heart, that God is not to be found outside ourselves but that He is our most intimate reality. In his book *All Religions Are One and There Is No Natural Religion*, Blake points out that "God becomes as we are, that we may be as he is,"[5] thus presenting life as an inner journey towards God. Our soul is like a mirror. The end of the journey would be the unveiling of the mirror which is our soul, until on this mirror we can contemplate the image of God. Similarly, in the poem "Stranger" Merton addresses God saying:

> Closer and clearer
> Than any wordy master,
> Thou inward Stranger
> Whom I have never seen
>
> Deeper and cleaner
> Than the clamorous ocean,
> Seize up my silence
> Hold me in Thy Hand! [6]

The Marriage of Heaven and Hell: going beyond the opposites

Besides this idea of the inner God, Blake taught Merton to love life, "to go beyond the dichotomy of life and death, and to be, therefore, a witness to Life."[7] Life with capital letters, that is Life which goes beyond opposites, beyond good and evil, beyond concepts, in order to achieve the virginal goodness and innocence of all that has been created. As it is said in the Bible: "And God saw every thing that he had made, and behold, it was very good" (Genesis 1,31). In his book *The Marriage of Heaven and Hell*, Blake attempts to purify man's perception until things appear to him as they really are:

> If the doors of perception were cleansed every thing would appear to man as it is, infinite
> For man has closed himself up, till he sees all things thro' narrow chinks of his cavern.

In the poem "Night," Blake believes that some day the contraries will "get married," and the lion (symbol of evil in Blake's poetry) will be "washed in life's river" and will sleep with the lamb, the symbol of innocence [8] and the symbol of Christ. The lion says:

> "And now beside thee, bleating lamb,
> "I can lie down and sleep;

"Or think on him who bore thy name,
"Graze after thee and weep.
"For, wash'd in life's river,
"My bright mane for ever
"Shall shine like the gold
"As I guard o'er the fold. [9]

In the same way, Merton believed in the reconciliation of the contraries as we can read in a translation he did of one of Chuang Tzu's poems, "The Kingly Man," for whom "Long life is no ground for joy, nor early death for sorrow" and whose glory is "in knowing that all things come together in One/And life and death are equal."[10]

Finding the Extraordinary in the Ordinary: a Sapiential Vision

Going beyond opposites would be the key to regain Paradise and to recover our innocence. However, to achieve this, we have to learn to look at things without prejudices and from the bottom of our hearts, or as Blake says, we must learn to observe the extraordinary in the ordinary:

To see a World in a Grain of Sand
And a Heaven in a Wild Flower
Hold Infinity in the palm of your hand
and Eternity in an hour.

Blake's sapiential vision of reality had a great impact on Merton's life and writings. Blake was aware that Western society had separated knowledge from love. In these verses, Blake unites the rational knowledge with a loving intuition of things which is attained by listening to reality carefully, with the ears of a child (what Merton will call "the paradise ear"), looking at things as if it were the first time. For him, love and imagination were two essential means of knowledge, and in his book *Europe, a Prophecy* he writes:

"If you will feed me on love thoughts & give me now and then
"A cup of sparkling poetic fancies; so, when I am tipsie
"I'll sing to you to this soft lute; and shew you all alive
"The world, when every particle of dust breathes forth its joy."

As we all know, Merton made of love and imagination a way of living and a way of being in the world. He was a very imaginative person and in his essay "The True Legendary Sound" he defines imagination as

the power by which we apprehend living beings and living creatures in their individuality as they live and move, not in their ideas and categories...it directs our eyes to beings in such a way as to feel the weight and uniqueness of their lives.[11]

In a French poem called "Le secret," Merton tells us that even our lives may be a product of God's expansive imagination and creative power, of God's dream:

Puisque je suis
Imaginaire
La belle vie
M'est familière

Et je m'en vais
Sur un nuage
Faire un serein
Petit voyage...

Sans figure
Et sans nom
Sans réputation
Ni renom,

Je suis un oiseau
Enchanté
Amour que Dieu
A inventé. [12]

Love and imagination lead us to a sapiential wisdom in Blake and Merton. Michael Higgins gives a good description of this kind of wisdom. He writes:

The wisdom that is sapiential is childlike; it is penetrative, immediate and unaffected. The child knows not only through the intellect but primarily through the imagination with the empathy and freedom it grants. Sapientia is the way of the poet, the child, the innocent dreamer and Christ: it is the way of knowing for the religious pastoralist, the Zen master, the visionary and the mystic. When the poet knows in the highest way and loves in the deepest way the poet has tasted the innocence of Wisdom."[13]

Once we have achieved this kind of wisdom, we are prepared to go beyond opposites and to perceive the hidden essence of the world and of ourselves which consists of the eternal desire for unity and love which is inherent in all creation, what Merton often refers to as "the hidden ground of love."

A search for the original unity: Love

In his *Songs of Innocence*, Blake wrote a wonderful poem about Love. The poem is called "The little black boy" and the mother of the little boy tells him:

"Look on the rising sun: there God does live,
"And gives his light, and gives his heat away;
"And flowers and trees and beasts and men receive
"Comfort in morning, joy in noonday.

"And we are put on earth a little space,
"That we may learn to bear the beams of love;" [14]

Blake was convinced that we are here in order to learn how to love. Love constituted for him the reason why we exist: "I cry, Love! Love! Love! Happy happy Love! Free as the mountain wind!" he exclaims in *The Visions of the Daughters of Albion*. Merton shared the same thought. He has a poem entitled "Freedom as experience" which expresses Dante's idea of Love being the force which moves the whole universe:

Because our natures poise and point towards You
Our loves revolve about You as the planets swing upon the sun
And all suns sing together in their gravitational worlds.

And so, some days in prayer Your Love,
Prisoning us in darkness from the values of Your universe,
Delivers us from measure and from time,
Melts all the barriers that stop our passage to eternity
and solves the hours our chains. [15]

Love saves us from death. As the poem suggests, the Creation is a loving dialogue between God and His creatures and the final aim of the universe is Unity in God. "My dear brothers," says Merton in his *Asian Journal*, "we are already one. But we imagine that we are not. And what we have to recover is our original unity. What we have to be is what we really are." It is only in the love of God found in my brothers that we can become one, and that we can be completely free.

Freedom and Void: recovering our innocence

Freedom is a recurrent idea in Merton and Blake. However, this freedom and happiness that fulfil a human heart can only be achieved by detachment from everything. Both authors were deeply influenced by Zen and the idea that we must learn to detach ourselves from the sensual voluptuousness, from the desire to be or the desire not to be. In his long poem *Cables to the Ace* (1968), Merton talks about this need for returning to a point of nothingness, of absolute void, the void of innocence, from which men will be able to see things as they really are, to see things for the first time; from this void, everything that occurs becomes a pure Gift:

> Desert and void... The Uncreated is waste land emptiness to the creature. Not even sand. Not even stone. Not even darkness and night. A burning wilderness would at least be 'something.' It burns and is wild. But the Uncreated is no something. Waste. Emptiness. Total poverty of the Creator: yet from this poverty springs everything...[16]

It is in this poverty that we reach perfect knowledge, perfect love, and perfect freedom and happiness. However, the journey into the void is not an easy one. God's ways are never easy. There is no road to follow: "The pathway dies/and the wilds begin"[17] says Merton's poem "Elias – Variation on a Theme." Our soul penetrates in the darkness of a knowledge which goes beyond any schema. And we begin to die in order to be born to a real life, we "forget ourselves on purpose, cast our awful solemnity to the winds and join in the general dance."[18] It is then that we recover the happiness of the innocent child, that happiness which Blake talks about in one of his *Songs of Innocence* called "Infant Joy:"

> "I have no name
> "I am but two days old."
> What shall I call thee?
> "I happy am,
> "Joy is my name."
> Sweet joy befall thee!

In a similar way, Merton wrote a nostalgic poem about the paradise of childhood called "Grace's House," Grace being the name of a little girl and also a synonym for "authenticity:"

> On the summit: it stands on a fair summit
> Prepared by winds: and solid smoke
> Rolls from the chimney like a snow cloud.
> Grace's house is secure.
>
> No blade of grass is not counted,
> No blade of grass forgotten on this hill.
> Twelve flowers make a token garden.
> There is no path to the summit –
> No path drawn

To Grace's House...

O paradise, O child's world!
Where all the grass lives
And all the animals are aware!
The huge sun, bigger than the house
Stand and streams with life in the east
While in the west a thunder cloud
Moves away forever.

Grace's House is the house of Truth, the house of Innocence, the new Jerusalem. It is the origin, where everybody wants to return, where everything is blessed, where everything is sacramental. However, there is "the uncrossed crystal water between our ignorance and Grace's truth." And there is no road, no path to her House because this house is nowhere and at the same time everywhere. As Anthony T. Padovano said,

> Grace and Love surround the human spirit as quietly, mysteriously and comprehensively as rain might have surrounded Merton's hermitage the night he wrote his essay on Rain and the Rhinoceros... Grace appears in the most simple, familiar, ordinary situations of life. Because the ordinary is mysterious, eventually infinite, inevitably divine.

I would like to finish by saying that Blake and Merton were aware that grace is everywhere and that God sends us messages through each of our senses:

Taste: Ripe peaches, cold spring water, the first cup of coffee in the morning, sharp cheddar cheese, Jesus extending himself to you in bread and wine, an ice-cream cone shared with a child.

Sight: Shimmering shades of grey in full moonlight, soft silver circles surrounding that moon on a moist night, undulating water ripples, mountains, rivers, lakes, seas, and the shape and smile of the one you love.

Hearing: Wind in the leaves before they fall, rustling feet in the leaves later on, raindrops falling from the branches when the storm has passed, church bells in the distance, fire crackling on the hearth, waves crashing, newborns crying, the words "I love you and I always will". And silence.

Smell: Steely air in your lungs on a winter day, fresh-mown grass, bread in the oven, the pages of a new book, a salt sea breeze, orange groves.

Touch: Rough tree bark, dewy grass on bare feet, moist earth at planting time, snowflakes on your cheek, spring sunshine warming your face, a child folded in your arms, yourself folded in the arms of another.

These are the notes of the symphony of God. We must defend our innocence in order to be able to listen to them. As Merton said in a letter to Latin American poets, "Come, dervishes: here is the Water of Life. Dance in it."[19]

Notes and References

1. In his essay "Poetry and the Contemplative Life" (Commonweal, 44, July 4, 1948), Merton relates the aesthetic experience to the mystical experience: "aesthetic experience transcends not only the sensible order...but also that of reason itself. In the natural order, as Jacques Maritain has often insisted, it is analogue of the mystical experience which it resembles and imitates from afar."

2. Blake's Poetry and Designs ed. Mary Lynn Johnson, New York, W.W Norton and Company, 1979, p.113

3. Extract from the poem "Stranger," The Collected Poems of Thomas Merton, New York, New Directions, 1977, pp.289-290

4. In his thesis, Merton defines Blake as a mystic who belongs to the Christian tradition of the Augustinians and the Franciscans.

5. W. Blake, "All Religions are One and There is No Natural Religion," in Blake's Poetry and Design, op.cit., p.15

6. Merton, "Stranger", Collected Poems, op.cit., p.290

7. Thomas Merton, Asian Journal, New York, New Directions, 1973

8. See the poem "The Lamb" in Songs of Innocence, where Blake identifies the goodness of God with the lamb and the child.

9. Songs of Innocence. In writing this poem, Blake followed the Bible very closely. The topic of the friendship between the lion and the lamb that we see in this poem reminds us of some verses from Isaiah, 11-6: "The wolf also shall dwell with the lamb, and the leopard shall lie down with the kid; and the calf and the young lion and the fatling together; and a little child shall lead them."

10. The Collected Poems of Thomas Merton, op.cit., p.911

11. In The Literary Essays of Thomas Merton, ed. by Patrick Hart, New York, New Directions, 1985, p.30

12.   Since I am
            an imaginary being
            Wonderful life
            is familiar to me
            and I set out on a cloud to make a quiet and small trip...
            Without figure
            and without name
            neither reputation
            nor fame
            I am

a delighted bird

Love invented by God.   (Author's translation)

13. Michael Higgins, "The laboratory of the Spirit: Pastoral Vision in the Age of Technology," *Cistercian Studies* 16:2, 1981, p.122

14. Blake: *Songs of Innocence*. op.cit.,

15. Merton: *Collected Poems*, op.cit., p.187

16. ibid. p.452

17. "Elias – Variation on a Theme," ibid, p.240

18. Thomas Merton, *New Seeds of Contemplation*, New York, New Directions, 1972, p.297

19. Thomas Merton, *Raids on the Unspeakable*, New York, New Directions, 1966, pp.160-161

Thomas Merton
poet · monk · prophet

Victor A. Kramer

Catherina Stenqvist

Michael J. Callaghan cm

David Scott

A Journal Turned Toward a World of Readers: Merton's Private Record and Developing Public Awareness

Victor A. Kramer

Editing *Turning Toward the World* (1960-1963), and study of the other complete journals, most recently *Dancing in the Water of Life* (1963-1965), and *Learning to Live* (1965-1967), make it clear Merton wrote simultaneously as recorder of selected events about his spiritual life, and as an artist fully aware of the need to sort out private issues along with wider concerns in relation to public responsibilities. All this is revealed in this enormous writing project. The complete journal documents this sorting process while it also takes on a unity which Merton realizes he both can and paradoxically should not control.

Part I: Process

In this paper I amplify one insight to examine parts of the complete journals which demonstrate Merton's prophetic awareness increasingly working on two, and often three, levels. (1) He is primarily concerned about his spiritual development; (2) however, he always is aware what he records in the journals will be read and digested by others later; (3) he often admits he needs to be faithful to facts he might even want to omit. Therefore, while his entries are always exceedingly private, as a literary performance they are so not so much as a retrospective record, but as selections of someone peering years into the future and anticipating readers of this literary project, a literary process which to some degree is taking on a life of its own.

This complete journal records the past while it anticipates future readers who may be able to learn from Merton's experiences. Merton is in process of revealing aspects of his life (which perhaps he might wish to shield) for the benefit of the journal project. This faithfulness is what I call level three. Perhaps this pattern which I suspected, before I read Volume Six, *Learning to Love*, is most evident there during the two years of 1966 and 1967.

Throughout the journals there are many references to the nature of keeping a journal, and quite significant is an entry made in July, 1956, which reveals Merton's insight into what is occurring just as he starts keeping a journal again after a lapse of three full years:

> I have always wanted to write about everything. That does not mean a book that covers everything – which would be impossible, but a book in which everything can go. A book with a little of everything that creates itself out of everything. That has its own life. A faithful book. I no longer look at it as a "book."[1]   (*A Search For Solitude* (S), p.45)

Merton was clearly becoming more aware of the complexity of the process of journal fabrication and its relationship to the readers who would follow as his public life, his literary reputation, and its connections developed. Analysis of his complex awareness of inter-relationships helps us see the complexity of his accomplishments as he watched his journal develop as a private record, but with an awareness of the reading public, and, finally, as his experiment in faithfulness.

Clearly Merton sought, above all, to be faithful to the truth of what he had experienced; yet as a writer he also knew – step by step – that his personal journal was both a record of that experience and a storehouse of materials which would inevitably have an effect upon many readers far in the future. His paradoxical need (as a writer) then became how to document the facts of his spiritual development, a reality which includes moments when one is either discouraged or encouraged as one observes life unfolding over an extended period of time.

Part II: Project

At the core of Merton's developing project is his systematic honesty. It is what makes these journals as a whole of significance as: raw material reflecting insight into this particular life; as the record of many plans, activities and incipient projects and disappointments which may be read precisely as written; and even more importantly, as Merton's record of actually dealing with the frequent darkness of his spiritual journey. He sensed all of this early, and it is no accident that he was fascinated with the work of St. John of the Cross already in the late 1940s. What Merton had come to recognize, to some degree like the T. S. Eliot of *Four Quartets*, was that life is always concrete – never theoretical – and therefore his own dark nights and frustrating contradictions had to be experienced, and lived through, and documented. Within that realization (as a born writer) Merton also came to the conclusion that he, therefore, had an obligation to record as much as possible of the honest truth — even if it was often not flattering to himself.

It is arbitrary, and I admit an over-simplification, but I would like to make an observation about how one can divide the complete journals into three basic groups:

(a) 1939-1952 — Pomposity and Certainty: Writing as a record of cleverness.

(b) 1953-1962 — Ambivalence about Self: Writing as a record of doubts.

(c) 1962-1967 — Increasing Honesty: Writing as a record of bold honesty and acceptance.

This is not to say that there is not considerable overlap between these three periods. All aspects are always there. The nature of any journal is to record honestly what one observes. What I want to stress is how Merton's sustained journal project while certainly honest, already at its beginning, is even more so once he realizes that he has a multifold obligation: to write for himself as record of a spiritual journey; to write for posterity; and as writer as honestly as he can manage, even when he does not particularly like what he feels he has to record.

This pattern becomes especially clear in Volumes Three and Four in the middle sections of the project. The beginning period, 1939-1952, is a time of great confidence: conversion, plans to write; vocation; preparation for ordination, etc. These twelve years reflect a certainty about earlier decisions. Less so is this the case at the end of his career: those final seven years from 1962 throughout 1968 reflect with greater and greater intensity Merton's questioning, and even uncertainty about his roles. There were many. He was monk, Novice Master, conference facilitator, editor, hermit, ecumenist, lover, photographer, reader, writer about war, and civil rights, and liturgy. He was poet, etc. All these conflicting roles and pressures make the final years difficult to label because Merton felt the need of doing so much. We might suggest in a very real sense these were years of turmoil.

In between are what I have labelled the "pivotal years," not so much just 1960-1963, (covered in Volume Four), but the almost decade of awakening, years of awakening from what he called his "dream of separateness" beginning as early as 1952 and 1953 and continuing throughout this middle period. Thus, we have thirty years of journal — three decades and roughly three periods. The first batch are years of confidence. This lasts about fourteen years. The second period is about a decade from 1953 to 1962. The remaining seven years reveal an acute awareness of the need to provide a detailed and complete record and an explosion of interests, contradictions, hopes and disappointments. These three periods are becoming shorter and the writing is becoming more energetic. It seems that there is a need to record honestly which becomes even greater as interests and responsibilities multiply. Merton is deciding to be honest in all kinds of ways that he could not so easily do when he started out with this sustained journal. The middle period of 1953 to 1962 is the moment when Merton, I think, consciously chooses to be unflinchingly honest. William H. Shannon's new book *Something of a Rebel: Thomas Merton, His Life and Works*, divides all of Merton's writing into a similar three part arrangement.

Part III: Reflections of Honesty

Merton's honesty about (one might say) his honesty becomes one of the most compelling sub-themes of his entire journal project. It is interesting that within *A Search for Solitude*, an entry, for August 18, 1952, he notes (as he is correcting page proofs for *The Sign of Jonas*) that the "Georgia censor" had attacked "the scruple which prompted me to say too many things I did not mean, but which I felt I had to say because they were things I did not like about myself" (S., p.9). Here Merton has been caught in his own observations so to speak.

He then comments about this comment, and this, retrospectively, helps us to understand what he is learning to do throughout his journal project: What one includes cannot just be a record of what one does or doesn't care for, but rather it is much more importantly, a matter of willfulness. Merton notes of the journal writer in general, and of himself:

> You have to distinguish what is ugly in you and what is willed by you
> and what is ugly – or silly – and not willed. The latter is never really
> interesting, because it is usually quite unreal and therefore not a matter
> for a journal — gives a false picture. (S., p. 10)

Thus, we can assume that what this ambitious monk-writer often chooses to do as a journal writer past this moment of finishing The Sign of Jonas in 1952, and into 1953, is to try in the future to select incidents and details which will provide a "true picture" of what is willed. It is the element of willfulness that is crucial. This is what reveals the tension in the life and what provides the tension in the literary record.

The entries for September 3rd and September 13th, which follow, are especially interesting when studied in the light of these strategic comments. Merton realizes that he functions best in solitude and he wants to be called into more silence; but he also realizes that he cannot easily, either in life or in the journal which reflects his selections about life, separate human "willful" actions and his desire to transcend such venality. In fact he cannot. Luckily, this inextricability makes for very good journal writing and, as well, later, journal reading. Therefore, Merton can in the immediate pages accuse himself of paying too much attention to his scholastics, and therefore, he can, as well, announce he has been making serious mistakes. Thus, he comments, he needs a

> Complete new attitude. I have been fooling myself about my
> 'compassion' for the scholastics — my interest in them is uselessly
> human, and the job itself, even when most supernatural, is something
> less than I need and therefore – practically speaking – an obstacle — an
> occupation that complicates my mind too much for the simplicity of
> God. (S., p. 15)

But of course what makes such an entry, and all related entries, doubly interesting is the contradiction and suspense. We know retrospectively that Merton kept that job as Master of Scholastics, and a similar one as Novice Master for thirteen more years. The entry is archetypal Merton. His consciousness remains at the center. He follows the preceding comment with a statement about his inability to write a book about St. Bernard: Why to do so, he jokes, would be "as if someone who just made a vow of virginity was told to get married" (S., p. 16). Here we react, "All right, no more such books."

But, of course, we also know that he did write just such a book, The Last of the Fathers, and it appeared only two years later.

There is no doubt Merton does often feel caught between his desire for solitude and his hope for experience of the transcendent, along with his also quite strong desire for writing about all this: "real tribulation — ground between millstones" (S., p. 15). What is important, in the present examination of how all this plays into the journal is that he keeps asking questions of himself: Why even write all this down? You do so, he explains, because it may help with one's desired spiritual transformation, but you also do it, he ironically admits, because you've got a contract for other books similar to The Sign of Jonas. The recently published correspondence of Merton and James Laughlin, one of his publishers, provides even more evidence of these conflicting concerns.

The entries which follow for September 15th and September 26th are also archetypal Merton, and continue his debate, one which will continue to his death. It is significant that this particular tortuous debate apparently leads to a hiatus of approximately three years for which we have no journal entries. Between September 26, 1952 and March 10, 1953 only seventeen entries survive, and then there is silence until the July 12, 1956 entries which I mentioned earlier (and this is approximately when he assumes a new job as Novice Master).

He apparently feels compelled to write again. Maybe at this moment he thinks he can be drawn more inward because his new job will be primarily spiritual formation, but we know, as journal readers, that his preoccupation with himself and willfulness is the real drama.

Still better and more provocative examples of Merton's consciously choosing to write about his "willfulness" and doing so as honestly as he can manage are the detailed episodes of the years 1966-1967 in Learning to Love. This is strong medicine (for Merton and the reader) but it is exactly what allows this journal writer to function on all three levels at once. He had to be honest. He knew the journal would remain in manuscript for twenty-five years after his death, but he suspected it would be published, most likely exactly as he chose to write it. In Learning to Love we have the most explicit evidence of Merton's compulsion to be honest about what he is living through, yet also the most extreme example of his wish to put down the facts not just for his personal benefit but for many other reasons, and ultimately, perhaps most importantly over the long haul, his hopes that all this documentation will be made available for readers decades forward.

The same drive to keep detailed records, not just for self, but for eventual publication is evident in Volume Five, *Dancing in the Water of Life*. He writes on August 16, 1963 of a beautiful "cool, dazzling bright afternoon...an entirely beautiful, transfigured moment of love for God." But note how Merton both praises God and then castigates himself:

> ...a transfigured moment of love for God and the need for complete confidence in Him, without reserve, even when nothing can be understood. A sense of the continuity of grace in my life and an equal sense of the stupidity and baseness of the infidelities which have threatened to break the continuity. How can I be so cheap and foolish as to trifle with anything so precious? The answer is that I grow dull and stupid and turn in false directions... It is usually a matter of senseless talking, senseless conduct, and vain behaviour...   (D., p. 9)

What is interesting about this entry is its tie to the related one following wherein Merton extends his concerns to questions about order within religious life (He is reading Romano Guardini's commentary on Jean Pierre de Caussade.) with regard to "the responsibilities of the individual called by what does not yet exist and called to help it exist in, through, and by a present dislocation of Christian life" (D., p. 10). Merton realizes he cannot know what all this means, yet he feels caught and even confused while he also knows, however, that he must record these particular dislocations.

Part IV: A Running Narrative

Merton's journal project is clearly one which fairly early on in its production reflects that he was aware of its many uses, not just for himself, but for others during years to come. Thus the entire project is, on its primary level, a record of selected events which for the writer are of value as a documentation and as a running narrative of a private spiritual journey — troubles, trials, and consternation. To be of use to him these selections have to be accurate and honest and representative of how he felt at particular moments. It is so.

At the same time the writer's process of selection is affected in at least two ways as the journaling occurs. The writer knows, and again fairly early on, that what he chooses as raw material may later be crafted into other works, for this is precisely what he did in The Sign of Jonas, Secular Journal, and Vow of Conversation. Thus, he chooses (maybe unconsciously to some degree) incidents which will be of literary value later.

However, secondly, Merton, as writer, also knows that there is an extremely good chance that all these "raw" complete journals, will, as well, eventually be published complete. Therefore, he is also writing for readers who will come to his honest record decades or centuries later and therefore absorb the journal entries in their honest completeness, not just as a private spiritual record or as material to be crafted, but as the planned selection of thoughts and events which are (to some degree) valuable and enjoyable precisely because this man of letters saw part of his responsibility as the job of selecting material which would in itself – of itself – provide a compelling narrative because it honestly revealed his willfulness, errors, mistakes, etc.

Merton's function as journal writer, then, works on several levels and more intensely so as he achieves maturity: It is a record of spiritual development, or change. It is also a systematic filing system as are his reading or working notebooks, which he also used for leading into other literary projects. It is finally, however, a depository for Merton's running narrative which he knows must eventually be read as a work which he to some degree consciously planned and consciously wrote to reveal how he (in retrospect) perceived his role as spiritual seeker within the larger context of society, church, monastery, personal relationships, etc., as these events "inexorably moved on towards crisis and mystery" which, of course, most importantly he could not control — yet which in the very act of making a detailed journal for those thirty years he did in fact control as writer.

Many more examples could be provided: one of the most interesting places occurs in Turning Toward the World and records the shift observed in late 1961 as the writer becomes more accepting of mystery as he moves into 1962. Another is in 1959, when a disappointing and firm letter arrives from Rome which states he must stay at Gethsemani. He quickly accepts that decision.

Still another example is the somewhat surprising strategy employed throughout the various materials of 1966-1967 including the private "A Midsummer's Diary for M." (written for his loved one, the nurse) that were later edited as appendix to the journal, *Learning to Love*. Especially in this tumultuous volume, the entries remain exceedingly private; and clearly it is also raw material Merton most likely would have refined. Yet it is always the honest record of Merton's turmoil, seeking, and finding peace, a model for other readers later.

Notes and References

Parts of this paper have been incorporated in the bibliographical essay which will be included in *The Merton Annual*, Vol. 11, forthcoming.

The page references to the Harper San Francisco Complete Journals are cited within the body of this paper in the following manner:

> Volume Three, *A Search for Solitude*, (S);
> Volume Four, *Turning Toward the World*, (T);
> Volume Five, *Dancing in the Water of Life*, (D);
> Volume Six, *Learning to Love*, (L).

How postmodern is Thomas Merton?

CATHERINA STENQVIST

To BE ABLE TO answer the question of this paper we need to go into what postmodernity is about. But first let me make a general outline of Merton's life during the decade of the sixties.

1968 – the year of Merton's death – is also, roughly, the year of the dawning of postmodernity.

The sixties were for Merton a decade of change and transformation, a time of breaking away from traditional Christianity. He sought new ways and came close to the views of Zen Buddhism. Merton had grown out of the old belief, of which perhaps the Epiphany of Louisville is a good expression. From now on he is trying to find new ways while still retaining what is best of his old beliefs.

We know that Merton felt close to the youth of the Sixties. He liked their ways of questioning traditional or conventional values. He appreciated their freshness and spontaneity. He felt akin. How could this be? Merton a monk in his fifties and these hippies in their teens? There is of course not a simple answer, but if I should try to give a spontaneous answer it will concern Merton's empathy and his yearning for authenticity. He saw in the hippie movement something of himself. And I would like to argue that this brought him close to what postmodernity is in general about: a deep dissatisfaction with Western philosophy, culture and views on the human being.

Merton's ability to empathise made him unusually perceptive of what was going on in his time. Although he was not familiar with the term "postmodernity" he caught its wind.

Another answer is rooted in Merton's dissatisfaction with the isolation and outer observance of monastic life. He writes: "What the monastic life should provide, then, is a special awareness and perspective, an authentic understanding of God's presence in the world and His intentions for man. A merely fictitious and abstract isolation does not provide this awareness."[1] These lines disclose Merton's dissatisfaction with abstraction and his longing for lived life: do not think, live! This attitude of his is certainly in accordance with the hippies' drive for life not hindered by what society claims.

What is postmodernity?

Postmodernity is in its essence − if there is any essence − a philosophy which is characterized by its questioning of Western civilisation and the idealistic philosophy from Plato down to our time. The critique concerns one main area: metaphysics. Predominantly, metaphysics is perceived as dualism. Dualism, in this context, is the idea of two worlds, where this world of human beings has a lesser value, sometimes no value, in comparison with the other world, the world of reason, concepts and spirit. Our world, the world of the material, in so far as it has any value, derives its value from the world of spirit. The consequence of this kind of reasoning is that our material world appears as void of meaning. It derives its meaning and purpose from the other world, but lacks intrinsic value. This concept is questioned by postmodern philosophies. It puts the word "philosophy" in the plural, and thereby indicates that postmodernity is not one philosophy: it is characterized by diversity, multiplicity and a stress on the concrete and the variety of experience.

Another characteristic of postmodernity is deconstructivism. It ought to be labelled a concept — although postmodernity is critical of conceptualization. Deconstructivism aims at exactly what the word connotes, deconstructing what has hitherto been held as true, the objective truth of life, reality and knowledge. What is found after the project of deconstruction? Nothing really; or what used to be described as substance or essence is shown to be an illusion. Some philosophers claim there is no other reality than what language creates.

The kernel, perhaps, of postmodernity is a deep mistrust of essentialism. This mistrust has to do with what was earlier said about dualism. If the belief is that there are not two worlds, and that this world has a value of its own, anti-essentialism is a natural result.

Two main ideas have been the target of the postmodern deconstruction. The deconstruction of the self and of the concept of truth. (I have taken the following from Rosemary Tong and her book *Feminist Thought*, p. 219):

> So total is the anti-essentialism of the deconstructionist, that he or she questions two of the assumptions that almost everyone holds: that there is an essential unity of self through time and space termed *self-identity* and that there is an essential relationship between language and reality termed truth. The notion of a unified, or integrated, self is challenged by reference to the idea that the self is fundamentally split between its conscious and unconscious dimensions. In turn, the notion of truth is challenged by reference to the idea that language and reality are variable and shifting, missing each other in a Heraclitean flux. Words do not stand for things, for pieces of reality. Rather, reality eludes language...

The point is that there is no fixed, objective world where truth, reality and the self are one and the same through time and independent of history and cultural formation. There is no substance behind the flux of time, culture and history which is the essence that gives identity and upholds appearances. Appearances, so to speak, are all there is. Truth is only partial; it is popular to speak of "contextualization." What we experience, and what we label as true are dependent upon my attitude, the perspective I bring to my experience, the context I am surrounded by, the culture I am part of, my ethnic belonging and my gender. What I am is not given. What I am is something I become; it is obvious here how alike postmodern thinking is to prevalent ideas of existentialism. That in itself is not surprising. Postmodernity succeeds existentialism and both are French phenomena, although the "father" of existentialism is the Danish philosopher Sören Kierkegaard.

What postmodernity discloses is the illusion of something given. We believe we are born into something fixed, almost God-given: this is a naive and realistic position, but which nevertheless has had a strong hold in our history. It is as if we "eat" and digest the meaning of life *presented* to us. We believe and act as if language mirrors an objective reality. We act as passive subjects with the only task to receive what is already there. This is in part a consequence of dualistic thinking. Now, postmodernity challenges this view but does not really put something in the void which is created when the old thinking is declared dead. Absence and void are in themselves part of life and a description of reality and must not therefore be pretended to be otherwise. We only know presence through absence, and vice versa.

Postmodernity takes apart and disrupts and is reluctant to build anew and make a synthesis as that, the argument goes, is to falsify the character of reality. Postmodernity has, on these grounds, been reproached as having fragmentized life and the individual: there are no truths, no reality, no assurance, no fidelity. Everything is absurd and as such we are not obliged to feel responsible for anything. This is correct but not altogether because what is forgotten in this picture is the complete freedom given to man. Man is released from a prison where he has been put by those in power claiming the authority of interpreting truth and objectivity. Postmodernity has given human beings their freedom back and handed over the possibility to start all over, no longer as a prisoner of what is claimed to be eternal truths. I think existentialism is right when talking about anxiety following the realization of complete freedom. In a sense, human life as a whole, can be described as escaping freedom. God "himself" is complete freedom, according to Kierkegaard, and this is what causes anxiety! What is free cannot be controlled. Postmodernity has let loose a way of experiencing life the way life "is," uncontrolled.

Furthermore, postmodernity is characterized by a Freudian Renaissance. One of the modern followers of Freud is Lacan. A psycho-dynamic outlook prevails in most postmodern philosophers, and a few even practise as psychoanalysts. This reveals, I think, that what philosophy is, is actually a question of who we are, how our knowledge has its origin in self-knowledge, and the activity of the subject; to become is a process. We are not born ready-made. We are not concepts of human being, we become humans.

Final point; postmodernity concerns itself with language and, in perhaps a simplistic way. It can be said that the stress is on the verb as compared to a language mainly using substantives.

Thomas Merton and the atmosphere of postmodernity

As far as I have read Merton, he is critical of two main concepts: dualism and the prevalent figuration of the subject originating in René Descartes (1596-1650). His critique of dualism becomes obvious in his agreement with Zen Buddhism and in his opinions concerning traditional Christianity and monastic life. His beliefs concerning the subject becomes clear in his critique of the Cartesian *cogito ergo sum.*

Zen Buddhism and Merton

I would like to argue that Merton in an implicit way carries out a critique of Christian metaphysics by approaching Zen Buddhism. Buddhism is actually a philosophy of reality, of metaphysics, associated with postmodernity. First and last, Zen Buddhism is characterized by its monistic outlook; there is just one reality and *satori*, enlightenment, and that is to come to grips with this "truth" concerning reality.

Zen Buddhism denies abstract thinking as not being authentic thinking; the only reality is lived experience; there is no abstract, logical truth. Or, abstraction is there, but it is an illusion to believe it to be the substance of the subject and reality. The purpose of life, for the individual, is to reach the bottom of herself or himself. At this bottom is realized that what I "is" is emptiness, that is to say, there is no substance. What is, is what is not; this is the paradoxical way of expressing that reality which can never be defined in a rational and logical way.

My opinion is that these briefly sketched views of Zen Buddhism are in accordance with essential features of postmodernity, features that Merton actually embraced. Further, Zen Buddhism expresses itself by using verbs instead of substantives, in expressing reality as something ongoing, not as something "there." To give an example. If you become a doctor, you are not a doctor rather you practise as a doctor. You can never "own" an ability as an essence, you can only make it actual by living it.

Subjectivity

Merton in his critique of René Descartes, in his kinship with Zen, is against a dualistic perception of reality, his apprehension of the contemplative experience is in line with postmodern thinking.

Let us look into what Merton says of Descartes. There are many instances in his material where he articulates a deep dissatisfaction with Descartes' basic formula *cogito ergo sum,* "I think, therefore I am." I would like to argue that this dissatisfaction discloses something essential in Merton's apprehension of reality and the human being. In *New Seeds of Contemplation,* Merton writes:

Nothing could be more alien to contemplation than the *cogito ergo sum* of Descartes...This is the declaration of an alienated being, ...compelled to seek some comfort in a *proof for his own existence* (!) based on the observation that he 'thinks'... He is reducing himself to a concept... He arrives at his own being as if it were an objective reality, that is to say he strives to become aware of himself as he would of some 'thing' alien to himself. And he proves that the 'thing' exists.[2]

These lines by Merton are written in the sixties. He is critical of Descartes by using what has become a Marxist vocabulary, 'alien.' Being alienated sums up a basic experience of our century, it occurs again and again: in Marxism, in psycho-analysis, in existentialism, in postmodernity. It has to do with a person's experience of being objectified, not treated and apprehended as a subject. This has been pointed out as a tragic feature in our modern era as a consequence of technology and industrialization. This alienation also has a philosophical root, which is the passivity of the subject. The subject is treated as a monad, an atom, circulating without any emotional contact with other atoms or human beings. The human being is treated as something to be proved, as a concept, in a way, beside the body, the ordinary life, and the daily routines. The subject as perceived as a free-floating reason and a reason, furthermore, equated with male reason. Merton is clear on this point. He stresses the subjectivity of the human being. Further, he is convinced in his critique of the old dualism, of the human being as regarded as part body, part soul. When Merton refers to a person he looks upon him or her as a whole. And in his concept of "the true self" it becomes clear that he is not dealing with a concept, an entity; it is lived experience.

He does not make a distinction between consciousness and being conscious which is comparable with the old distinction between object and subject. Not to use this distinction is to overcome alienation and to perceive oneself, not as an atom, but as a subject in process. Merton arrives at this through his contemplative experience and through how he himself apprehends himself and reality:

Contemplation... is the experiential grasp of reality as subjective, not so much 'mine' (which would signify 'belonging to the external self') but 'myself' in existential mystery. Contemplation does not arrive at reality after a process of deduction, but by an intuitive awakening in which our free and personal reality becomes fully alive...[3]

It is further clear in *Contemplation in a World of Action* that he thinks and argues in a context of psychodynamic reasoning, for example in his chapter "The Identity Crisis." I find this kind of reasoning typical of the climate of postmodernity. Increasing fatigue with positivism and a static view of reality, bring into focus the idea that human beings and the world that they inhabit have, in fact, no reality independent of one another:

> When 'the world' is hypostatized... it becomes another of those dangerous and destructive fictions which we are trying vainly to grapple... The world as pure object is something that is not there. It is not a reality outside us for which we exist. It is not a firm and absolute objective structure which has to be accepted on its own inexorable terms. The world has in fact no terms of its own. It dictates no terms to man. We and our world interpenetrate. If anything, the world exists for us and we exist for ourselves.[4]

I find these words enlightening. When Merton writes "we and our world interpenetrate" he is indeed hitting the core of postmodernity. And further, when he writes that "the world has in fact no terms of its own" he is indeed doing away with the objectivity of something out there to which the human being must be submissive. Instead humans are their own masters, or in Merton's own favourite words towards the end of his life: "to stand on my own two feet." That, to me, is the message of postmodernity, to give humans their authority, creativity and self-confidence back, although along with an anxiety which seems to follow the release from traditional metaphysics.

Merton's deepest concern was the restoration of the contemplative life. He returned to the early sources of Western monasticism and brought them into modern life. In this restoration he once more came close to postmodern thinking; he wants life to break through and not to be captured by old structures. He asks for a new outlook and a new faith:

> What is needed is not only new rules but new structures and new life. The new life stirs, but faintly, incoherently. It does not know if it can exist without the old structures. What is also needed is a new outlook and a new faith in the capacities of modern men to be monks in a new way.[5]

It is, of course, necessary to point out that postmodern thinking is not religious, or at least that it does not take account of religion.

It can be interpreted as if religion is regarded as an old structure, the old metaphysics. But I would like to stress that religion, in this sense, is also an issue for Merton. Reading the following lines, where Merton refers to Thomas Aquinas, is clarifying: "However, this view too is static rather than dynamic, hierarchic, layer upon layer, rather than on-going and self-creating, the fulfilment of a predetermined intellectual plan rather than the creative project of a free and self-building love."[6]

Is Merton postmodern and in what sense?

Now to my question: is Merton postmodern and in what sense? If I look at the phenomenon of postmodernity and its situation in time; no, Merton is not postmodern. What we now view as postmodernity was not fully articulated and labelled as postmodernity while Merton lived, although there are expressions like "post-Christian" in *Contemplation in a World of Action*. But if I look upon postmodernity as something in the air; yes, Merton was postmodern. He was not postmodern in a strict philosophical sense as the French philosophers like Lyotard, Derrida, Foucault and Kristeva. But Merton was not a philosopher! He was a well-educated, well-read Trappist monk with a keen interest in his time and curious about what was going on, but as that, never losing his identity as a monk. He always ·speaks and talks as a monk, even though his awareness of himself as a monk shifts, transforms and deepens. But I dare to say, it is exactly in this sense that Merton is most truly postmodern: he develops his own thinking, he stands on his own two feet, he challenges old ways of thinking and beliefs, he is bold in his move into Zen Buddhism, firmly believing that the truth of yourself is always truer than the truth of objectivity and what is imposed on a person. Merton's postmodernity is a lived example of what postmodernity might do to you!

Notes and References

1. Thomas Merton: *Contemplation in a World of Action*, p.27 [New York, Doubleday, 1971, p.8]
2. Thomas Merton: *New Seeds of Contemplation*, p.8 [Wheathampstead, Hertfordshire, Anthony Clarke, 1972, p.6]
3. Ibid., pp.8-9 [Anthony Clarke, p.7]
4. *Contemplation in a World of Action*, op.cit., p 169 [Doubleday, p.154]
5. Ibid., p.29 [Doubleday, p.9]
6. Ibid, p. ? [Doubleday, p.147]

The Influence of the English Mystical Tradition on Thomas Merton's Life and Writings

Michael J. Callaghan CM

THESE COMMENTS TEND TO paint, in broad strokes, a picture of Merton's reading of the English mystics. The factors which motivated Merton's reading the English mystics stem from a desire to re-connect with a spirituality which first opened him to God, to share the joy of that openness with those living the Cistercian life in a time of change, and to establish, in a vitalized and refreshing way, a common ground with twentieth century pilgrims in the pursuit of God.

By 1963, Merton, having been director of novices since 1951, centred precisely on the problems facing those being formed in the monastic life. It would be difficult not to read into his comments a similarity with the nature of the problems the mystics faced living in fourteenth century England. Writing to Archbishop Paul Philippe, Merton records problems faced in monasteries as "problems of *spirit* and not merely of institution."[1] In that same letter of April 5, 1963, he observed that monastic life needed "men who are alive with the Spirit of the Risen Saviour and are not afraid to seek new paths guided by the light of perennial tradition and the wisdom of Mother Church."[2] These qualities of seeking "new paths" guided by "perennial wisdom" were precisely the qualities Merton found in the English mystics of the fourteenth century. It was no surprise, then, that Merton, writing to the Carthusian Denys Rackley, mentioned Hilton, and the author of *The Cloud*, as part of "penetrate[ing], with deeper understanding the good things [monks] already have [for liturgical and monastic life]."[3]

Merton developed a theology of living from Hilton's teachings on restoration, particularly "restoration in feeling." Contemplatives, according to Hilton, had the special ability, identified as restoration in feeling, to "recognize the workings of grace."[4] This was the special awareness allowing Merton to live his life deeply centred in God, to continue, however imperfectly, living as a monk. This spiritual life-style was what Merton wanted for all who were attracted to contemplation. Merton learned from *The Scale of Perfection* that the God who gives the gift of life is the same God who touches lives with grace. Hilton's orthodox teachings, especially those linked to the sacraments of baptism and penance, appealed strongly to this relatively new convert. Hilton's certainty of the power of God's life of grace would have appealed to Merton's awareness of how grace worked continuously in his own on-going conversion. When Merton read Book Two of *The Scale*, he would have noted gladly that baptism and penance, for Hilton, had the power of "maintaining [the soul] in grace... [as well as] to save [the soul] from hell."[5] Another way in which Merton would have easily identified with the teachings of *The Scale*, was through Hilton's numerous references to Pauline anthropology, especially those passages in the letter to the Romans concerning the restoration of the life of God in mankind through the sacrifice of Christ. This notion of restoration is best developed by Merton in his book on grace and restoration entitled *The New Man*: "We become 'spiritual' men, (*pneumatikoi*) by believing in Christ and by receiving baptism."[6]

Of relevance, as well, is the fact that Hilton's teaching on "reformation in feeling" can be easily identified with the title of Merton's outstanding treatise on prayer, *The Inner Experience*. Real living takes place interiorly. Merton's inner experience while reading Hilton was eye-opening. Merton desired that spiritual eye which could perceive God's secrets. He desired to be numbered among those to whom God would show His secrets "which can only be seen by sharp eyes."[7] Merton felt at ease with the flexibility of Hilton's approach: "*The Scale of Perfection* is a 'ladder' and hence, it has steps or degrees, but Hilton...does not insist too much on analysing and measuring out the precise stages through which the spiritual man is assumed to pass, on his way to mystical union."[8] The plainness and directness of Hilton's approach to contemplation spoke worlds to Merton's living situation:

> It does not matter what exercise a man makes use of, he has not reached reform in feeling nor come truly to contemplation, unless he has attained this humble self-knowledge and is dead to the world as far as

his affections are concerned. From time to time he must feel himself in this peaceful darkness in which he is hidden from the world and sees himself for what he is.[9]

During times of real crisis, Merton found great consolation in the teachings of the author of The Cloud of Unknowing. He learned from the teachings of The Cloud that crises in identity or faith are part of living, part of the journey in faith, part of the contemplative vocation. He noted that "this [the work of The Cloud] is not merely a way of prayer, a manner of devotion: it is a way of life."[10] His best description of the "work" of prayer described by the Cloud-author was similar to the way he might have explained his reason or his need to remain in the contemplative vocation: "It is a pure response to the mysterious appeal of a hidden and incomprehensible God."[11] In those many moments when Merton's life made no sense, at least to himself, he reached out to the God of crises whose answer was that the hidden God is the answer and the critical question: "this perfect stirring of love that begins here in this life is equal with that which shall last eternally in the bliss of heaven, for they both are one."[12] Sometimes Merton felt the 'bliss' in the centre of the crisis. Somehow in the economy of the apophatic way of The Cloud of Unknowing, crisis made sense; worry did not. From the dark spirituality of The Cloud of Unknowing, he learned that perseverance in crisis was a breakthrough to the greater joy of life with God. The best summary Merton gave of the work of The Cloud was stated in "Part V" of The Inner Experience. This section is entitled "Infused Contemplation." Here he captured all that the theology of The Cloud meant to him:

> Even when there is no very definite experience of a hidden presence in the darkness of contemplation, there is always the positive and urgent movement of love which, on the one hand, wants to forget and 'trample down' all clear knowledge of everything that is not God, and on the other strives to 'pierce the cloud of unknowing' with the 'sharp dart' of its own longing. And the anonymous fourteenth century writer gives his explanation, which is also that of St. Thomas and St. John of the Cross. Though the essence of God cannot be adequately apprehended or clearly understood by man's intelligence, we can nevertheless attain directly to Him by love, and we do in fact realize obscurely in contemplation that by love we 'reach Him and hold Him close.' And when love reaches Him we are satisfied. Knowledge is of no importance. We know Him by love.[13]

Whenever Merton wrote about The Cloud of Unknowing, he was never far from seeing its connection to Zen. For example, Merton wrote to William Johnston on January 25, 1965, and he noted a reference in Johnston's edition of The Cloud as having similarities to Zen practice: "For instance, on p.166 that thing 'which is hid betwixt' two opposites would give a very suggestive point of entry into the Zen experience and point up the similarity, on a certain level, between it and the experience of The Cloud."[14] Previously, in 1964, Merton wrote to Fr. Aelred, an Anglican priest in Oxford. He told Fr. Aelred of "an interesting ms. from a Jesuit in Japan treating The Cloud in its relation to Zen."[15] There was definitely a correspondence between Merton's crisis of self-discovery, the teachings of The Cloud of Unknowing, and the practice of Zen.

Merton's comments regarding Lady Julian centre around the years 1961-63. He aligns Julian with women of courage like Raïssa Maritain. Christine Bochen, editor of The Courage for Truth, Merton's letters to writers, expressed the nature of Merton's association with the Maritains: "With Merton, they shared a commitment to art, wisdom, and social action. Like Merton, they recognized contemplatives as the source from which all else flowed."[16] The correlation between Raïssa and Lady Julian is noted by Merton as based upon his notion of "Hagia Sophia," God's holy wisdom portrayed as a caring mother.

Merton's feelings about and response to Julian's Revelations of Divine Love are manifold and always positive. More than to any other mystic, he responds to the person of Julian of Norwich as much as he does to her teachings on prayer. Merton hailed Julian as "the best known and most charming [of all the English mystics]... one of the greatest English theologians."[17] He ranks the Revelations of Divine Love as a description of an experience of God "equal to those of St. Teresa of Avila or St. Margaret Mary."[18] Merton's love for Julian and her teachings could very well stem from the clarity of orthodox doctrine in The Revelations which appealed so much to his experience of being a convert to Catholicism. He described the revelations recorded by and reflected upon by Julian as "a document that bears eloquent witness to the teaching and tradition of the Catholic Church...a meditative, indeed a mystical, commentary on the basic doctrines of the Catholic faith."[19] His love for Julian stemmed on the one hand, from her orthodoxy. On the other hand, Julian's teaching never placed the institutional trappings in the way of the individual's experience of and pursuit of God. Julian presented Merton with a view to the reality of an approachable God. For this, he was eternally grateful and eternally loyal. Julian's teachings captured all that Merton wanted to say about his own love for God. Merton became infatuated with Julian's certainty that "love is our Lord's meaning...before God made us, he loved us."[20] The degree of intimacy he felt for Julian was expressed so well in his essay "Day of a Stranger," which appeared in *The Hudson Review* in 1967:

> There is a mental ecology, too, in living balance of spirits in this corner of the woods. There is room here for many other songs besides those of birds... Here should be, and are, feminine voices from Angela of Foligno to Flannery O'Connor, Theresa of Avila, Juliana of Norwich, and, more personally and warmly still, Raïssa Maritain. [21]

There were two things which impressed Merton about Richard Rolle: he was "one of the first English vernacular poets [and] he is a genius of fire and light."[22] At the same time, Merton was careful to note that "[Dom David] Knowles tends to question his [Rolle's] mysticism."[23] As early as 1939 Merton read and was impressed by Richard Rolle's emotional teachings about unitive prayer and the methodology Rolle suggested for those committed to that life-style. Living on Perry Street in Greenwich Village, Merton recorded his thoughts about wanting to continue to read the works of Richard Rolle. The remarks were part of a journal entry for Monday, October 23, 1939. Characteristically, Merton wrote with a desire to read: "I do not turn around to see the good fire I have lit, because I am writing very fast and presently want to read Richard Rolle."[24]   Rolle's teachings became especially important when Merton faced the crisis of being asked to withdraw his application to the Franciscans and had to learn to abandon the rest of his life to the will of God. This was a time when Rolle's teachings on heat, sweetness and song were a soothing remedy for his young yet tired soul: "If a man be tempered in his flesh, he shall then cast down the flesh, that the spirit be not overcome."[25] He learned from reading Rolle's *Mending of Life* and *Form of Living* that God often communicates his love for his creatures in a sensual fashion. He found much consolation in Rolle's teachings on the psalms: vocal prayer is fed and sustained by "offer[ing] all the syllables of our prayer with a fervent desire up to God." [26] He needed the heat, sweetness, song, the insuperable and inseparable and special experience of Rolle's methodology to find his way back to discerning the will of God for him. Rolle's equation of contemplation as love, love as contemplation was Merton's invitation to solitude and to a special kind of prayer: "A strong, sweet love ravishing and burning willful and unfleschable draweth all the soul into the service of Christ, and it suffereth it to think upon nothing but upon Him."[27]

Merton's chosen pathways of mystical prayer involved reading and reflecting upon the teachings of Meister Eckhart, the English mystics, and St. John of the Cross. Through this process, Merton's friends, Fr. Daniel Walsh, Professor Mark Van Doren, Robert Lax, Edward Rice, Naomi Burton Stone, Jacques and Raïssa Maritain, Robert Giroux, and Dom Jean Leclercq, to name but a few, lighted his intellectual pathway along the interior dimensions of faith. He read the English mystics, and their characteristic simplicity and directness were special and therapeutic in his life. These mystics, English men and women, gave Merton a temporary experience of the timeless childhood of grace which was his for the asking, the praying, and the living.

Notes and References

1. William Shannon, Silent Lamp. (New York: Crossroads, 1992) , p.195
2. Thomas Merton, The School of Charity: Letters on Religious Renewal and Spiritual Direction. ed. Patrick Hart, ocso (New York: Harcourt, 1990), p.166
3. Ibid., p.187
4. Walter Hilton, The Scale of Perfection. ed. Gerard Sitwell, osb (London: Burns and Oates, 1953), p.154
5. Ibid., p.161
6. Thomas Merton, The New Man. (New York: Farrar, 1963), p.200
7. Ibid., p.308.
8. Thomas Merton, Mystics and Zen Masters. (New York: Farrar, 1967), p.136
9. Sitwell, Scale, op.cit., p.219
10. Merton, Zen Masters, op.cit., p.138
11. Ibid., p.139
12. The Cloud of Unknowing. trans. Ira Progoff. (New York: Julian Press), 1957, p.110
13. Thomas Merton, "Inner Experience: Infused Contemplation (V)" Cistercian Studies 19. (1984): p.71
14. Thomas Merton, The Hidden Ground of Love: Letters on Religious Experience and Social Concerns. ed. William H. Shannon, (New York: Harcourt, 1985), p.441
15. Merton, The School of Charity, op.cit., p.254
16. Thomas Merton, The Courage for Truth: Letters to Writers. ed. Christine Bochen, (New York: Harcourt, 1993) , p. 22

17. Merton, *Zen Masters*, op.cit., pp.140-41

18. Ibid., p.141

19. Ibid.

20. Julian of Norwich, *Revelations of Divine Love* ed. James Walsh, S. J. (New York, Harper, 1961), p. 209

21. Thomas Merton, *The Literary Essays of Thomas Merton*, ed. Brother Patrick Hart. (New York: New Directions, 198), pp.xv-xvi.

22. Merton, *Zen Masters*, op.cit., p.136

23. Ibid.

24. Thomas Merton, *Run to the Mountain: the Story of a Vocation*. ed. Patrick Hart, OCSO Vol. 1. (San Francisco: Harper, 1995), p.69

25. Richard Rolle, *The Mending of Life*. ed. Dundas Harford. (London: H. R. Allenson, 1913), p.43

26. Rolle, *Mending*, op.cit., p.49

27. Ibid., p.77

28. Merton, *The Hidden Ground of Love*, op.cit., pp. 549,611

29. Ibid., p.611

30. Ibid.

31. Ibid., pp.549, 551-52

An Apophatic Landscape

DAVID SCOTT

I WANT TO BRING three things into conjunction, for no other reason than that they are swimming around in my head, and break the surface of the pool quite frequently when I think of Thomas Merton. They are: The Cloud of Unknowing; the landscape of Oakham; and the mystical tradition, which is given the esoteric title of apophaticism. Other things might surface too, but it is the conjunction of these three that speak a feeling in my mind, and I call it 'The Apophatic Landscape.'

Oakham is a market town in Rutland, England, where Merton went to school from the autumn of 1929 to the Christmas of 1932:

> Today, a fine rain, very grey, a little raw outside, like days in England.

Oakham is the last hilly place before you get towards the flat eastern side of England, looking towards Cambridge, and the Fens. It is what we might call the East Midlands. Dr. W. G. Hoskins in his guide to Rutland describes it like this:

> ...limestone walls shining from afar in the clear winter sun and the rows of stacks in the corners of the great ploughed fields; fields that themselves gleam like a rich, brown velvet, ready for the barley and the wheat.

Merton opens his chapter in The Seven Storey Mountain on Oakham like this:

> In the autumn of 1929 I went to Oakham. There was something very pleasant and peaceful about the atmosphere of this little market town, with its school and its old fourteenth-century church with the grey spire, rising in the middle of a wide Midland vale.

and again, "the grey murk of the winter evenings in that garret where seven or eight of us moiled around in the gaslight." 'Moiled' is an interesting word there, quite an uncommon one: one of its meanings is to work in wet and mire,' and a 17th century commentary on Leviticus 18.20 uses the word in a rather different way, of David's relationship with Bathsheba, "As David, how he did moil himself with Bathsheba."

Merton's experience at Oakham School as described in *The Seven Storey Mountain* (the American version of his best selling autobiography *Elected Silence*) is full of psychological drama, and intellectual snobbery. Much of it reflects the grey light in which so much of that period is described. It is where he hears of his father's death by telegram in the Headmaster's study. The father who had been such a companion to him. Merton's reaction as recalled in the *Seven Storey Mountain* was partly one of relief that it was all over, partly huge sadness and depression, and then after a while a sense of freedom to do just whatever he liked. This freedom, he recalled, was used to make a greater captivity.

His School Chaplain takes a bashing for basing his whole theology on the premise that 'Love' in St Paul's First Letter to the Corinthians chapter 13, could be replaced by the word 'gentleman.' Whatever became of 'Buggy' Jerwood? More correctly, the Reverend Frederick Harold Jerwood: Jesus College, Cambridge B.A. 1903, Cuddesdon College 1910, deacon 1911, priest 1912, Curate of All Saints Northampton 1911-1914, Chaplain and Assistant Master at Oakham School from 1914. So he had been at the School for 15 years when Merton arrived, and was still teaching them how to row on top of the desks because there was no stretch of water in the town.

The description of his illness in his last year at school, is given in Dantesque terms, 'but now I lay on this bed, full of gangrene, and my soul was rotten with the gangrene of my sins and I did not care whether I died or lived.' Whether it was really as bad as all that we shall never know, but that is what Merton remembered it as eighteen or so years later in the autobiography. It provided for the author a significant lead up to the visit to Italy, shortly after he had left school, where he began to experience the reality of Christ through the Byzantine mosaics of Rome. The light had to come out of an intense darkness to be even more illuminating. Yet he did not have to wait for Rome to trace the seeds of his burgeoning faith. There was a moment in his school experience when his reading of Blake's poems, and the knowledge of his intellectual life and ideas, that coalesced in an epiphany, latent and subdued though it was:

One grey Sunday in the spring, I walked alone out of the Brooke Road and up Brooke Hill, where the rifle range was. It was a long bare, hog-back of a hill, with a few lone trees along the top, and it commanded a big sweeping view of the Vale of Catmos, with the town of Oakham lying in the midst of it, gathered around the grey, sharp church spire. I sat on a stile on the hill top, and contemplated the wide vale, from the north, where the kennels of the Cottesmore hounds were, to Lax Hill and Manton in the south. Straight across was Burley house, on top of its hill, massed with woods. At my feet, a few red brick houses straggled out from the town to the bottom of the slope.

And all the time I reflected, that afternoon, upon Blake. I remember how I concentrated and applied myself to it. It was rare that I ever really thought about such a thing of my own accord. But I was trying to establish what manner of man he was. Where did he stand? What did he believe? What did he preach…

The Providence of God was eventually to use Blake to awaken something of faith and love in my own soul in spite of all the misleading notions, and all the almost infinite possibilities of error that underlie his weird and violent figures. I do not therefore want to seem to canonize him. But I have to acknowledge my own debt to him, and the truth which may appear curious to some, although it is really not so: that through Blake I would one day come, in a round-about way, to the only true Church, and to the one living God, through his Son, Jesus Christ.

The association of that place and that walk up Brooke Hill with the influence of Blake is so archetypically true of what goes on in adolescence when the influences are so all-surrounding, and art is infused with the environment and both with the growing body. "In three months, the summer of 1931, I suddenly matured like a weed…" and all that again with the expanding mind. Notice, too, the aloneness and the reflection in the open air, and the intensity with which he questions himself, and the big questions to which he was always returning: what manner of man, where did he stand, what did he believe, what did he preach.

The weather was 'grey spring,' muted, and soft. "I myself am part of the weather and part of the climate and part of the place, and a day in which I have not shared truly in all this is no day at all. It is certainly part of my life of prayer." (Journal 4, p. 300). His memory of Oakham was one of greyness. The cloud of dank, dark autumn and winter days. 1929, low watt light bulbs, rugby matches finished in the dark. There was a rugger side to Merton. Longing in the cloudy greyness and the dark, searching and reaching, because the end was always beyond, and the now always just a symbol of what was to come.

One or two other flashes of the Oakham climate of prayer come back to Merton much later in his life. One a poem, untitled, in which he recalls a contrast between the heightened tragic emotion of Euripides's writing and the "Sons of a cool & gentle England:"

When class was in the garden at Greylands
And we tried to translate Euripides
Not knowing Greek

We cared little for a dead hero
However mad
Or for his mad language

Prefects and cricketers
We were alive & sane and careless in our own strength.
We spoke English.
We smiled
At the master's cat.

Holidays came
We left the crazy Titan
Before the hot shirt
Drove him to kill his own children.

We were alive & sane
Sons of a cool & gentle England.

That was in 1931. Since then
There have been hotter seasons
We go on translating
More & more Euripides
With less and less Greek.

The fury of Herakles
Has swollen beyond bounds.
And now we are never out of danger
We have forgotten our smiles & our strength.

It is as if the world had got far more dangerous since the days at school, more serious. The stories are becoming true, and there are no holidays in which to forget them, or to realise that they are only stories.

The third epiphany is described in *Journal No. 4*, an entry of September 29, 1962:

> This morning, in John of Salisbury, ran across a quote from the *Georgics* which has entered into the deepest part of my being since I learned it thirty years ago at Oakham and was moved by it then, studying I think one June morning before the Higher Cert., by a brook behind Catmose House.

> *Felix qui potuit rerum cognoscere causas*
> *Atque metus omnes, et inexorabile fatum*
> *Subjecit pedibus, strepitumque Acherontis avari.*

> (Happy is he who can have known the causes of things, and has placed under his feet all fears and inexorable fate and the rumbling of greedy Acheron.)

> Inexhaustible literary, spiritual, moral beauty of these lines: the classic ideal of wisdom. What a gift to have lived and to have received this, as though a sacrament, and to be in communion of light and joy with the whole of my civilisation - and my Church. This is indestructible, Acheron (whose strepitus (rumbling) was never so full of ominous rumblings) has nothing to say about it.

And John of S. — glossing this with words about faith as a way to the highest truth, adds:

> *Impossibile est ut diligat et colat vanitatem quisquis et toto corde quaerit et amplectionem veritatis.* (It is quite impossible for someone to seek and foster vanity and wholeheartedly at the same time to seek also for the embrace of truth.)

And me, glossing Merton, glossing John of Salisbury, glossing Virgil, to say how he remembers the place and the month of June, and how he recalls the significant within a climate, as though the words and the weather interacted, and came out of air and were to go back to air, but leaving their imprint, their scent on the soul.

The Cloud of Unknowing is a book, a treatise or series of pieces of advice on the contemplative life. I mention it now because it surrounds itself with all the ingredients I am dealing with in this paper. It was written by an anonymous country parson in this area of England, the East Midlands. Merton knew the work well, wrote about it in *Mystics and Zen Masters* (1966), and wrote an introduction to William Johnston's *The Mysticism of The Cloud of Unknowing* (1967). It is also a prime example of the influence of the apophatic way of thinking (though 'thinking' is not at all the right word) for a way which clouds out thinking. We might today say accessing God. Another connection is that throughout the middle years of Merton's time at Gethsemani, one of the tensions in his life was between the Cistercian way and the Carthusian way. *The Cloud of Unknowing* was known to have had a great influence on the Carthusians in the 14th century, and speaking to them it spoke also to Merton's contemplative and eremitical spirit.

So we have a bundle of jostling influences, stretching across time and place: 14th century — 20th century; Oakham — Kentucky; coenobitic — eremitical; Cistercian — Carthusian. No one area of influence takes centre ground, and to deal with them all in a paper like this is difficult. I am reminded of how T.S.Eliot, confronted with a similar bundle of influences, when trying to bring them into some sort of unity, wrote *The Four Quartets*. Similarly, David Jones wrote *The Anathemata*, both modernist poems, attempting to hold together disparate ages and cultures, while allowing each their separate genius. I believe our post modern age has given up the struggle on this one, and Merton's own attempt in his poem, *The Geography of Lograire* suffers from having a toe in the postmodern waters, in which nothing can really relate to anything else.

Holding things together in a grand design was not Merton's way. He was a very unsystematic theologian. What did hold his work together was partly his skin, although that often cried out for mercy at the sight of yet another request for an article, or an introduction. But what I value most in Merton is his capacity to enthuse, and excite, and embrace such a wide range of concerns and people, and to hold them together at the point of contemplation, where all things are held but also all things are allowed to slip away. To know that this activity of loving, because love was the impetus for his voracious enthusiasms, was also around in Oakham in the 14th century. As all things are gathered into the fellowship, or *koinonia*, of those who 'list' towards God, and enjoy God's love which initiates all attempting. Anthony T. Padovano puts it like this:

> Merton was consistently aware of the anonymous community we forge with people whose spirit is bonded with ours. Often, we never meet them; sometimes their agenda is adversarial, at least on the surface. Nonetheless we form together the company of those who defend life under siege and we collaborate with them without knowing clearly the identities of those who make common cause with us."

All that to say that time and centuries should not constrict us in our sense of fellowship with the communion of saints, and The Cloud is as contemporary as you like. The message of The Cloud is expressed in the first three chapters, and this from Chapter 3:

> Lift up your heart to God with humble love, and mean God himself, and not what you get out of him.

> Do not give up then, but work away at it until you have that longing (list). When you first begin you find only darkness, and as it were a cloud of unknowing.

That cloud which surrounded Moses in Exodus, and Elias in the Book of Kings, was a cloud of unknowing in which language ceases to be able to express the glory, and in which talking to God goes on, without seeing Him. "One of the ways of attacking this problem," says Merton, "has been opened up by so called apophatic theology, the theology of 'unknowing,' which describes the transcendent experience of God in love as a 'knowing by unknowing' and a 'seeing that is not seeing.' The language of apophatism is not peculiar to Christianity, and it had currency in Asia long before Christian times (for instance in Lao-Tzu and in the Upanishads)... For centuries mystics have groped for words in which to account for the supreme reality of this experience which not only illuminates a man's mind and fills his heart with new strength, but really transforms his whole life." (Mysticism of the Cloud, vii).

Apophatism took an interesting contemporary turn with Merton. Certainly he knew all the history. His book on St John of the Cross, the classic exponent of apophatic theology, was written in the cauldron of Merton's apophatic days, The Ascent to Truth. More interesting is how it affected his whole way of thinking and communicating. If you listen to the tapes of Merton teaching, they are a strange mixture of authority and irony. His delivery is quite forceful and combative, punchy, it's that rugger side of him again, and yet every so often, he breaks out into a joke, or a swipe at himself, or a tangential thought which he follows just for fun. He could spot the humour in the moment. So he was talking about music and plainsong, and a bird sings outside the window, and he breaks off his talk and picks up the connection very playfully.

What has this got to do with The Cloud and apophatic theology? Merton knew a tremendous amount, but he was also continually aware of a greater reality than knowledge, which puts all human knowing into the perspective of humility. If we know we can only know nothing, really, of what God is, then our reading, writing, thinking, planning are all done in a cloud. We can put no ultimate trust in them. We can be deceived by them. We can lose our way in them. So the cloud disorientates us to reorientate us towards the one thing that does really matter above all others, which is the love of God. We learn about that love in the cloud:

Lift up your heart to God with humble love and mean God himself.

An English public boarding school in the 1930s was not unlike a Cistercian monastery. I guess that something of the community life, the downright awfulness of much of it, the rugger side of things, the thrashings, the bad food, and the wondrous delight of getting away from it, out into the countryside, up Brooke Hill, or into the pages and poems of William Blake, rather than putting him off, in a strange way drew him back. It was an institutional and emotional world he knew and had conquered. Nothing would ever be so bad again. School was the place where he had experienced and survived the news of his father's death and that he now was really alone in the world. It may have been dreadful but it was a part of the reality of his experience, and one which he may have been wanting to recapture, in a redeeming way, in the monastery.

Looking back on Oakham in the *Conjectures* period he saw the countryside, the landscape, as one of his many angels: "all the villages and fields and hedges and corners of woods around Oakham, The tower of Oakham Church and the broad vale." For these he was truly grateful. The rebel he was in the sixth form was also the rebel he was in the monastery, the same rebellious need to be other, an individual in community, outside as well as inside.

"It had become evident to me that I was a great rebel. I fancied that I had suddenly risen above all the errors and stupid idiots and mistakes of modern society...and that I had taken my place in the ranks of those who held up their heads and squared their shoulders and marched into the future." (*Seven Storey Mountain*, p.93).

By nature I think Merton must have been claustrophobic, always searching to be outside, physically in the woods and close to natural things, and intellectually out there in front, going where no-one has gone before, and always imagining that the grass was greener on the other side of the enclosure. *The Cloud of Unknowing* had a great influence on the Carthusian movement in England. Some have thought that its author must have been a Carthusian, but Evelyn Underhill is not convinced:

> It has been thought that the author was a Carthusian. But the rule of that austere order, whose members live in hermit-like seclusion, and scarcely meet except for the purpose of divine worship, can hardly have afforded him opportunity of observing and enduring all those tiresome tricks and absurd mannerisms of which he gives so amusing and realistic a description in the lighter passages of the Cloud .

The seduction of the hermit or Carthusian life to Merton was intense in the late 40s and early 50s. He was in correspondence with Dom Humphrey Pawsey, a Carthusian monk of St. Hugh's Charterhouse in England and who went on to be Superior of the Sky Farm foundation in Vermont, and Dom Jean-Baptiste Porion from La Grande Chartreuse. He discussed with them his desire "to embrace the eremitical life." That desire took various forms through the years, until it found some reconciliation in the hermitage. Perhaps there his Carthusian spirit, the spirit of the Cloud, found its home. The hermitage within the monastery grounds provided a greater degree of solitude without breaking off the Cistercian belonging. An ideal answer and a happy one.

Did that mean that the whole notion of apophaticism slipped away in a new found happiness and release from the darkness of the Oakham moiling? St. John of the Cross seemed to become less quoted, and the South American poets took over. The boarding school gloom was being dispersed. The holidays were coming. The smell of cabbage and brimstone were being replaced with the smell of wood smoke, and the heart and the mind were looking beyond the walls to the world.

One thing he did not lose from his apophatic past was the love of the night, and the lights shining in the darkness. The night was always for Merton darkness redeemed, not light obscured. ('Six Night Letters,' *Eighteen Poems*, cf. also 'Night Flowering Cactus.')

It begins to sound strange speaking of someone I have never met in such intimate terms as if I knew all the answers about him. Such presumption!   So perhaps all I am talking about is myself, which is only one step less embarrassing. So I'll stop.

THOMAS MERTON
poet · monk · prophet

COLIN ALBIN

JOHN WU, JR.

PATRICK EASTMAN

DANNY SULLIVAN

Thomas Merton and Inter–Faith Dialogue: Exploring a Way Forward

Colin Albin

Introduction

RELIGIOUS TRUTHS ARE A source of both passion and of conflict. Because of this, religious people need to find ways of understanding one another and of living in tolerance with one another, in order to ensure some sort of harmony in multi-faith societies, such as our own, as well as on the religiously plural global landscape. Religious tensions in Britain, Israel, the Balkans and elsewhere alert us to the need for action as well as words. Hans Küng has warned us that there will be 'no peace in the world until there is peace between the religions.'[1] In a more pointed argument, Samuel Huntington[2] has spoken of the danger of a clash between civilizations. The two main potential enemies of the West, in Huntington's view, are Islam and Confucianism. However, if his appeal lies in the realm of security and the protection of interests from a perceived enemy, Thomas Merton's lies in the realm of reconciliation and the value of learning from a perceived friend. Merton believed that if the Western world continued to neglect 'the spiritual heritage of the East,' it could 'hasten the tragedy that threatens man and his civilizations.'[3] This paper is about Thomas Merton's dialogue with Eastern religions and the lessons we can learn from him.

Preliminary Reflections on Inter-Faith Dialogue

There are well-established principles for the conduct of inter-faith dialogue as well as key theological categories which have tended to guide scholarly debates. The principles were outlined in 1979 when the World Council of Churches produced 'Guidelines on Dialogue with People of Living Faiths and Ideologies.' In 1983, the British Council Of Churches distilled the wisdom of the W.C.C.

document in a publication entitled 'Relations With People Of Other Faiths: Guidelines For Dialogue In Britain.' This has been widely accepted by Christians and people of other faiths throughout the world. The principles are as follows:

1) Dialogue begins when people meet each other.
2) Dialogue depends upon mutual understanding and mutual trust.
3) Dialogue makes it possible to share in service to the community.
4) Dialogue becomes the medium of authentic witness.

The main theological categories which have been set out are exclusivism, inclusivism and pluralism. These have been elaborated in detail elsewhere[4] and within a very short space of time they have been widely accepted as key definitions around which debates are centred.

Nevertheless, although the principles and theological approaches are helpful, there is a growing feeling that these are all, in some way, inadequate. In short, there is considerable uncertainty about the best way to approach inter-religious encounters. To find a way through this current impasse, I want to suggest that we look more closely at the inspiring figure of Thomas Merton. In his religious quest for truth, for enlightenment and for God, he was willing to listen to, to learn from and to love those of faiths and traditions other than his own. He moved beyond perceptions and dogmas and touched something of the heart of other religions and of the devotees of those religions. In order to do this he himself had to undergo the most thoroughgoing transformation. Merton's pilgrimage took him from secular-minded and disinterested Protestantism, through an initially pious Catholic monasticism, to a man at home in the metaphysics and mysticism of Zen and other religious schools of thought and practice. Thomas Merton did not suggest that all religions were the same. Indeed, he was keen to admit and to value differences. He was very aware that the mystical path was one in which much common ground could be discovered, but was aware that no faith, even his own, had a complete monopoly on truth or on God. He believed himself to be on a journey, rather than having arrived. By examining Merton's fascinating journey, I believe that we can find a model for inter-faith dialogue which will prove to be invaluable in our age of religious conflict and misunderstanding.

His sense that truth is provisional has now gained a much firmer foundation, in science as well as in religious studies, in the light of present day knowledge. But, given his great interest in poetry, it is perhaps more fitting to use a poem to illustrate something of the direction of his life. The poem 'Truth', by Ann Lewin, aptly summarizes Merton's approach to the religious quest.

> For some, Truth is a fortress, square and strong,
> In which, once entered, safety lies.
> Only like-minded people dwell there, none disturb
> The calm and certain sureties of belief
> Outside, the world pursues its way, its noise and
> Clamour offering small attraction to those
> Whose knowledge keeps them safe beyond the
> Drawbridge of conviction. If any try to breach the
> Bastions of tradition, they are repelled with
> Boiling scorn. Truth is impregnable.
> For others, Truth is both journey and
> Discovery, a Way which leads and
> Urges without rest.
> No castle for retreat, but
> Camps, where fellow pilgrims join
> To take refreshment in each other's
> Company. Assorted in experience, they
> Enrich, enlighten, challenge and
> Go on further exploration.
> Travelling light. Knowing that in this life
> All is provisional; seeking fulfilment,
> The end and explanation of the quest. [5]

The radical shift in the Roman Catholic position in respect of non-Christian religions (as expressed by the Second Vatican Council) sat well with Merton's later thinking. One suspects that he might also have felt comfortable with recent Anglican statements[6] on inter-faith understanding. However, the modern position which I believe most closely reflects Merton's own understanding is that of Professor John Bowker. In his fascinating book, *Is God A Virus? Genes, Culture And Religion*,[7] Bowker moves beyond exclusivism, inclusivism and pluralism to propose a fourth solution, a position he has called 'differentialism.' This is suggestive of a very helpful way forward in terms of both good theology and good inter-faith relations, allowing for 'differences to be carried to their ultimate conclusion.' It[8] does not attempt to force the 'approximate and corrigibly expressed accounts of ultimacy in each religion' into the claims of any one of them, 'since more than one may be correct.' Neither, he argues, does it 'allow an indefinable category of "ultimacy"' to force all religions into 'approximate accounts of the same thing' because differences are real and 'lie deeper than semantics.' Bowker argues that this admission of legitimate diversity in differentialism allows for 'equal outcomes of value which cannot be translated into each other.'[9] According to David Bosch[10] the three main positions leave no room for 'embracing the abiding paradox' of asserting one's own ultimate religious commitment and 'genuine openness to another's...' Differentialism, on the other hand, does leave such room and it is into this 'abiding paradox' that Thomas Merton speaks very powerfully. It allows for the symbolic and provisional nature of religious language, which Merton clearly recognised.

Reflections on Eastern Spirituality and Identity

Thomas Merton's life reveals a dogged search for identity. His affinity with Eastern spirituality was a key factor in this. He read widely about the major religions of the world. But the impact of personal contact with people of non-Christian religions was, for him, probably of far greater significance. Lipski highlights the fact that his initially 'negative impressions' of Oriental mysticism 'were partially neutralized by his encounters in June 1948 [1938: Ed.] with an Indian yogi,' whose 'calmness and worshipfulness deeply impressed Merton.'[11] His spiritual experience was greatly enhanced through his contact with people of other faiths. And, as spiritual experience grew in influence, rigid adherence to doctrine became less significant. In addition, it is important to realize that his life of contemplation and dialogue was largely a search for his true self. His writings show how he realized that the discovery of one's true self was the same process as the discovery of God and 'the other.' Merton's spiritual journey led him to a surprising sense of wholeness in which he saw inter-connections between the self, God and the other. His journey eastwards was a crucial part of this voyage of discovery.

Although Merton was a committed Christian, it was because he did 'not believe anything is final or conclusive'[12] that he moved beyond the books and letters and discussions and actually went to Asia. He was, in fact, very honest about his desire to learn from Eastern spiritual traditions. He said that he sought 'to learn more (quantatively) about religion and monastic life' and also 'to become a better and more enlightened monk (qualitatively).' He was looking for a 'full and transcendental liberty which is beyond mere cultural differences and mere externals...'[13] Furthermore, he referred to his Asian trip in a remarkable way, by saying that 'I am going home, to the home where I have never been in this body...'[14] There is little doubt that he regarded Eastern religious spirituality as central to his sense of identity, to his life of faith and to his spiritual calling as a monk. As Merton's spiritual exploration turns further towards the East, he comes to a fuller, deeper and richer understanding and experience of what his true identity is. He clearly became comfortable with the imagery of the religious thought patterns of the East and was open to all that these could teach him.

In this process of discovery, change and spiritual growth I see two aspects of Merton's complex nature which particularly inform his approach to other religions: the artistic and the apophatic. These inspired his inter-faith explorations and enabled him to inwardly grapple with and outwardly express the conflicting, contrasting and intermingling aspects of his spiritual journey. Hence, his contemplation became deeper and his dialogue wider. Furthermore, it seems to me that Merton's radical thinking about the inter-relationship between God, self, and 'the other' is suggestive of a model of dialogue which I have called 'explorational.' This is quite different to what may be called a functional approach. By functional I mean official dialogue between representatives of various religions and organisations, with definite objectives in view. By explorational I mean open-ended dialogue between spiritual people on an unofficial level, even a personal level, with only limited or even no particular objectives in view. Merton, in my opinion, personifies the latter. Before we examine the explorational model in more detail, let us first cf all look at these two important aspects of Merton's evolving personality which I believe to be largely responsible for his openness to Eastern spirituality and his ability to engage in fruitful dialogue.

Finding God, Self and 'The Other' in Art

Thomas Merton had a sense of pride in the fact that both of his parents were artists. He even acknowledged that he had inherited something of his father's vision of the world.[15] Their artistic awareness had been transmitted to Merton and as his spiritual journey developed he became conscious of the link between art and spirituality. Ross Labrie makes a convincing argument for Merton's artistic orientation and comments that his mind 'was intuitive and tentative.'[16] He points out that, for Merton, mystics such as William Blake and St. John of the Cross had woven together threads of both the artistic and the contemplative life. In Labrie's view, Thomas Merton's writing 'was intimately connected with his sense of identity,'[17] a sentiment echoed by others as well as by Merton himself Although he, at times, doubted his monastic call, he knew that he could not doubt his call to be a writer. 'I was born one and will most probably die as one,' he once remarked.[18] This was, I believe, the creative urge of the artist within him. It was because of his artistic leanings that he was often frustrated about being over busy. Furlong records his comment that, 'It is not much fun to live the spiritual life with the spiritual equipment of an artist.'[19] His appreciation that different forms of artistic communication were akin to religious experiences was a common thread through his later writings. He believed that 'Poetry is not ordinary speech, nor is poetic experience ordinary experience. It is closer to religious experience.'[20]

Moreover, Merton's thinking on the interrelationship between art and spirituality was crystallized during his visit to Polonnaruwa in 1968, which was 'such an experience' that he 'could not write hastily of it.' Indeed, it was such a profound and defining experience for Merton that he felt inadequate to speak of it at all. He describes a fellow visitor, the vicar general, sitting under a tree reading, 'shying away from "paganism,"' whilst he approaches the enormous Buddhas 'barefoot and undisturbed.' His linguistic collage which portrays this momentous event evokes images of Moses at the burning bush:

> Then the silence of the extraordinary faces. The great smiles. Huge and yet subtle. Filled with possibility, questioning nothing, knowing everything, rejecting nothing, the peace...that has seen through every question without trying to discredit anyone or anything – without refutation – without establishing some other argument. For the doctrinaire, the mind that needs well-established positions, such peace, such silence can be frightening. I was knocked over with a rush of relief and thankfulness at the obvious clarity of the figures, the clarity and fluidity of shape and line, the design of monumental bodies composed into the rock shape and landscape, figure, rock and tree... Looking at

these figures I was suddenly, almost forcibly, jerked clean out of the habitual, half-tied vision of things, and an inner clearness, clarity, as if exploding from the rocks themselves, became evident and obvious... All problems are resolved and everything is clear...everything is emptiness and everything is compassion. I don't know when in my life I have ever had such a sense of beauty and spiritual validity running together in one aesthetic illumination... I know and have seen what I was obscurely looking for. I don't know what else remains but I have now seen and have pierced through the surface and have got beyond the shadow and the disguise... It says everything; it needs nothing.[21]

Merton was approaching the figures at Polonnaruwa positively, not as a misguided form of paganism. The result was overpowering. Hugo Meynell says that, 'The appreciation of art in general tends to counteract the rigidity of our habits of perception and understanding.'[22] We certainly see here Merton's fascination with aesthetics and with the spiritual power of art forms to break down his own false perceptions, misunderstandings or barriers to enlightenment of any kind. I tend to agree with Monica Furlong's assessment that it was at Polonnaruwa that Merton underwent his most transforming spiritual experience and found something he'd been seeking all his life. In the introduction to his biography, she makes the interesting observation that 'these great holy figures' somehow released 'joy and love in his heart' and gave him the feeling that 'he had come home, and the home was God.'[23]

Finding God, Self and 'The Other' in Darkness and Emptiness

Thomas Merton spoke about a 'transformation of consciousness' which is required in order to leave the 'false self' and discover the 'true self.' The notion of transformed consciousness which evolved in his mind was enriched by both his artistic orientation and by Christian mystics of the apophatic (from the Greek apophasis: denial, negation) tradition, such as St. John of the Cross, St. Gregory of Nyssa and Meister Eckhart as well as by Taoism, Sufism, Judaism, Hinduism and Tibetan Buddhism, but especially by Zen. John Teahan has rightly highlighted the 'appropriation of the apophatic tradition in Christian mysticism' as a 'dominant concern' of Merton's.[24] Much that he discovered in Taoism and Zen resonated with treasures he'd unearthed from the apophatic tradition in Christian mysticism. Teahan helpfully identifies and clarifies 'Merton's apophaticism,' particularly with reference to the symbols of darkness and emptiness. These, he believes, are highly significant symbols in apophatic literature as well as being constantly recurring themes in Merton's writings. This important strand in Merton has, as Teahan argues, direct 'relevance to the meeting of East and West.'[25] Teahan explains that '"negative theology" refuses to assign attributes to God' and that the 'apophatic mystics further claim that it is impossible to reach God through reason alone.' Apophatic mysticism attempts to 'approach God by transcending ideas, images and sense impressions.'[26]

Merton claimed 'that contemplation transcends the theological enterprise'[27] and 'reveals a God beyond concepts, a God known by unknowing.' John Wu, Jr. believes that Merton intuitively realized that 'wisdom and the search for the inmost self did not lie in the gaining of knowledge' but rather 'in the losing of it.'[28] Furthermore, Teahan argues that Merton had an 'aversion to technical theology, even of the apophatic variety,' and this 'increased in the last fifteen years of his life.'[29] He asserts that Merton was 'more at home with the metaphorical language of darkness and emptiness than with complex reasoning.' Teahan draws attention to the fact that, for Merton, 'The essence of God is beyond human knowledge,'[30] but this was in his understanding a very positive discovery.

Emptiness was another important motif for Merton. According to Teahan, Merton described emptiness in 'two major ways: as realization of spiritual destitution and finitude and as liberation from attachment to selfish obsession.'[31] D.T. Suzuki sought to correct what he believed to be Merton's misunderstanding of emptiness, at one stage, and maintained that Zen emptiness is 'not the emptiness of nothingness', but the 'emptiness of fullness', in which 'zero = infinity.'[32] Commenting on the correspondence between Suzuki and Merton, Teahan says that, for Merton, emptiness came to indicate 'a potential for fullness, though the contemplative may not always recognize it.'[33] Just as I argued that Merton's artistic orientation accelerated his openness to Eastern spirituality and ability to dialogue, so I want to also argue that his way of darkness and emptiness furthered this endeavour. Teahan puts it this way:

> The theme of openness to all modes of dynamic spirituality permeated the final decade of Merton's life and writings. To be empty of egocentricity is to be open to others, to the possibilities that arise only when defensiveness and discrimination are replaced by compassion and communion.[34]

Explorational Dialogue - A Model for the Future

Merton came to believe in the need to enter upon a way which meant he had to 'leave all ways and in some sense get lost,' an insight he gleaned from studying Chuang Tzu.[35] Yet, for Merton acceptance of 'the other' never meant rejection of his own tradition. He believed that:

> genuine ecumenism requires the communication and sharing, not only of information about doctrines which are totally and irrevocably divergent, but also of religious institutions and truths which may turn out to have something in common, beneath the surface differences. Ecumenism seeks the inner and ultimate spiritual "ground" which underlies all articulated differences. A genuinely fruitful dialogue cannot be content with a polite diplomatic interest in other religious traditions and beliefs. It seeks a deeper level, on which religious traditions have always claimed to bear witness to a higher and more personal knowledge of God than that which is contained simply in exterior worship and formulated doctrine. [36]

Merton speaks of a 'universally recognizable' spirituality, which has a 'very real quality of existential likeness.'[37] He perceived 'the growth of a truly universal consciousness in the modern world,' 'a consciousness of transcendent freedom and vision.'[38] However, whilst readily admitting that God may well 'impart His light to other men,'[39] he is alert to the dangers of syncretism and is keen to distance his own approach from that particular option. Merton strongly rejected the tendency of those who 'identify all religions and all religious experiences with one another.' He believed that this would guarantee that the interfaith dialogue would end in confusion.'[40] The extent of Merton's exploration is, perhaps, best revealed by his obvious affinity with people of other faiths. He found it astonishing that he had 'much more in common' with a Japanese Zen Buddhist than with fellow Christians, 'who are little concerned with religion, or interested only in its external practice.'[41] This affinity with 'the other' and the superficiality of many within his own tradition obviously concerned Merton, for he wanted fellow Christians to share the joy of his discoveries. 'Our task now,' he said:

> is to learn that if we can voyage to the ends of the earth and there find ourselves in the aborigine who most differs from ourselves, we will have made a fruitful pilgrimage. That is why pilgrimage is necessary, in some shape or other. Mere sitting at home and meditating on the

divine presence is not enough for our time. We have to come to the end of a long journey and see that the stranger we meet there is no other than ourselves – which is the same as saying that we find Christ in him.[42]

In this section, then, I want to draw attention to those aspects of Thomas Merton's explorational approach which are distinctively characteristic of him and from which we can learn vitally important lessons.

Valuing Pure Exploration

Merton saw a profound innocence in the artistic enterprise of contemplation and dialogue. Recognising the link between art, poetry and spirituality, he said that the art of the poet 'depends on an ingrained innocence which he would lose in business, in politics, or in too organized a form of academic life.'[43] This is why I prefer to think of him as an artist rather than an academic, even though his intellectual capabilities were immense. When Merton was asked directly about art and freedom, his answers were very revealing. He was profoundly aware that the artist 'is responsible first of all for the excellence of his work' and should not need to justify itself in any functional frame of reference. 'The artist,' he believed 'must serenely defend his right to be completely useless.'[44] He argued that it is 'better to produce absolutely no work of art at all than to do what can be cynically "used."'[45]

Humility

Merton's spiritual journey is one of remarkable humility. He was readily willing to change his mind and to admit the fact. William Johnston comments that, 'When questioned about one of his early works, Thomas Merton remarked: "The man who wrote that book is dead."'[46] He adds that Merton 'died and rose many times.' It seems to me that an important part of this process for Merton was the willingness to enter the dark night of the soul. I also see something of the inspired artist in this humble process of change. Labrie notes that:

> The artist, Merton believed, went out to the object before him – a rose or a grain of sand – with complete humility, not subjecting the object to the classifying habit of the mind, but so identifying with it as to look out of it as though the artist fulfilled the role of consciousness not only for himself but for the object as well. [47]

Holding Together The Contradictory

In this study I have suggested that Thomas Merton was a religious artist. I regard his pilgrimage as a form of wrestling with God, just as Jacob wrestled with the angel in the book of Genesis. The poem 'Art,' by Herman Melville[48] uses this imagery and speaks of how 'unlike things must meet and mate' to produce art. In Merton's own spirituality, the 'unlike things' certainly did 'meet and mate' and form a very powerful picture of spiritual reality. Amos Oz says that the ability to hold together, with 'integrity,' those things which appear contradictory is the sign of the writer. It is, if you like, the artistic gift. This skill is simply a different form of art and it may be described as the ability to see the unity in diversity, to find the wholeness in that which is different.[49]

One of the remarkable things about Merton was this ability to hold together a range of apparently conflicting ideas in his own person, his own identity. Here is a classic example of how he expressed something of his multi-dimensional being in his own words:

> the more I am able to affirm others, to say "yes" to them in myself, by discovering them in myself and myself in them, the more real I am. I am fully real if my own heart says yes to everyone. I will be a better Catholic, not if I can refute every shade of Protestantism, but if I can affirm the truth in it and still go further. So, too, with the Muslims, the Hindus, the Buddhists, etc. This does not mean syncretism, indifferentism, the vapid and careless friendliness that accepts everything by thinking of nothing. There is much that one cannot "affirm" and "accept," but first one must say "yes" where one really can. If I affirm myself as a Catholic merely by denying all that is Muslim, Jewish, Protestant, Hindu, Buddhist, etc., in the end I will find that there is not much left for me to affirm as a Catholic: and certainly no breath of the spirit with which to affirm it.[50]

Openness

In the Preface to the *Asian Journal*, the consulting editor, Amiya Chakravarty said that:

> Readers of Thomas Merton will know that his openness to man's spiritual horizons came from a rootedness of faith; and inner security led him to explore, experience, and interpret the affinities and differences between religions in the light of his own religion.[51]

In other words, for Merton, his own faith was not a barrier to openness but rather a springboard for it. Thomas Merton was a remarkably open person, who learned to approach people of other faiths with a reverence and willingness to learn. He said that, 'To give priority to the person means respecting the unique and inalienable value of the other person...'[52] Furthermore, he clearly believed that insights shared with others were more likely to result in 'certainties' than the imagined certainty of isolation, which Lewin's poem[5] speaks of as the 'fortress' of truth.

Insider Perspective

Merton's aim was not to stand back and observe other religions and judge, but rather to look at that particular faith from the inside. This is clear from his preface to Mystics And Zen Masters. He says:

> The author has attempted not merely to look at these other traditions coldly and objectively from the outside, but, in some measure at least, to try to share in the values and experience which they embody. In other words he is not content to write about them without making them, as far as possible, "his own."[53]

Jim Forest refers to Merton's 'insider perspective' with reference to his correspondence with the Muslim, Abdul Aziz. For Forest, Merton's letters to him were 'a perfect example of this gift Merton had of writing to people from almost within their own skin.'[54] It seems to me that he possessed an absolutely remarkable intuitive perception of and insight into them. This fact is borne out by scholars and respected followers of those religions who praised his appreciation of their particular faith. These include such respected figures as D.T. Suzuki[55] Chatral Rinpoche[56] and the Dalai Lama.[57] Although it is never possible to gain a perfect 'insider' perspective as an 'outsider,' the response of prominent members of other faiths to Merton's understanding of their faith bears ample evidence to suggest no small measure of mastery on his part.

Recognition Of Interdependence

Merton wrote that, 'Every other man is a piece of myself, for I am a part and a member of mankind.' He added: 'Nothing at all makes sense, unless we admit with John Donne, that: "No man is an island..."'[58] Merton became aware of the interdependence between man, God, and all things in the universe. Reflecting on the wisdom of the Vietnamese Buddhist, Thich Nhat Hanh, he recognized the unity of humankind:

> To set up party, race, nation or even official religion as absolutes is   to erect barriers of illusion that stand between man and himself...[59]

Then, in *Zen And The Birds Of Appetite*, speaking of Zen and art, Merton points to a unity between existence and being, a broader interdependence between all things. He calls man 'a soul in the form of art,' and 'a solitary being full of meaning and close to the essence of things.'[60] He was concerned that we should be 'Piercing the illusions in ourselves which divide us from others' through 'unity and solidarity' and 'openness and compassion.' Such love, he says, 'can transform the world.' This wider transformation is, for Merton, a direct result of an inner transformation. He argued that, 'In order to see rightly, one must recognize the essential interdependence, impermanence, and inconsistency of phenomena.'[61]

Conclusion

In conclusion, let me simply list current initiatives with which I believe Merton would have felt a kindred spirit. Space forbids me from doing more than simply naming them:

- The Kagyu Samye Ling Tibetan Centre's Inter-Faith Symposia and Holy Island Inter-Faith Project.
- The World Congress Of Faiths, with its emphasis on world peace.
- The Christian Meditation Centre, with its John Main Seminars — notably the 1994 one, at which the Dalai Lama gave his reflections on the Gospels.
- The Thomas Merton Society, of which I need say no more.

Notes and References

This paper is a summary of Cohn Albin's M.A. Thesis, entitled 'Dialogue With Asian Religions: Exploring "A Way" With Thomas Merton' – available at Lancaster University.

1. Hans Küng, *Judaism: The Religious Situation of Our Time*, London, SCM Press, 1992.
2. Samuel Huntington, *The Clash of Civilizations and the Remaking of the World Order*, Herts, Simon and Shuster, 1996.
3. Thomas Merton, *Mystics and Zen Masters*, New York, Farrar, Straus, Giroux, 1967, p.46
4. Alan Race, *Christians and Religious Pluralism*, London, SCM Press, 1983.
5. A. Lewin, *Candles and Kingfishers*, Winchester, Optimum Litho, 1993, p.1

6. Inter-Faith Consultative Group of the Board for Mission and Unity, *Towards a Theology for Inter-Faith Dialogue*, London, CIO Publishing, 1984. Doctrine Commission of the General Synod of the Church of England, *The Mystery of Salvation:The Story of God's Gift*, London, CIO Publishing, 1995.

7. John Bowker, *Is God A Virus? Genes, Culture and Religion*, London, S.P.C.K., 1995, p.181

8. ibid. ,pp.181-2

9. ibid., p.182

10. David J. Bosch, *Transforming Mission: Paradigm Shifts in Theology of Mission*, New York, Orbis, 1993, p.483

11. Alexander Lipski, *Thomas Merton and Asia: His Quest for Utopia*, Michigan, Cistercian Publications, 1983, p.6

12. Thomas Merton, *Asian Journal of Thomas Merton*, London, Sheldon Press, 1974, p. xxiii.

13. *Mystics and Zen Masters*, op. cit., p. xxiv.

14. *Asian Journal*, op. cit., p.5

15. Thomas Merton, *The Seven Storey Mountain*, London, Sheldon Press, 1975, p.3

16. Ross Labrie, *The Art of Thomas Merton*, Fort Worth, Texas, Christian University Press, 1979, p.8

17. ibid., p.4

18. Monica Furlong, *Merton.A Biography*, London, Collins, 1980, p.237

19. ibid., p.170

20. *Asian Journal*, op. cit., p.204

21. ibid., pp.233-236

22. Hugo A. Meynell, *The Nature of Aesthetic Value*, London, Macmillan Press, 1986, p.99

23. Furlong, op. cit., p.xix

24. John F. Teahan, 'A dark and empty way. Thomas Merton and the apophatic tradition' *Journal of Religion* 58, July 1978, pp.263-287, (p.263, 264).

25. ibid., p.264

26. ibid., p.264

27. ibid., p.266

28. John Wu, Jr., 'The Zen in Thomas Merton', in *Your Heart is My Hermitage*, Southampton, Thomas Merton Society of GB & I, pp.90 103, (p.92)

29. Teahan, op. cit., p.266

30. ibid., p.269

31. ibid.,p.277

32. Thomas Merton, *Zen and The Birds of Appetite*, Boston, Shambhala, 1968, p.274

33. Teahan, op. cit., p.279

34. ibid., p.286

35. Thomas Merton, *The Way of Chuang Tzu*, Tunbridge Wells, Burns and Oates, 1995, p.12

36. *Mystics and Zen Masters*, op. cit. p.204

37. *Asian Journal*, op. cit. p.312

38. ibid., p.315

39. *Mystics and Zen Masters*, op. cit.., p.207

40. ibid., p.208

41. ibid., p.209

42. ibid., p.112
43. Thomas Merton, *Raids on the Unspeakable*, Tunbridge Wells, Burns & Oates, 1977, p.119
44. ibid., p.125
45. ibid., p.128
46. William Johnston, *Lord Teach Us To Pray: Christian Zen & The Inner Eye of Love*, London, HarperCollins, 1990, p.19
47. Ross Labrie, *The Art of Thomas Merton*, Fort Worth, Texas, Christian University Press, 1979, p.14
48. M.L.Rosenthal (Ed.), *Poetry in English: an Anthology*, Oxford, Oxford University Press, 1987, p.686
49. Amos Oz, *Israel, Palestine and Peace*, London, Vintage, 1994, p.1
50. Thomas Merton, *Conjectures of a Guilty Bystander*, Tunbridge Wells, Burns & Oates, 1995, p.144
51. *Asian Journal*, op. cit., p. vii.
52. *The Way of Chuang Tzu*, op. cit., p.17
53. *Mystics and Zen Masters*, op. cit., p. ix.
54. Jim Forest, 'The Panel of Friends,' in *Your Heart is My Hermitage*, op. cit., pp. 12-31, (p.30).
55. *Asian Journal*, op. cit., p. xxvii.
56. ibid., p.143
57. ibid., p.125
58. Thomas Merton, *No Man Is An Island*, Tunbridge Wells, Burns & Oates, 1955, p. xxi.
59. *Mystics and Zen Masters*, op. cit., p.286
60. *Zen and the Birds of Appetite*, op. cit., p.192
61. *Mystics and Zen Masters*, op. cit., p.287

Thomas Merton:
the Once & Future Paradigm

JOHN WU, JR.

> Mine...is a piety without a home; it survives
> the obsessive, annihilating image of universal
> disjointedness and, fortunately, allows me no
> safe superiority.
>
> Czeslaw Milosz

> A man has only to persist in refusal (to give his love
> to false gods), and one day or another God will
> come to him.
>
> Simone Weil, *Science, Necessity and the Love of God*

I. *A True Man of Countless Titles*

If the Zen master D. T. Suzuki was "True Man of No Title" as Thomas Merton once said of him in *Zen and the Birds of Appetite*, we might very well regard the monk/writer himself as "True Man of Countless Titles." To the outsider, the monk seemed to have been trying on numerous hats for size to see if they would fit; yet a reading of his writings would convince even the casual reader of the depth Merton was naturally able to enter into whatever tradition he was taking a fancy to at the moment.

Much as he assiduously studied the different traditions, what distinguished the American Trappist from others was that he savoured and cherished and was able to cull from them their richest fruits. Perhaps he was able to enter the richness of those traditions because he had the gift of understanding the natural gap between *knowing* and *loving* knowledge. His identification with others, particularly with the socially and politically downtrodden and those living on cultural fringes, appeared at times so direct and naturally unadorned that he must have suffered intensely when he finally tasted the gift of their destitution. And I deliberately say *gift* because without it, the monk himself would have remained an outsider looking in and his writings would not have been filled with the compassion and anger that characterise them.

If the sense of oneness with others seemed second nature, Merton rarely, one felt, came upon this identification in any artificial or self-conscious way. For his openness, an inborn trait that with time transformed into meekness of heart, naturally appealed to those seeking a spiritual master. Yet, as his extensive correspondence suggests so well, he sought solace and insight from others as much as they did from him. In Merton, no matter how brilliantly he expostulates on a subject, one never quite gets the feeling that he has given you the definitive final answer. This is especially true in his strikingly bold Journals where there are as many questions as there are answers. My contention is that this apparent uncertainty lies in his ever-growing Christology and selfhood (neither of which can be understood without an understanding of the other) as well as deep belief in dialogue which he saw as an essential function of *being*. In one of many writings that reveal his simplicity of heart and faith in the necessity of dialogue anchored on the revelation of truth alone, he warns Christians of complacency and, in doing so, establishes new parameters in the practice of piety:

> It is my belief that we should not be too sure of having found Christ in ourselves until we have found him also in the part of humanity that is most *remote* from our own. Christ is found not in loud and pompous declarations but in humble and *fraternal* dialogue. He is found less in a truth that is imposed than in a truth that is *shared*.[1] (Emphasis added)

The monk, driven by a deep conviction that Christ lived and breathed in all of us, especially among those most abandoned, possessed a toughness of mind that refused to accept mere contingencies for the authentic; on the other hand, he possessed a heart that could not help but love what he touched, beginning with his own Christianity. Some extraordinary spiritual tentacles led him to the vintage only, whether sweet, sour or bitter, which he found in hidden places; and he had the natural instinct for uncovering not only the esoteric but the obvious and the ordinary, though at times he may have taken some rather extraordinary routes to get to where he got.

His knack for the discovery of universal spiritual treasures came from a strong resistance in refusing to settle down into any specific well-worn grooves or niches that were likely to shield the vintage. As a Christian monk, the heart of Christ was his 'Eternal Tao,' which in all its surface shabbiness he knew held the unimaginable splendour of the sacred and which informed and enlightened the heart of each person. This conviction made him live and love ever more nakedly and, obviously, solitarily, in the presence of the fully unfathomable New Law of the Gospels.

If Merton was unconventional and prophetic as a monk, it was not so much his odd idiosyncrasies but the ambiguous unconventionality of the ever radical and renewing Word of God that made him so. And what makes him all the more challenging for a Christian to grasp is that he regarded all authentic secular, intellectual and aesthetic worlds as signposts – one may even regard them as divine ciphers – leading him ever deeper into the heart of Christ. Further, his being ill-at-ease in seeing the world dualistically helped him to see the divine in the multifarious cultural manifestations. This atypical faith in the works of humankind also set him apart from other men and women of the spirit.

Constitutionally, Merton was unsettled, as it were, in the Emersonian sense of always being an outsider. What he saw he faithfully recorded without the usual pietistic sentiments that one would ordinarily associate with the religious. This faithfulness to his vision was unsettling to many who knew him personally or through his writings. Yet, in remaining true to himself he became, in time, the very paradigm of that full-grown man we see described by Lao Tzu in the *Tao Teh Ching*, who "sets his heart upon the substance rather than the husk; /Upon the fruit rather than the flower," and preferring "what is within to what is without."[2] On the other hand, one may justifiably ask, Should a monk or anyone else be anything else but a true man or woman of *Tao*?

The substance, the fruit and the within became so much an unfailing lighthouse that, almost by reflex, lit up from the inside whatever the monk touched, and made an otherwise dead past part and parcel of an ever-revealing Present, that asked for nothing more than to be itself. He took his willing friends and readers into his formidable and sometimes knotty moral and spiritual world, not in order to make them over into little Mertons but challenging them to redefine their worn-out notions of culture and spirituality. The real boon of travelling with him on the crest of his noble and often evocative insights was the continuous discovery and, more truly, recovery of self in new yet strangely ordinary ways.

So far, we have suggested he did not deliberately lead anyone along some esoteric paths that put one above the masses; if he had an objective, it lay in the re-invention of what is in this particular point in one's history, individually and communally. He would have been one with his friend, Czeslaw Milosz, who wrote so plainly and profoundly on the matter of piety – which the future Nobel laureate felt was not a choice but a gift – and the almost always difficult consequences of trying to live out such a life. Note too how Milosz shares Merton's "unsettledness" in the following:

> It seems to me that we are born either pious or impious, and I would be glad were I able to number among the former. Piety has no need of definition – either it is there or it is not. It persists independently of the division of people into believers and atheists, an illusory division today, since faith is undermined by disbelief in faith, and disbelief by disbelief in itself. The sacred exists and is stronger than all our rebellion... My piety would shame me if it meant that I possessed something others did not. Mine, however, is a piety without a home; it survives the obsessive, annihilating image of universal disjointedness and, fortunately, allows me no safe superiority.[3]
> (Emphasis added)

All the roles Merton played, including the principle ones of monk and writer, too, seemed more in the nature of distinct callings and their subsequent responses, rather than something derived from his own choosing, which would have narrowed their scope and objectives. Had they not been directed and commanded by some compelling voice from within – most assuredly, a Christian form of the Greek daimonion – he most surely would have been in danger of either condescension or masquerading in hats and outfits that he had hardly any business wearing. He seemed to have drunk so deeply from the well of humanity – almost indiscriminately putting on the variegated and seemingly clashing garments of humanity – and literally believed that the paschal Christ, in divesting himself of his divinity, had regained paradise for and made the brotherhood and sisterhood of humanity no longer mere possibility but the *essential regained nature* of the human person, demanding full exploitation within the dimension of the New Man.

We may say that Merton recognized both the privilege and the cost of discipleship. The haunting words of Jesus in answer to the prophecy of Isaiah to his disciples must have both humbled and frightened the monk:

> Blessed are your eyes, because they see, and your ears, because they hear. Truly, I say to you, many prophets and righteous people longed to see what you see but did not see it, and hear what you hear but did not hear it. (Matt. 13: 16-17)

By gently insinuating his love and compassion upon humankind, Christ makes it possible for each person to have a radical change of heart. This *metanoia,* or *reformatio vitae,* was, for Merton, the one essential element in any social, political or religious revolution. For it took the form of a continuous line heading outward, yet also inward, in its ever-expanding concern and search for the hidden, suffering Christ,crying to be heard in the more obscure and forgotten races and traditions both past and present, that Merton, the spiritual sojourner, was able to decipher in their purest cries of joy and agony.

To Merton, living the Christian life meant being privileged to witness the continuing work of Christ's redemption through God's creation, not so much from above but, as it were, *from below.* Our eyes and ears, particularly in the light of faith, are enlightened and informed in ways that ancient prophets and other men and women of good will were not privy to. For through collective human experience, of Christians and non-Christians, believers and non-believers and even atheists, we see and hear the contemporary message of Christ in a manner that would be alien even to the original disciples and eyewitnesses of the Paschal Mystery. This is no claim that we are greater than they were, only that we today are in a *privileged* position to view the unfolding consequences of the Incarnation and the dramatic, ongoing process of God's redemptive plan of personal and universal love from a broader and deeper historical perspective.

The scope of the brother-and-sisterhood of humanity today has grown immeasurably larger and more complex than in the past, even the proximate past when such a recent inhumane practice as slavery, being rarely questioned except by a handful of courageous individuals, was accepted by whole races of people; or, when not long ago it was still fashionable to blame the death of Jesus on the entire Jewish race, which curiously, in the eyes of countless multitudes, justified their collective murder. Christians in our time are finally coming to terms with the universality of Christ, not through some proud and chauvinistic and, therefore, empty, claim but one that fully places the burden of good faith squarely on their shaky, often hypocritical historical shoulders; at the same time, Christians are asked to live concretely the painful ambiguities of belief that is an essential aspect of their life of faith in a God, Who, for reasons that only He knows, very often chooses to remain far more hidden than manifest.

If Christ is neither East or West, nor North or South, then what exactly is he? Among contemporary believers, there exists much confusion and pain. This surely stems from the hard fact that, first, Christians are now asked to hold a good deal more in their hearts and minds than what had been demanded of them in the past two millennia, and, secondly, the vast majority of Christians have not yet been able to come to terms with the full meaning – as defined by both the privilege and cost – of discipleship that this newer and existentially more challenging notion of universality demands of them. In fact, this confusion extends also to non-Christians, agnostics and atheists as well, for the model of the historical Christ in all its diverse levels and intricacies and ambiguities of meaning – whether the various *realities* of Christ are acknowledged or not – forms a critical part of our *inseparable collective human consciousness.*

There is no denying we have all come together, for the most part, unwittingly and probably unwillingly, finding ourselves suddenly responsible for one another; moreover, we come to realize we shall either die or survive as one mass humanity. This would be the mark of a growing humanism in the broadest sense; in the moral, spiritual Christian realm, we have simply hit upon the very traditional idea of the Mystical Body of Christ.

What is difficult to avoid is the reality of the paradigm of Jesus as a historical figure claiming to have taught a universal message to and for all humanity irrespective of race, country or religious belief. For the believing Christian seeking his or her divine Saviour, Christ as the Everyman speaks, in a hidden way through each man and woman, the language – both linguistically and culturally – that rises from the very soil in which we find ourselves in our concrete lives. And, blessed indeed are those who are able to see and hear beyond all the cultural trappings and then to communicate back and share *substantially* what they have seen and heard.

The truly *seeing* Christian, it would seem, can no longer merely regard the other as even "like" Christ for, in his heightened state, he sees each person as Christ himself in both his passion and death and glorious risen state. In the end, it becomes quite clear that it is neither cultural accumulations nor deprivations that matter, as they can weigh us down. Rather, what does matter is that, in sharing our essential qualities with others, our authentic self is set free. It is this close and warm identification with the other in the sweet embrace of love and compassion rather than through some facile intellectual synthesis that brings about personal emancipation and selfhood. Was this not the truth that the life of solitude had brought home to Merton? The process may indeed begin with the will, but it ends with the will of the individual subsumed under *a greater likeness than itself*, which remains secret and hidden and to which we come to regard as *more us than we are ourselves*, as perhaps either Meister Eckhart in the West or Dr. Suzuki in the East might have said.

II. "Stop seeking. Let it all happen!"

Particularly in his later anti-poetry, Thomas Merton seemed to have put on the vastly different and multiple lives – both consecutively and simultaneously – found among races of people, some very obscure, that few cared for, let alone understood or identified with. Yet, he was able to enter deferentially into their often long-forgotten and broken lives as one would expect a poet of compassion to do. Without self-consciousness the monk became the Desert Father, the Geshe, or the Sufi, or Chuang Tzu, Ishi, even the Zen master.

There is delight and surprise in following the manner in which Merton, shedding excess baggage and dead skins, became as it were increasingly more *weightless* and, paradoxically, more universal, the more he "put on Christ," which became synonymous with putting on the numerous faces of humanity. From being accused of having a "strident ascetic tone"[4] as a young monk, Merton had soon travelled

millennia to become a trusted, warm, living, flesh and blood
spokesman of the disenfranchised, of people agonizing to
understand a world gone awry. Like John the Baptist, the harbinger,
we see him as if crying from out of the wilderness and touching the
raw chords of our own solitude, beyond words, beyond thought,
even beyond conventional affectivity, in the midst of a fractured
paradise he had fought so hard to regain in his own life. That
recovery held the real key and gave his writings authentic weight. In
Cables to the Ace, he wrote,

> I think poetry must
> I think it must
> Stay open all night
> In beautiful cellars.[5]

Which is what he did for many: by keeping his capacity for inner
experience in his own "cellar" open, he encouraged his readers to
keep their own inner life active and well-lit even in darkest times. In
many voices, he spoke with hope and a comfort becoming a man of
the spirit so that those who could hear, as he wrote rhapsodically,
would "gladly consent to the kindness of rays and recover the warm
knowledge of each other we once had under those young trees in
another May." (*Cables*, 53, #76) Here in such simple images, Merton
appears to say, the soothing and consoling hymns from that forgotten
kingdom ("cellars") are there for our asking, for paradise is as much
with us as we are prepared or would allow ourselves to receive it, or
to simply live in the nourishing milk flowing ever so richly from its
bosom. If there is a central message in the monk, it is that Christ the
New Adam has long ago recovered paradise — not for Christians
alone but for *all humankind* and that enlightenment begins with the
recognition of this paradise within each human person.

We begin a journey at birth that may at times take us so far away
from ourselves that memories of our original home – our true
human lineage – start to fade. Further, that remembrance, in which
we belong to a time of *Unborn*, to a place of *No Place* that, though
ordinary and the everyday, is one to which we sadly become strangers.
As such memories of paradise recede from us, the more we settle
along conventional paths leading everywhere but home, we lose
our way, the more we find ourselves settled and enamoured
in momentary forms, in the contingencies of life that ever more
gravitate us earthward. For the greater we become intoxicated to

such seasonal excellences, the greater the degree of self-entrapment we are liable to find ourselves mired in.

By way of contrast, Merton teaches us the simplest and noblest lesson of a mystic when he says matter-of-factly, "The way that is most yours is no way" (*Cables*, 27, #38), advising us to "stop seeking. Let it all happen. Let it come and go. What? Everything: i.e., nothing." (*Cables*, 27, #37) And what does the monk mean by the very *taoistic*-like paradox, "to seek without seeking?" He goes on to explain:

> For each of us there is a point of nowhereness in the middle of movement, a point of nothingness in the midst of being: the incomparable point, not to be discovered by insight. If you seek it, you do not find it. If you stop seeking, it is there. But you must not turn to it. Once you become aware of yourself as a seeker, you are lost. But *if you are content to be lost you will be found* without knowing it, precisely because you are lost, for you are, at last, nowhere. (*Cables*, 58, #84. Emphasis added)

So, be not like a wilderness, but be wilderness, void and emptiness – without form, without place, without time and without name – for, as Meister Eckhart has said, "The true word of eternity is spoken only in the spirit of that man who is himself a wilderness" (*Cables*, 59 #86) that is without sand, without stone, even without darkness or night, and so *poverty-stricken* that there is not even any room for God Himself. You see, Merton seems to tell us, God wants the whole wilderness to Himself, for the universe is His playground by right. And perhaps from this perspective, man must be so abject in spirit and helplessly dependent on God – as Job finally became – that he must free himself even of the wilderness, and to be detached from whatever he may consider detachment to be. For the wilderness *is* paradise.

For no tainted happiness can ever be completely full. It is a reaching back, more truly, perhaps, a travelling without travelling, to a time before, to the no-time of the *Uncreated*, to the "Total poverty of the Creator," yet "from this poverty springs *everything*... Infinite zero" (*Cables*, #84), which echoes perfectly Dr. Suzuki's

zero=infinity,   infinity=zero[6]

For the zero – which is infinity and, therefore, a no-thing and a no-place and a no-time – is "a storehouse or womb of all possible good or values," perfect act, or action encompassing being and becoming, knowledge and innocence, the *action* of the Creator. It is, therefore, "actionless action," or *wu wei*, the mysterious workings of *Tao* but mysterious only insofar as our puffed up fullness and narcissistic pull keep our sights and visions earthbound, shadowy and barely half-awake.

In everything, we seem to need and to keep much more than we have a right to, and are greatly troubled that in refusing or discarding anything, our very souls would be joined to the garbage heap; but most things we prize so dearly have in fact little to do or be in common with us *essentially* and lack the status that would raise them above what corrupts and cannot last. We forget that even a Van Gogh *Sunflower*, Chartres Cathedral, or the Great Wall of China, regardless of their status as great works of art and extraordinary engineering feats, will one day come to dust once their natural time has run full circle. Yet, we live as though temporary things were meant to last forever. This is not only vanity but idolatry.

To Abdul Aziz, his Sufi friend, Merton wrote on December 9, 1964:

> I see more and more clearly that even the believers are often far short of having true faith in the Living God. *The great sin remains idolatry, and there is an idolatry of concepts as well as of graven images.* The minds of men (sic) are made vile and corrupt by the images they worship under the pretext of 'science,' 'politics,' 'technology,' etc.[7] (Emphasis added)

No doubt the monk had in mind certain philosophical turnings occurring in the nineteenth century when politics and technology, then followed rapidly by economics, were uncritically raised above that of the merely *instrumental* and given suddenly the status not very much lower than the position previously held by theology and the theological virtues themselves.

As the third millennium closes in on us, we continue to live more than ever in such a philosophically-depraved positivistic milieu. However, if for the most part large, unwieldy utopian political and economic enterprises have, in the twentieth century, through horrifying, apocalyptic experiences lost their appeal among the great masses of the world, it nonetheless is difficult to dispute the high status of technology (and now, hi-tech) and behavioural sciences as disciplines that are enjoying unprecedented popularity as continued sacred cows or idols.

Living in an increasingly technologized world, it becomes ever more difficult to remain authentic, for such a task, the natural work of being, becomes difficult when the inner eye is mislaid. And for those solicitous of the disquieting effect that technology has had on the self, there is no greater enigma than how the shrinking person can be retrieved.

Merton had his solutions and he battled such demons in his own way. Particularly in his correspondence, the monk shows the depth of anxiety that he had begun to feel by increasingly identifying with both Christ's sufferings and the despair of the modern world. His solutions, though they may at times be couched in intellectual terms, were not intellectual at all. For he saw the problems in deeply personal terms and faithfully identified with the suffering masses, particularly "the excluded ones" in the world. Merton's prophetic bent helped him anticipate the many problems he would find himself facing throughout the last decade of his life as he broadened his contacts with the world through letters and the wide regimen of readings he forced upon himself.

In a letter to Louis Massignon dated July 20, 1960, Merton, besides commenting on the Sufi authority's meditations on the desert and the God of Agar and Ishmael, also remarks on Massignon's idea of "Le point vierge" ("the virginal point, the centre of the soul, where despair corners the heart of the outsider"). Typical of his interest and ability in appropriating ideas to himself, Merton writes from the heart though perhaps a bit over-dramatically:

> We... have to reach that same "point vierge" in a kind of despair at the hypocrisy of our own world. It is dawning more and more on me that I have been caught in civilization as in a kind of spider's web, and I am beginning to say "No" louder and louder, though surrounded by the solicitude of those who ask me why I do so. There is no way of explaining it, and perhaps not even time to do so.[8]

While "despair at the hypocrisy of our own world" and being "caught in civilization as in a kind of spider's web" do not directly refer to technology, they were to my mind oblique descriptions of Merton's own despair and feeling of entrapment in a religious community which he increasingly found overly weighted down with pragmatic and organizational concerns that had little to do with the formation of monks and the building of true community life. The Journals, including Conjectures of a Guilty Bystander, are full of references expressing this vexation brought on by a monastery that Merton felt had begun to reflect too precariously the neuroses of the outside world. In short, though he never quite said it explicitly, he could see impersonalism slowly creeping inside the monastic walls as more and more monkish candidates from the video generation came calling at the gates.

Our moral and spiritual desensitization runs deep and broad and it is difficult to deny that alienation today is more the rule than the exception. One cringes in realizing the profound destruction our century has done against the *sacred* and, consequently, the loss of humanity to self that has invariably followed. Obviously, no deep reflection is needed to understand that the *sacred* and humanity affect each other intimately and exist in a tight bond.

Yet, this uncritical, technologizing way of thinking, convention-ally and, I might add, conveniently, thought of as originating in the West (*conveniently* because, if it comes from the West, it would seem that we in the East become *less morally culpable* for what we do), is intractably embedded and is now breeding its poison in Asia. Asians have thoughtlessly bought nearly the entire progress package, and then some, and one cannot be overly encouraged in imagining what all this might mean in future decades when China joins what we can now only euphemistically call the "civilized community of nations."

To Thomas Merton, what we are presently witnessing might be likened to the respective hollowness and cynicism of Gog and Magog finally joining forces (as he had so well predicted), whereby the blind leads the rest of us into an unimaginable state of moral and spiritual void. What makes it all the more frightening is that, lacking any formidable idea of Transcendence by which to perceive a Self beyond the self, we will then – both East and West – be carried off into the future by a relationship mutually fuelled not by paradisiacal but *parasitical* interests, wholly utilitarian and pragmatic and without any clear vision nor substantive goals or values. From this rather despairing point of view, Thomas Merton suddenly becomes a most welcome paradigmatic hope upon which to hang our fractured existences.

Notes and References

1. Thomas Merton, "A Letter to Pablo Antonio Cuadra Concerning Giants," *The Collected Poems of Thomas Merton* (New York: New Directions, 1977) pp. 382-83

2. Lao Tzu, *Tao Teh Ching*. Translated by John C. H. Wu. (Boston and Shaftesbury: Shambhala Publications, Inc., 1989), Chapter 38. Hereafter referred to in the text as TTC.

3. Czeslaw Milosz, *Visions from San Francisco Bay*. Translated by Richard Lourie. (New York: Farrar Straus Giroux, 1982) Pp.33-4

4. Dom Aelred Graham, *The End of Religion: Autobiographical Explorations* (New York and London: Harcourt Brace Jovanovich, Inc., 1971) p. 63

5. Thomas Merton, *Cables to the Ace* (New York: New Directions, 1968) p.37, #53. Hereafter referred to in the text as *Cables*.

6. Thomas Merton, *Zen and the Birds of Appetite*, (New York: New Directions, 1968) p. 107

7. Thomas Merton, *The Hidden Ground of Love: Letters of Religious Experience and Social Concerns*. Selected and edited by William H. Shannon (New York: Farrar Straus Giroux, 1985), p. 60

8. Thomas Merton, *Witness to Freedom: Letters in Times of Crisis*. Selected and edited by William H. Shannon (New York: Farrar Straus Giroux, 1994), p. 278. Hereafter referred to in the text as *WF*.

For the Sake of the World

PATRICK EASTMAN

THESE TIMES HAVE BEEN described by some as the new axial age or in the terms of a book recently published by Frank Tuoti, *The Dawn of the Mystical Age*. Whether those are the words we would use to define our times or not, we would probably all agree that this is a time of rapid change and great challenge. Such change and challenge are not excluded from the spiritual arena. The writings of contemporary scientists, the burgeoning of feminist theology and the seeming dissatisfaction of many with institutional religion as they exhibit a growing interest in spirituality all provide a profound challenge to those concerned with the spirit. Professor Mary Grey puts her finger on this well in her book *Prophecy and Mysticism* where she writes persuasively of the urgent need for communities that are both mystical and prophetic. She writes:

> This book reflects on what mysticism and prophecy might mean today. I argue that the days of the angry prophet of the Hebrew Scriptures as individual, together with the image of the levitating mystic – and their counterparts in other cultures – have had their day; what is needed is "the community as prophet." But to be "prophetic," I argue, is inseparable from being a "mystical" community.[1]

In this paper I want to explore whether the contemplative monastic life is merely a relic from a bygone age or whether it can give us some direction for those who are trying to build communities that are both prophetic and mystical. Is monastic life simply a self-indulgent opting out of a society that is deemed to be irredeemably corrupt? In this paper I hope to establish that authentic contemplative monasticism is not a "forsaking of the world," but "for the sake of the world." I wish to suggest that the apparent withdrawal of those who inhabit monasteries or follow a contemplative lifestyle are really following a path that leads to a closer engagement with the life of the larger community. The findings of this paper then may encourage us to see how monastic life can be used as a pattern for a broader based prophetic and mystical community for our world today. First, I will look at the basis for the monastic *fuga mundi* in terms of both the Christian and the Buddhist traditions. I will then indicate how that is manifested in the well-known figures of the Christian monk, Thomas Merton, and the Vietnamese Buddhist monk, Thich Nhat Hanh. These two figures I will suggest are models of the mystical and prophetic to inspire us today.

We look first then to the Christian tradition. If we start with the gospels we can clearly see that the central message of Jesus is about a "kingdom" which is essentially a "this world" reality. At the opening of Jesus' ministry in Luke's gospel we read:

> The spirit of the Lord is on me,
> For he has anointed me
> To bring the good news to the afflicted.
> He has sent me to proclaim liberty to captives,
> Sight to the blind,
> To let the oppressed go free,
> To proclaim a year of favour from the Lord.

The commitment to the fulfilment of these words from the prophet Isaiah together with that of the subversive Song of Mary is not only reflected in the ministry of Jesus the Carpenter, but it is consistently central to the activity of the early church. Peter Phan, commenting on the contemporary social teaching of the Catholic Church in his Introduction to *Social Thought in the Early Church Fathers*, writes:

> It would be wrong, however, to claim that social concern is the exclusive and original discovery of socialism or that the social doctrine of the church is simply a belated attempt to respond to the challenges of modern social upheavals. On the contrary, it must be said that social consciousness belongs to the very essence of Christianity since the salvation it proclaims affects not only the individual but also the whole human society, indeed, the whole universe itself, in its sociological, economic and political dimensions.[2]

Within the Roman Catholic Church tradition, commitment to the social and political issues that are the natural outcome of the proclamation of the gospel became most explicit in the last century with the encyclical *Rerum Novarum* by Pope Leo XIII in 1891. Since that time, the Catholic Church, under the leadership of successive Popes, has linked its spirituality and prayer to economic and the social injustice of oppression, racism and the infringement of human rights. Many of the documents of the Second Vatican Council in the 1960s emphasized the inextricable link between prayer and prophecy. As Daniel Berrigan writes, "the time will come, indeed it is upon us already when contemplation will be seen as a purely subversive activity."

A similar commitment can be found in the Anglican Communion as pointed out by Ken Leech in *True Prayer*: "In the Church of England, there is a long tradition in which the Eucharistic worship of the church has been seen as the basis of social action and social criticism."[3] To expand this to include other traditions we can refer to many of the documents of the World Council of Churches. Indeed there have been accusations by some that this body is too political. I do not wish to get into any details on that issue, but simply draw your attention to the fact that an authentic Christian spirituality needs to have a lively awareness of social justice and peace. The Christian monastic or contemplative is not exempt from this, but must be part of this tradition.

It must be admitted that this connection has not always been made clear, as Grace Jantzen points out in her book, *Power, Gender and Christian Mysticism*. She demonstrates that a male dominated mysticism gives rise to a spirituality that is intellectual, and against the body. It becomes merely a way of coping with the hard things of life rather than an awakening to the social dimension of the Gospel. Prayer is reduced to a means of promoting psychological well-being, and healthy sexuality. The success of so many contemporary spiritual self-help books which do nothing more than "ease the pain" indicates how urgent is the felt need for such resources to cope with life. Admitting that, Jantzen goes on to say:

> ...this does not address the question of where the stresses of life origi-
> nate, or whether there are unjust structures in society which generate
> the oppression and anxiety for which help is sought. (She then rightly
> points out that)...this is deeply worrying. To the extent that prayer and
> meditation and books on spirituality actually help to cope with the
> distresses of life that arise out of unjust social conditions, without
> challenging those conditions themselves, to that extent they act as a
> sedative which distracts attention from the need to dismantle the struc-
> tures that perpetuate the misery. If books and practices of spirituality
> help to calm jangled nerves and release anxieties and renew courage to
> re-enter the world as it is, then whatever the good intention of the
> authors and practitioners (and these are usually not in doubt) what is
> actually happening is that the structures of injustice are being rein-

forced. The social and political policies that make for starving children, battered woman and the evils of rising fascism are still there unchallenged as people learn through prayer to find the tranquillity to live with corrupt political and social structures instead of channelling their distress and anger and anxiety into energy for constructive change.[4]

Let us now take a few minutes to look at the Buddhist tradition. For this I draw on a paper by Daniel Palmer from the Philosophy department of Purdue University entitled 'Maso Abe, Zen Buddhism and Social Ethics.' In this paper, after explicating the detailed examination of the Buddhist concepts of nirvana and sunnyata done by Maso Abe, Palmer concludes that, although criticisms can be made "that certain Buddhist doctrines are incompatible with the development of any positive social ethic" the hermeneutical strategies adopted by Abe enable one to uncover the positive social implications of Zen doctrine. It leads, as he says, to an awareness that sunnyata is "the ground and not the end of Buddhist life." Such an understanding has given rise in recent years to the term "Engaged Buddhism" which has been used a lot recently by the Dalai Lama himself.

In an approach that is rather more practical than philosophical, Ruben Habito, a Christian Zen Roshi trained by Yamada Koun in Kamakura in Japan, writing of the apparent gap in the connection between Zen meditation and social concern goes on to say:

> The significant point for us here is to realize precisely that it is a lacuna, that is, something expected to be there but which is missing. And this is because the practice of Zen is a struggle with many stages, aimed at rooting out the fundamental self-centeredness in us that prevents us from seeing "things as they are." It is a long struggle that calls for an "inward turn," and unfortunately this inward turn, which is but an initial stage, can be so protected as to engage one for years and years, before one is able to free oneself of inner shackles. We can perhaps regard this as a "novitiate" period where we need to cut out distracting social ties in order to devote our full energy to this task of self-liberation.
>
> But it must not be forgotten that this prominently ascetic part of Zen practice is only an initial stage that is meant to be outgrown.[5]

I suggest, then, that there is a solid basis within the spiritual and thereby monastic traditions of both Buddhism and Christianity for an engagement in the social and political implications of contemplation.

> While monks and nuns have specialized in disciplines aimed at radical
> personal transformation...many, such as Antony and Hildegard,
> Bodhidharma and Sanghamitta, have stood out as moral and spiritual
> exemplars, not only for other monastic persons, but also for laity.[6]

It is now time to turn to the more contemporary exemplars of
Thomas Merton and Thich Nhat Hanh whose lives and teachings
embody a contemplative monasticism that is "for the sake of the
world."

One of my favourite stories about Merton is of a time when he
was walking down one of the hallways in Gethsemani with Jim
Forest who was visiting him. Apparently there was a monk in a little
niche reading an article by Merton which he had picked up from a
small table. The article was on some social issue by Merton. As the
anonymous monk saw Merton approaching he screwed up the
article, and threw it in the trash with a disgruntled grunt and walked
off. Merton, Forest reports, could not contain his amusement and
after a hearty laugh pointed out that this monk had berated Merton
in his early years for being too "other worldly" and pietistic, whereas
now he took offence at his outspoken writing on the social ills of the
day. (A story reminiscent of the scriptural saying: "I played a tune
and you would not dance, I sang a dirge and you would not weep!")
That story, I think, illustrates the difference between the early Merton
— who wrote the best selling autobiography The Seven Storey Mountain
and "who had spurned New York, spat on Chicago, and tramped on
Louisville" — and the later Merton whose social essays are gathered
together, well edited and introduced for us by William Shannon in
the book Passion for Peace. In the Introduction to this collection of
essays, Shannon points out how prominent and influential Merton
was in Catholic circles. He was highly acclaimed when he spoke on
spiritual matters and a withdrawal from the wicked world. But, as
Shannon writes:

> Who of his thousands of readers could have anticipated that Merton, of
> all people, would ever start writing — and writing with deep passion —
> on such a worldly subject as war? Some of his many readers were
> scandalized and walked with him no more. Others shook their heads
> and asked themselves, "What in the world has happened to Thomas
> Merton? Why is he calling people to unite in a crusade to abolish all
> war? What does this have to do with his spirituality?" [7]

Merton changed over the years and not insignificant in that change was the well-known epiphany on Fourth and Walnut in the shopping district of Louisville recorded for us in *Conjectures of a Guilty Bystander*.[8]

Merton began to realize that what he said about prayer and spirituality had a great deal to do with the social problems of the time, including war. Again as Shannon points out:

> What had happened to him was that his solitude had issued into what all true solitude must eventually become: compassion. Finding God in his solitude, he found God's people, who are inseparable from God and who, at the deepest level of their being (the level that only contemplation can reach), are at one with one another in God, the Hidden Ground of Love of all that is. This sense of compassion bred in solitude (something like the "karuna" of the Buddha born of his enlightenment) moved him to look once again at the world he thought he had left irrevocably twenty years earlier, in 1941, when he had entered the monastery. He now felt a duty, "precisely because he was a contemplative," to speak out and to warn his fellow men and women about what he believed was the gravest possible danger threatening the civilized world. He confides his concern to Daniel Berrigan in a letter written on June 25, 1963: "What is the contemplative life if one does not listen to God in it? What is the contemplative life if one becomes oblivious to the rights of men [sic] and the truth of God in the world and in His Church?" (HGL, 79)[9]

Merton remarked of himself that "I find myself travelling toward my destiny in the belly of a paradox." It is a life of paradox but not of contradiction. He joined one of the most withdrawn of the Catholic monastic orders, yet he wrote sixty books of prose and poetry on topics ranging from Prayer to Politics, from spirituality to social issues and from theology to literary criticism. He was deeply rooted in his commitment to Christ and yet he often felt a deeper spiritual relationship to non-Christians, as his relationship with the Dalai Lama, D.T. Suzuki and Thich Nhat Hanh clearly show.

Merton needed to embrace the paradox or his life would be nothing. As he points out in *Thoughts in Solitude* either ALL of life is spiritual or none of it is. We are, in other words, a spiritual being on a human journey and "the inner quest for personal transformation is incomplete without active concern for the welfare of others, just as the struggle for social, political, and economic justice leads to violence and the breakdown of community when not rooted in the depth of one's spiritual quest."[10]

As indicated this does not mean that one launches directly into social action or that the contemplative has no part to play. Merton knows this and writes:

> "A certain depth of disciplined experience is a necessary ground for fruitful action. Without a more profound human understanding derived from exploration of the inner ground of human existence, love will tend to be superficial and deceptive."[11]

I am suggesting here that Merton was a pilgrim who went first to Gethsemani and later to Asia. A monk who entered community, but ended as a hermit. He was a pilgrim in much the fashion of the central figure in the Buddhist Ox-herding pictures. These begin with the boy, who having a presentiment of the ox, goes into the wilderness and forest to find it and ends with an old man returning to the market place. We read:

> Barechested and barefooted, he comes
> Out into the marketplace;
> Daubed with mud and ashes, how broadly
> He smiles!
> There is no need for the miraculous power
> Of the gods,
> For he touches, and lo! The dead trees are
> In full bloom.[12]

Merton's human journey brings him from his voluntary marginalization (in the wilderness and forest as it were) back to the world as a powerful critic of racism, Nazism, war, injustice and intolerance. In a letter written a few months before his death he affirmed:

> I am against war, against violence, against violent revolution, for the peaceful settlement of differences, for nonviolent but nevertheless radical changes. Change is needed, and violence will not really change anything: at most it will only transfer power from one set of bull-headed authorities to another. If I say these things, it is not because I am more interested in politics than in the gospel. I am not. But today more than ever the Gospel commitment has political implications, because you cannot claim to be "for Christ" and espouse a political cause that implies callous indifference to the needs of millions of human beings and even co-operate in their destruction.[13]

I find that Merton draws together and integrates his thought on the relationship between the world and the monastery best in his Introduction to the Japanese Version of *The Seven Storey Mountain*:

For one thing, when I wrote this book, [i.e., *Seven Storey Mountain*] the fact uppermost in my mind was that I had seceded from the world of my time in all clarity and with total freedom. The break and the secession were, to me, matters of the greatest importance. Hence the somewhat negative tone of so many parts of this book.

Since that time, I have learned, I believe, to look back into that world with greater compassion, seeing those in it not as alien to myself, not as peculiar and deluded strangers, but as identified with myself. In breaking from "their world" I have strangely broken from them. In freeing myself from their delusions and preoccupations I have identified myself, none the less, with their struggles and their blind, desperate hope of happiness.

But precisely because I am identified with them, I must refuse all the more definitively to make their delusions my own. I must refuse their ideology of matter, power, quantity, movement, activism and force.[14]

In the same Introduction, Merton goes on to say:

The monastery is not an "escape" from the world. On the contrary, by being in the monastery I take my true part in all the struggles and sufferings of the world. It is my intention to make my entire life a rejection of, a protest against the crimes and injustices of war and political tyranny which threaten to destroy the whole race of man [sic] and the world with him. By my monastic life and vows I am saying NO to all the concentration camps, the aerial bombardments, the staged political trials, the judicial murders, the racial injustice, the economic tyrannies, and the whole socio-economic apparatus which seems geared for nothing but global destruction in spite of all its fair words in favour of peace. I make monastic silence a protest against the lies of politicians, propagandists and agitators.[15]

Should we find that this sounds somewhat negative in tone, Merton corrects that by saying:

If I say NO to all these secular forces, I also say YES to all that is good in the world and in man. I say YES to all that is beautiful in nature, and in order that this may be the yes of a freedom and not of subjection, I must refuse to possess any thing in the world purely as my own. I say YES to all the men and women who are my brothers and sisters in the world, but for this yes to be an assent of freedom and not of subjection.[16]

With that clear voice of Merton resounding in our ears we should now proceed to look in a little more detail at the life and writings of Thich Nhat Hanh. Nhat Hanh is a Vietnamese Buddhist monk who has also been a University Professor. He is the founder of The School of Youth for Social Service in Vietnam and he headed the Vietnamese

Peace Delegation in Paris during the Vietnam War. He has served as Vice Chairperson of the International Fellowship of Reconciliation. A mark of his commitment to issues of justice and peace is the recognition given him when Martin Luther King, Jr. nominated him for the Nobel Peace Prize.

Today, Thich Nhat Hanh lives in a small retreat/meditation Center in France where he teaches, writes, gardens and works to help refugees from oppression worldwide. He travels widely to give mindfulness retreats for war veterans, psychotherapists, environmentalists, social change activists and many others. He is the author of over sixty books including *Peace Is Every Step: The Miracle of Mindfulness; Zen Keys;* and *Love In Action.* You no doubt recognize that Nhat Hanh and Merton had much in common. Both were monks, poets, and authors, and both were deeply concerned with nonviolence, social, political and economic injustice in the world.

Just as Jim Forest gave me the story which I used to illustrate Merton's changing orientation to the world, so Forest gives me a story that admirably illustrates the connection of contemplation and social concern in Thich Nhat Hanh.

During 1968 Thich Nhat Hanh was on a speaking tour in the United States. After a lecture in the auditorium of a large Christian church in the St. Louis area a man stood up and asked with a very sarcastic tone: "If you care so much about your people, Mr. Hanh, why are you here? If you care so much for the people who are wounded, why don't you spend your time with them?" When he had finished, Forest recounts that he looked at Nhat Hanh with apprehension. What would he say? Forest says that the spirit of the war itself had suddenly filled the room, and it seemed hard to breathe. There was a deafening silence.

> When Thich Nhat Hanh began to speak – quietly, with deep calm and a sense of personal caring for the man who had just attacked him. The words seemed like rain falling on fire: "If you want the tree to grow," he said, "it won't help to water the leaves. You have to water the roots. Many of the roots of the war are here, in your country. To help the people who are to be bombed, to try to protect them from this suffering, I have to come here." After this response, Nhat Hanh whispered something to the chairperson and walked quickly from the room...[17]

Knowing that something was wrong Forest followed him out and found Thich Nhat Hanh stood on the sidewalk struggling for air.

He eventually explained that he had been extremely upset and that he had wanted to respond with great anger but he had made himself breathe deeply and slowly so that he was able to respond in the way he did. In order to return to normal he had to leave the room. It was at this point that Forest realized that there was a real connection between the spiritual practice of simply breathing and the way one responds to the world.

Nhat Hanh's book Zen Keys illustrates well this connection between action and contemplation. He presents Zen as a practice that leads to awakening (you may remember that Merton's definition of Contemplation was "An awakening to all that is Real in all that is real"). This awakening or awareness is an awakening to the heart of reality, a necessary prior step to social action. Nhat Hanh concludes Zen Keys with a section on "Zen and the World of Today." He first outlines the problems of the modern world, speaking of overpopulation, famine, political repression, nuclear war and environmental pollution from industry and technology. He answers with "what we need is not another doctrine/system, but an awakening that can restore our spiritual strengths." We need a new civilization and he suggests that:

> The first phase of this civilization must be to establish social conditions in which life can be lived in a human way. "Awakened" people are certainly going to form small communities where their material life will be simple and healthy, and time and energy will be devoted to spiritual concerns. These communities of mindful living will be like Zen monasteries with no dogma. In them, the sickness of the times will be cured and spiritual health will be renewed.[18]

The basic solution then is to be a development of a new culture in which we can discover our true selves and thereby be thoroughly human. It will be a civilization where genuine community life is possible. Such community is needed to counter the impersonal dehumanizing effect of the urban megalopolis of today.

In short, we all need to follow the path that Thomas Merton and Thich Nhat Hanh propose. It is the path of the transformation of our consciousness through the spiritual discipline of silence and solitude. They challenge us to see the world not as something "out there" to be overcome, but within each one of us. Prayer should awaken us to our interconnectedness with the universe and this places a responsibility upon us. The direction the world takes in providing what is necessary for all to live with human dignity depends on the direction of our own lives. Merton and Thich Nhat Hanh teach us that in contemplation we recover our true self, which in turn provides the compassion which gives us our capability of living for the sake of the world.

My own experience over the last five years or so has revealed a need for the new civilization mentioned by Thich Nhat Hanh. We need the formation of communities that are both mystical and prophetic, encouraging and supporting those who are trying to live with a spiritual practice that is authentically contemplative. It was for this reason that I began The Monos Community, members of which are primarily, though not exclusively connected through our bi-monthly journal. In the face of a culture and church that is quite alien to contemplation we aim to support those who, inspired by the lives of Merton and Thich Nhat Hanh, endeavour to live a life of prayer that is not a forsaking of the world but precisely For the Sake of the World.

Notes and References

1. Mary C. Grey, Prophecy and Mysticism: The Heart of the Postmodern Church. T & T Clark, Limited, 1997, p.2
2. Peter C. Phan, Social Thought, Michael Glazier Incorporated, 1984, p.15
3. Kenneth Leech, True Prayer: An Invitation to Christian Spirituality, Harper & Row, 1980, p.91
4. Grace Jantzen, Power, Gender and Christian Mysticism, CUP, 1996, pp.19-20
5. Ruben L.F. Habito, Total Liberation: Zen Spirituality and the Social Dimension, Orbis Books, 1989, pp. xvi & xvii.
6. Donald K. Swearer & Patrick G. Henry, For the Sake of the World: The Spirit of Buddhist and Christian Monasticism, Fortress Press, 1989, p.19
7. Thomas Merton, Passion for Peace: The Social Essays, The Crossroad Publishing Company, 1995, p.2
8. Thomas Merton, Conjectures of a Guilty Bystander, Sheldon Press, 1977, pp. 153-4
9. Op.cit., p.3
10. Op.cit., p.21
11. Thomas Merton, Contemplation in a World of Action, Redwood Press, 1971, p.158
12. D.T. Suzuki, & W. Segal The Ten Oxherding Pictures, Green River Press, 1988, #X
13. Merton Midsummer Letter 1968 quoted in Henri J. Nouwen, Pray to Live — Thomas Merton, Contemplative Critic, Fides Claretian, 1972, pp. 56-7
14. Thomas Merton, Introductions East and West: The Foreign Prefaces of Thomas Merton, Unicorn Press, 1981, p.43
15. ibid., p.45
16. ibid., p.46
17. Op.cit., For the Sake of the World, pp. 31-32
18. Thich Nhat Hanh, Zen Keys: A Guide to Zen Practice, Doubleday, 1974, p.158

In Praise of Insanity:
revisiting Thomas Merton's
'A Devout Meditation in Memory of Adolf Eichmann'[1]

DANNY SULLIVAN

THIS VERY BRIEF ESSAY by Merton was written in the 1960s at a time when America was experiencing serious unrest. There was a serious questioning of long held values and an establishment that resisted any kind of real questioning. Merton was known for his commitment to civil rights, the peace campaign and social justice in general. He refused to be drawn into stereotyping and consistently challenged the American view of Russia and her people. He could be withering in his criticism of established Catholicism's facility to go with the Government tide and its inability to dig deep into its radical roots.

Merton begins the essay by saying that the most disturbing fact about Eichmann was that he was examined by a psychiatrist and found to be sane. If the Nazis had been psychotics some of their appalling cruelties would have at least been easier to understand. Merton asserts that Eichmann was:

thoughtful
orderly
unimaginative

and that he had a profound respect for systems and law and order. He was:

obedient
loyal
a faithful officer of the state.

He did not develop any psychosomatic illnesses, had a good appetite and he slept well. This is all the more disturbing given the evidence of Eichmann's involvement in the systematic murder of the Jewish people. Once on a visit to Auschwitz he was disturbed at what he saw but he was devoted to duty and proud of his job.

Merton asks why is Eichmann's sanity disturbing and answers the question for himself by reminding us that we equate sanity with a sense of:

justice
humaneness
prudence

and the capacity to love and understand other people. We rely on the sane people of the world, Merton argues, to preserve it from barbarism, madness and destruction. Merton then provocatively challenges us by saying that we then realise that it is the sane who are the most dangerous. It will be the sane ones who will push the nuclear buttons. They will have perfectly good reasons for this – indeed logical and well adjusted reasons. They will obey sane orders that have come down from the sane chain of command. As Merton says with not a little irony:

"When the missiles take off it will be no mistake."[2] Thus a concept of sanity where spiritual values have lost their meaning is in itself meaningless.

What is the meaning of a concept of sanity that excludes love, considers it irrelevant and destroys our capacity to love other human beings, to respond to their needs and sufferings, to recognise them also as persons, to apprehend their pain as one's own? In inimitable Merton style he is not content to leave it at that and asks the question: but what about Christianity and sanity? What business have we to equate sanity with Christianity?

"The worst error must be to imagine that a Christian must try to be sane like everyone else, that we belong in our kind of society."[3]

There have been plenty of sane Christians in the past. Torture is nothing new, is it? He again provocatively suggests:

"We ought to be able to rationalise a little brainwashing and genocide, and find a place for nuclear war, or at least for napalm bombs, in our moral theology. Certainly some of us are doing our best along these lines already. There are hopes. Even Christians can shake off their sentimental prejudices about charity and become sane like Eichmann. They can even cling to a certain set of Christian formulas and fit them into a Totalist Ideology. Let them talk about justice, charity, love and the rest. These words have not stopped some sane people from acting very sanely and cleverly in the past."[4]

Merton then argues that most of America would agree with Time magazine that it is the pacifists and the ban the bomb people who are quite seriously a little crazy. He concludes that sanity is no longer an end or value in itself. If the modern person of the 60s were to be a little less sane, a little more doubtful, a little more aware of their own absurdities and contradictions then there might be the possibility of survival. But if we remain too sane then perhaps in a society like ours the worst insanity is to be totally without anxiety, totally sane.[5]

A brief essay then which is filled with an astonishing range of insights. The hermit sitting at the edge of society and radically challenging the current values. As Merton said in another essay, the monk and the authentic hippy share the same vocation which is to sit on the edge of society and be critical. A noble vocation desperately misunderstood in the world of the 60s if, in fact, ever understood in any time or place.

Merton, the social commentator, in touch with the issues of the day and more than happy to bring a sense of irony to anybody's pious platitudes. Whilst he never at anytime considered himself a theologian he knew enough to be scathing of those who would hide behind a facile and superficial moral theology and tried to give a Catholic gloss to what was ultimately morally reprehensible.

But perhaps, most importantly of all, we have the uncomfortable insights of the prophet. If we think back to the context of America and the American Catholic Church in the 1960s, to take the sanity of Eichmann and apply its implications to American political life and the essence of institutional Christianity and Catholicism must have been quite shocking. No wonder some lovers of The Seven Storey Mountain found it exceedingly difficult to deal with the Merton of the 60s. There were no indulgences to be gained from going on peace marches, fighting for racial justice or standing with the poor and attacking the systems that seemed to generate an inherent underclass. And anyone who could speak of the Russians as a people to be loved, and not nuked for the dangerous and subversive Reds that they were, must be suspected of subversiveness themselves. Such is the vocation of the prophet.

And, of course, the authentic prophet speaks for all time. So, thirty years on, do Merton's prophetic insights hold true?

A lot has happened in thirty years. In the West we continue to elect sane leaders who have involved the world in a range of wars and military conflicts. The arms industry cannot survive without these conflicts and politicians never disappoint them. Our own Foreign Secretary only this year has given perfectly sane and rational reasons why arms should be continued to be sold to East Timor despite the clear and unequivocal evidence of the high levels of suppression of its people. At one of Mrs. Thatcher's election campaigns the biggest cheer of the night was for the comedian who suggested bombing the Russians. Billions of pounds are spent on nuclear satellite shields so that we might all sleep safely in our beds. And weren't the women of Greenham Common more than just a little bit crazy? Why were they not at home being proper mothers and/or wives or at least behaving in the way that proper women should. What a scandal for our country that we should embarrass our American military friends with the presence of these women who lived in such an undignified and insane manner.

The gap between rich and poor has widened considerably in the past thirty years and in Britain we have never been able to meet the minimum figure for overseas aid which is actually minuscule compared to our gross national product. And politicians have tried to hi-jack the Gospel to their own ends. Mrs. Thatcher assured us that the Good Samaritan could only be helpful because he had generated the money to be so. Our present government, we are told, is littered with Christian socialists who have no difficulty at all in targeting the most vulnerable and exposed because we all must worship now at the temple of spending limits. The streets must be cleared of our beggars and homeless for this is no symbol of a dynamic new country. And our Prime Minister tells us that, of course, there will still be room for compassion but that it must be a compassion with hard edges. Revisit the story of the prodigal son and reflect on the total and unqualified compassion and love shown to the wandering child who had returned home. No casting up of guilt, no hard edges, just unequivocal, unreserved love.

Lord Longford is painted by the media as a clown and buffoon for arguing that Myra Hindley should eventually be paroled and not doomed to the rest of her life in prison. He challenges the underlying assumptions of vengeance which lie behind the sane rationalisation of never truly rehabilitating a fellow human being.

He is naive, being conned and above all insensitive to the feelings of the victims' families when all he is doing is questioning a theology and a society that cannot bring itself to offer authentic forgiveness. And now that we no longer have the Russians to satanise we can find plenty of other candidates, be they Iraqis, Muslims, Libyans, gay people or Aids sufferers. In France, because of Jean Marie Le Pen's National Front's stigmatising of gay people, no French town or city would risk opening a hospice for people with Aids related illnesses. There is now just one in Paris and one opening in Provence to serve the needs of the whole country. In our own country we treat genuine asylum seekers as if they were spongers and keep them in the most inhumane conditions sometimes for as long as a year at a time. Merton's concept of sanity which he found so disturbing is clearly alive and well.

And what of Christianity? How has it fared in the thirty years since Merton's essay? Well, institutionally it remains as sane and rational as ever which would be much to Merton's disappointment but, I am sure, not to his surprise. The institutional Church seems to be having a dialogue of the deaf, for it seems incapable of listening to and hearing what ordinary people are saying, and the gap is being filled by fundamentalist groups and New Age philosophies. While these at times may have serious links with people's authentic search for the spiritual, they fail to connect to a radical sense of social justice. And it seems to me that one of the most powerful aspects of the contemplative tradition for us ordinary people is that our silence and meditation must take us to a radical sense of the needs of the other — our fellow human beings.

My own tradition, Roman Catholic, rationalises the exclusion of women from real ministry. It excludes its own members from eucharist if they are divorced and in a second marriage and has no concept of eucharistic hospitality towards our fellow Christians whom it still has the arrogance to describe as non-Catholics. It explains this sane and rational approach to hurting people by an appeal to Church Law and Doctrine and to the concept that the Church has to think in centuries. Which is indefensible, given that we have to live in the eternal now and deal with our day-to-day brokenness and fallibility.

And the Churches are working together to make the millennium a real Christian celebration. They argue that Christianity should be at the heart of this and we can be fairly confident that they will avoid embarrassing the Government. How can the Churches influence politicians if they do not play the politician's game? Oh for a Christianity that would be so insane and irrational as to hive off its riches for the poor at the millennium, that would provoke our government to a radical programme of overseas aid and whose members could be found on the 31st December, 1999 sitting on pavements with the homeless or in inhumane institutions with the forgotten or in our prisons with some of the 60,000 plus prisoners, 50,000 of whom at least do not need to be there. Of course, there will be Christians who will do this for they are already doing it but you can be pretty sure that they are regarded as a little crazy. Meanwhile our institutional Church leaders will bless the new century side by side with the politicians and the law makers who give us such a sane and comfortable life. Why be party poopers?

Oskar Schindler has been a very uncomfortable hero for many Catholics. For although he rescued many Jews and, when confronted with a stark choice between good and evil, chose good, he was also known to be a womaniser and bit of a drinker. This human fallibility does not qualify you for plaster sainthood or Butler's *Lives of the Saints*. Lacking perfection, how could Schindler possibly be a role model for others? And yet in an ironic way he epitomises Merton's plea for us to be a little less sane, a little more doubtful, a little more aware of our absurdities and contradictions. What Schindler did was irrational, insane and highly dangerous. But, when pushed on it, he said that actually the choice was so stark that there was no choice. For all his fallibility and absurdities and contradictions he had the insight to see his Jewish workers as his fellow human beings, to love them and to be able to respond to their needs and sufferings, to apprehend their pain as his own.

Merton would have been able to relate to who Schindler was and to what he did, for he would have recognised a fellow prophet. And Merton would rejoice in the dictum of John of the Cross that in the evening of our lives we will be judged on love. Not religious practice or dogma or doctrine or Church Law but that radical sense of love which lies at the heart of the gospel and which makes God's kingdom a possibility here and now, if we were but mad and insane enough to realise it.

Notes and References

1. Thomas Merton, *Raids on the Unspeakable* (Tunbridge Wells, Kent: Burns & Oates, 1977) pp.29-33
2. Op.cit., p.31
3. Op.cit., pp.31-2
4. Op.cit., p.32
5. Op.cit., p.33

An Introduction to
'Un Pas de Deux, Un Pas de Dieu'

CHRISTINE JENSEN HOGAN

ALTHOUGH THOMAS MERTON AND Anne Bradstreet were centuries apart and lived vastly different lives, similarities in their understanding of life and of God are striking. They were both seekers. They sought wholeness, integrity, through a constant questioning of life and of God which is manifested in their writing. They were both independent thinkers, quite unafraid to let their minds take them into unknown territories. Their art, their poetry, in its straightforward eloquence, shows that these authors were both pioneers; pioneers of the mind, pioneers of the spirit.

Anne Bradstreet was born in 1612, during the latter days of the Elizabethan era. Elizabeth I had ruled from the middle 1500s until the turn of the century and her influence was felt well into the 1600s. Bradstreet was well aware of the influence of the former queen. The Elizabethan women were appreciated for their intelligence, for their strength of character, more than women had been before in the history of England. Anne was raised in Tattershall Castle and at Sempringham Manor, where her father worked with the Earl of Lincoln. Her father's position was steward or manager for the vast estate. The Earl was a wealthy and learned individual, and there was a library with extensive holdings and, most likely, a great deal of stimulating and interesting conversation in the noble household. The growing influence of Calvinist ideas and the backlash from those who had followed the Catholic Queen Mary, the Restoration and the Reformation, were all brewing during this period. As the unrest grew, the people of England came to feel the heavy burden of taxes levied by the monarchy to quell rebellions.

The life that Anne Bradstreet found in America was very different from the one she had left in England. Her father was a leader of the colony, but her life, even though the family was of noble background in England, was no longer one of gentility and leisure. All the settlers of the new colony suffered from want of everything during those first few years. Nobility of birth did not protect them from the harsh winters, the scarcity of food, the diseases, the wolves, the Indians. In *An American Triptych: Anne Bradstreet, Emily Dickinson, Adrienne Rich*, Wendy Martin writes:

> Once in New England she uprooted her household several times to move to increasingly more distant, uncivilized, and dangerous outposts so that her father and husband could increase their property as well as their political power in the colony. (16)

Perhaps Martin's tone is somewhat harsh toward the men in this case. The possibility is that Bradstreet recognized the need for these moves even though there was hardship. Hardships, under the circumstances of pioneer life, were to be expected if not to be enjoyed. In addition, the Puritans believed that hardships were a blessing. God afflicted those he loved as a way to remind them of their purpose in life. Bradstreet interpreted her sufferings as God's punishment and God's lesson, in hopes of being one of the elect predestined to gain the reward of heaven.

Anne and her husband, Simon, had eight children, all of whom lived well into adulthood. He was away a great deal of the time, on business for the colony at first, and then, later, as its governor. Although she was a pioneer, Bradstreet strove to maintain the civility of her former life in England.

Born in 1915, Thomas Merton grew up living a rather sophisticated nomadic existence with his artist parents, in France and in the United States. His mother died when Thomas was five years old and his father raised him with little supervision. His father became ill when Thomas was fifteen, and they returned to the United States to his maternal grandparents home in New York. Orphaned by the time he was sixteen, he journeyed about Europe alone, leading the life his father had led before. Although he had a certain financial security from relatives, and from his father's estate, he had no guidance in his life. He attended school in England, where his godfather lived, and then went to Cambridge. While there, he became involved in drinking, carousing, and general dissipation. His godfather withdrew support, and Merton returned to New York and to Columbia University. His escapades continued for some time but he was able to complete his Bachelor of Arts and go on then to finish a Master of Arts degree in English. He had begun writing novels while still in his youth and was an editor and writer as well as graphic artist for the Columbia University literary journal and the humour magazine, *The Jester*. He also edited the Yearbook.

Through the study of philosophy courses with Dan Walsh, a devout Catholic, and through self-searching, which he began while at Columbia, Merton's life took on a deeper character. He began to read philosophers of the Church, St. Ignatius of Loyola, St. John of the Cross, and began to see a need in himself for order and for spiritual growth. He turned to Catholicism which took him from the life that hereafter he referred to as decadent, to one of peace and discipline and, ultimately, joy. After achieving his degrees, he taught in a small college in upstate New York and began his serious writing. Seeking more stability for his life and greater spiritual freedom, he entered a monastery in Kentucky where he continued his writing along with the rigorous schedule of prayer, physical labour, and study as a cloistered Trappist monk. His life at Gethsemani brought him peace, although his hermitage, ironically, became a meeting place for Merton and the world. He was visited by Civil Rights leaders, by artists, by poets, by religious leaders, all seeking his guidance, his warmth of friendship, his brilliance.

The solitude that Merton sought at Gethsemani was elusive. The days were busy with study, with farming, with prayer. His writing, which he had begun at Columbia, was not given high priority. He had chosen his life of asceticism. He chose it with the thought that he might never have the opportunity to write again, that the monastery would curtail his writing. This did not happen. He was encouraged to write, yet he was given little time in which to do it. Merton made time. Before he was given permission to live as a hermit on the monastery grounds, he would write after prayers, in the very early hours of the morning, filling many notebooks with poems, thoughts, and essays.

Unlike Merton, who chose solitude, for Bradstreet, the isolation of the colony with its loneliness, its difficulties, was not a choice. This arduous existence was thrust upon her. That she used it, that she did not revel in misery in her poems, is to her credit. The poems quoted in my play show her humor, her wonder, her delight in life. The thought of a room of her own in which to work was repeated in her prose and poetry often. She would rise from bed while her household slept, to compose her verse.

Adrienne Rich gives an interesting view of Bradstreet's work saying it was

> ...an act of great self-assertion and vitality. To have written poems, the first good poems in America, while rearing eight children, lying frequently sick, keeping house at the edge of wilderness, was to have managed a poet's range and extension within confines as severe as any American poet has confronted. If the severity of these confines left its mark on the poetry of Anne Bradstreet, it also forced into concentration and permanence a gifted energy that might, in another context, have spent itself in other, less enduring directions. (xx)

Perhaps the isolation spurred her to the thoughtful verse, the personal lines which are so universal in feeling. In a most eloquent simplicity she shares her responses to the life around her, to her own artistic life within her. It is these poems, written during such difficulty, which have made Bradstreet retain readers over the centuries.

Adrienne Rich's comments about Anne Bradstreet are echoed in an article written by Victor Kramer regarding Merton. This article appeared in the *Dictionary of Literary Biography*:

> The years Merton spent from 1941 to 1968 as a cloistered monk are best characterized as a continual and systematic investigation of ways to combine contemplation and writing...

> Ultimately the activities of the contemplative and the writer reinforced each other, for while he entered a monastery, he would never forget that he was by temperament an artist. (220)

And so, although Merton's isolation and ascetic life were by design, whereas Bradstreet's were not, there were choices that the poets made within their lives which are similar. Victor Kramer makes further comments about Merton's life of solitude, "although a hermit, Merton severed many connections with the world while in artistic ways he was extending connections." (225) Merton published very little before he entered the monastery and afterward his publications list grew to such an extent that he stated his concern in an article quoted in *Contemporary Authors*:

> In the first place I think I have written too much and published too much. Some early work resulted in my being classified as a spiritual writer, or, worse still, an 'inspirational writer,' a category to which I

seriously object, but which I have perhaps not worked hard enough to avoid. However, it is certainly true that my work, both poetry and prose, represents a monastic view of life and implies a rather strong criticism of prevailing trends toward global war, totalism, racism, spiritual inertia, and crass materialism. This criticism is not something I want to repudiate, though I regret an occasional note of acerbity. (777)

It is true that Merton sought publication for his works before he became a monk and, although he did not actively seek it afterward, he was pleased to have his works appreciated and in print.

It is paradoxical that Bradstreet may not have intended for her work to be published at all. Her volume printed during her lifetime was done so through the actions of her brother-in-law and sister, who took the manuscript with them to England, possibly without the author knowing about it. In her poem, "The Author To Her Book," she refers to her 'illform'd offspring that was taken and exposed to publick view.' After this publication, her corrections and additions were added to the work when it was published after her death. In essence, however, both Bradstreet and Merton wrote for themselves, for their souls, and for those they loved.

For her children, Anne Bradstreet wrote poetry and prose as a means of sharing with them her hard-won understanding of life and of God. These are conversational in tone and are touching in that she even shares her doubts about the existence of God, knowing that all intelligent young people have doubts, some of which, like hers, are never clearly resolved. There are beautiful poems written to her husband, Simon, who was a man dedicated to his family and to the colony which he helped govern. In "To My Dear And Loving Husband," the author proclaims,

> If ever two were one, then surely we.
> If ever man were lov'd by wife, then thee;
> If ever wife was happy in a man,
> Compare with me ye women if you can.

She was a loving mother, a loving wife, a loving author, sharing her words, her thoughts, to make life under the tenets of Puritanism happier for her children, her family. Many of her lines were written for their edification and for their comfort after her death.

Although he did not have a family of his own to write for, Merton found one in the world of his readers. The correspondents he had, the novices he taught, all were like his family, his children. His writing is personal. In his autobiographical works he talks of his doubts about God, of his concerns with religion, with faith. He shares the pains of his life with candour and talks of his early life of extreme liberality in his famed work The Seven Storey Mountain. All his books are personal, directly and simply written for all their beautiful prose and poetry. They can be seen as compassionate lessons to the reader, Merton's only family. Bradstreet's family was her relatives, her children, her husband, and now the world of her readers. Merton's family was his friends, his fellow monks, and the world that he cared so much about.

Though plagued by occasional physical illnesses, both of these authors were basically quite strong, which helped them through their difficult daily lives and gave them the stamina to write when others would have rested. Although Bradstreet wrote several poems while she lay ill in bed, I think that her sicknesses were a surprise to her and that the time spent resting gave her the opportunity to write and to reflect on God's purpose in afflicting her. She had borne eight healthy children and lived to be over sixty years of age, criteria, I believe, for being considered remarkably healthy some 350 years ago in the harshness of early New England.

Merton had been ill as a child, as had Bradstreet, and he was bothered with minor aches and colds throughout his life. His teeth were not good and caused him much pain as well as keeping him from serving in the military during World War II. He was, however, physically strong enough to overcome the several years of abuse to his body from his raucous life in college, both at Cambridge and at Columbia. He also was able to manage the rigours of life as a farmer/monk at Gethsemani.

In the play I have chosen to depict Anne in her middle years. It is the time after the publication of her book, The Tenth Muse. It is also the time during which her inner questioning and her work began to join more and more. Her work from this time on is like a window into her mind and her soul. Her later works still question God although, as in all her writing, she seems resigned to the power of an authority greater than hers.

Thomas is shown in his early fifties, at the peak of both his career and his inner life. Actually, this is the age he was at his death. He had been touring India and was then in Thailand speaking on

'Contemplative Thought in Eastern Philosophy and in Christianity.' His list of writings and his schedule during the last years of his life are phenomenal. His trip to Asia had brought him to an even deeper awareness of spirituality, self, and man's responsibilities to himself, God, and others. His death was due to electrocution caused when he touched the exposed wires of an electric fan on that very hot afternoon in Bangkok.

Merton had come full circle. He had gone over the mountain and the mountain had vanished. He was in tune with the person he had been before he became a monk. The monastery and its discipline had refined him and ultimately it gave him the freedom to be what he was meant to be. His concerns that grew later in his life, about the world, the cruelty, the love, the heroism, the meanness, were there in the poetic, dream-like writing of *My Argument with the Gestapo* written before he went to Gethsemani. In it are autobiographical vignettes and sequences in which he projects himself into war-torn Europe, in which his personality and his concerns are shown vividly. Merton wrote the novel while he was teaching at St. Bonaventure College in upstate New York. He was in his early twenties. It wasn't published then, although he sent it to several publishers. He cared enough about the book, what it said to the world about war, and what it said about him, to have kept it after destroying most other works he had done before entering the monastery. It is as though he were protecting this book which showed his young self, his tender, yet strong self, still vulnerable, still naive. The manuscript remained with him until the last year of his life when preparations had begun for the work to be published. Naomi Burton Stone, the editor of many of Merton's books, writes:

> Far from changing his youthful ideals... [he] now felt more than ever obliged to speak out against the unmorality and callousness of nuclear warfare, to urge, whenever and wherever he could make himself heard, the urgent necessity of world peace, of a true understanding of the inherent dignity of man, all men, everywhere... I admit to having some qualms. Early works are often better left in the attic... As I read the book, I was delighted with it. I had forgotten how many scenes from his boyhood were in it, and doubt if I had even noticed originally the signs of his growing interest in the monastic life.

Merton looked forward to the publication of his work. He fretted over the typing of a few minor corrections and was thrilled at the prospect of it finally being printed.

This full circle, from before his turning from the world to his entering the monastery to do the bidding of the church, to the re-emergence of the person he had been in his earlier years, shows the man as striving for wholeness and integrity. He had found a peace in the monastery, an understanding of God, of simplicity. The strength of that peace allowed him to question the deepest aspects of life throughout his years and to give to his writing this contemplative spirit. This was his way to God.

It was also Bradstreet's way; however, her questioning was not as free as Merton's. Hers was certainly striking for the mentally closed time in which she lived and for the fear that must have been always with her about overstepping the boundaries of outspokenness in a rigid Puritan society. The story about her father's banishment of Sarah, Anne Bradstreet's sister, which is an important point in the play, is true. It is discussed in a biography of the poet, by Elizabeth Wade White. Although Anne never wrote about the situation, it must naturally have struck her deeply, and so I chose to make it a part of 'Un Pas de Deux, Un Pas de Dieu.' I believe that she would have and likely did respond in the way represented in the play. The private grief, the guilt for having a contented household while her sister was ostracized, and the guilt for feeling anger toward her father and the Puritan way, must have been unbearable. It would seem that she must have felt fear and constraint and that her strong and intelligent personality, at this point, turned inward more and more to seek the answers to the cruelty present in the situation. I also feel that, unlike Merton, she may never have completely become free of this guilt, this confusion of her father, authority, and God, and the harshness of the Puritan society. Her writing certainly became more personal after this terrible incident which was also the time in which the family moved to Andover, a settlement even more removed from the other towns. This was to be her monastery, so to speak, her room of her own, her chance to let her mind explore and her pen to heal through her poetry.

Anne Bradstreet lived some 300 years before Thomas Merton. She was a Puritan. He was a Catholic monk. Their artistry, their brilliant minds, their need for solitude, their seeking of wholeness, integrity, brought them together in my mind and in my writing. Seeing them come alive again, in the performance of my play, is a thrilling experience for me.

*Christine Hogan's play was performed by the author
and Michael Woodward on the first evening
of the Oakham Conference.*

Notes and References

Books in Print. New York: Booker, 1989.

Contemporary Authors: A Biobibliographical Guide to Current Writers in Fiction. General Non-Fiction. Poetry. Journalism. Drama. Motion Pictures and Other Fields: 1963 -1969. Detroit: Gale, 1970.

Ellis, John Harvard, ed. The Works of Anne Bradstreet in Prose and Verse. New York: Peter Smith, 1932.

Kramer, Victor. 'Thomas Merton'. Dictionary of Literary Biography: 1981 Yearbook. Ed. Matthew J. Bruccoli. Detroit: Gale, 1982.

Martin, Wendy. An American Triptych: Anne Bradstreet. Emily Dickinson. Adrienne Rich. Chapel Hill: University of North Carolina Press, 1984.

Merton, Thomas. The Collected Poems of Thomas Merton. New York: New Directions, 1977.

Rich, Adrienne. Foreword. The Works of Anne Bradstreet. Ed. Jeannine Hensley. Cambridge: Belknap Press of Harvard University Press, 1967.

Stone. Naomi Burton. Introduction. My Argument With The Gestapo: A Macaronic Journal by Thomas Merton. New York: New Directions, 1975.

Notes on Contributors

COLIN ALBIN is an Anglican priest who has recently retired from parish work to explore other forms of ministry.

CANON A.M. ALLCHIN is Honorary President of the Thomas Merton Society and a friend and correspondent of Thomas Merton.

CHRISTINE M. BOCHEN is Professor of Religious Studies at Nazareth College of Rochester, USA. She edited the fourth volume of Merton's letters, The Courage for Truth and Learning to Love, the sixth volume of his Journals.

MICHAEL J. CALLAGHAN CM is a Vincentian priest at St. John's University in New York. He has recently received his doctorate from New York University for his thesis on Merton and the English Mystics.

LAWRENCE CUNNINGHAM is Chair of the Theology Department at the University of Notre Dame in the US. He edited Thomas Merton, Spiritual Master and the third volume of The Merton Journals, A Search for Solitude.

PATRICK EASTMAN is a parish priest in Tulsa, Oklahoma. He is editor of the spirituality newsletter Monos and a frequent lecturer and writer on spirituality and monasticism.

PATRICK HART OCSO is the General Editor of The Merton Journals. Merton's last secretary at Gethsemani Abbey, he is the monastery's representative on Merton affairs.

CHRISTINE JENSEN HOGAN is a poet and writer who lectures in English Composition at the University of Notre Dame.

VICTOR A. KRAMER is Professor of English at Georgia State University. Founding editor of The Merton Annual, he edited the fourth volume of The Merton Journals and is author of Thomas Merton: Monk and Artist.

LINDSAY NEVIN is a founding member of the Thomas Merton Society. Her drawings appear frequently in The Merton Journal.

TOMMIE O'CALLAGHAN was a close friend of Merton's; he frequently visited the O'Callaghan home in Louisville. She is a Trustee of the Merton Legacy Trust.

PAUL M. PEARSON is Librarian of the Institute of Laryngology in London. He is secretary to the Thomas Merton Society and an international advisor to the International Thomas Merton Society.

M. BASIL PENNINGTON OCSO is a Cistercian monk from St. Joseph's Abbey, Spencer, Massachusetts and has written many books on the spiritual life, and on Centering Prayer in particular.

SONIA PETISCO recently completed a doctoral thesis on Merton's poetry and is currently translating Merton's poetry into Spanish.

DAVID SCOTT is Rector of St. Lawrence's in Winchester. A poet, he is a founding member and past chairman of the Thomas Merton Society and poetry editor of *The Merton Journal*.

CATHARINA STENQVIST is Associate Professor of Theology at Lund University in Sweden. She has written and lectured extensively on mysticism, Simone Weil and Thomas Merton.

DANNY SULLIVAN is a founding member of the Thomas Merton Society and editor of *The Merton Journal*.

BONNIE THURSTON is Professor of New Testament Studies at Pittsburgh Theological Seminary. A founding member of the International Thomas Merton Society, she was its third President.

ESTHER DE WAAL is the author of *A Seven Day Journey with Thomas Merton*, Esther has also written and lectured extensively on the Benedictine life and Celtic Spirituality.

ROWAN WILLIAMS is Bishop of Monmouth. He is a theologian, poet and the author of numerous books and articles.

JOHN WU, JR. is Professor of English and Philosophy in Taiwan. He is the son of Merton's friend John Wu, and was himself a correspondent, visitor and friend of Merton.

MADE AND PRINTED IN WALES BY
GWASG DINEFWR PRESS
LLANDYBIE FOR
THREE PEAKS PRESS
9 CROESONEN ROAD, ABERGAVENNY,
MONMOUTHSHIRE NP7 6AE